THE ESSENTIAL GUIDE TO COLOR KNITTING TECHNIQUES

THE ESSENTIAL GUIDE TO COLOR KNITTING TECHNIQUES

MARGARET RADCLIFFE

Storey Publishing

The mission of Storey Publishing is to serve our customers by
publishing practical information that encourages
personal independence in harmony with the environment.

Edited by Gwen Steege and Erin Holman
Art direction and book design by Mary Winkelman Velgos

Cover photography by John Polak Photography, except for author photo by Mars Vilaubi
Interior photography by John Polak Photography, except for © Dunja Dumanski,
    Lighthouse Photographers, 39, 91, 139, 143, 171, 230, and 269; Mars Vilaubi, 25 and 195
Charts by Leslie Anne Charles/LAC Design
Illustrations by Alison Kolesar, 244 and 292–303; Ilona Sherratt, 37, 93, 131, 132, 198, 222,
    229, 278, 282, and 283
Indexed by Sunday Oliver

Storey Publishing
210 MASS MoCA Way
North Adams, MA 01247
www.storey.com

Printed in China by R. R. Donnelley
10 9 8 7 6 5 4 3 2 1

Library of Congress Cataloging-in-Publication Data

Radcliffe, Margaret (Margaret K. K.)
  The essential guide to color knitting techniques / Margaret Radcliffe. — [2nd edition].
    pages cm
  Includes bibliographical references and index.
  ISBN 978-1-61212-662-3 (pbk. : alk. paper)
  ISBN 978-1-61212-663-0 (ebook) 1. Knitting—Miscellanea. 2. Color in art. I. Title.
TT820.R225 2015
746.43'2—DC23
                      2015007486

Contents

AN INVITATION:
Going Beyond Knits and Purls

On the one hand, the beauty of knitting is its simplicity; it is made up of just knits and purls. On the other hand, the lasting interest of knitting, for those of us frankly addicted to it, lies in the complexity that comes from the interplay of color, texture, fiber, and pattern to create a limitless number of unique fabrics. Unfortunately, it is this very complexity and the inexhaustibility of the choices open to us that knitters sometimes find daunting.

While the main focus of this book is on color, I have considered it in relation to texture, fiber, and pattern, because knitting always includes all of these elements. Throughout *The Essential Guide to Color Knitting Techniques,* you'll find general information on color and color techniques, combined with specific practical advice and step-by-step explanations of the techniques and their variations. You'll also find inspiration in the many photos of knitted swatches and finished pieces. Be sure to make use of the Appendix, which includes basic techniques that may be unfamiliar to you, explanations of how to use charts in color knitting, and specific chapter bibliographies, where you'll find additional sources of information and inspiration.

I hope that *The Essential Guide to Color Knitting Techniques* will make your choices less intimidating, your knitting more enjoyable, and the end results much more successful.

—Margaret Radcliffe, 2008

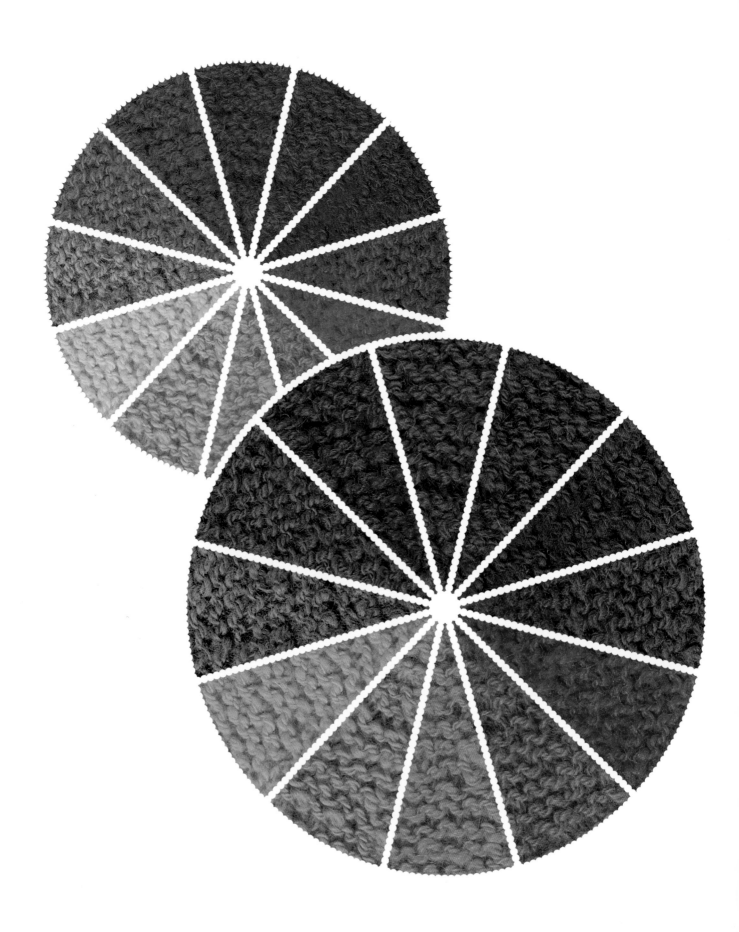

1 COLOR BASICS

Everyone perceives color a bit differently, and our responses to certain colors or groups of colors are a matter of personal preference as well as psychology and perception. Some people love bright colors, some are attracted to pastels, some adore grays and blacks, and others are happiest when a wide variety of colors are combined. Color can make us feel excited, calm, happy, or wretched. Lighting also affects the way we perceive colors. Incandescent, fluorescent, and halogen bulbs make colors look more yellow, purple, or blue than they really are. Colors even look different in daylight depending on the time of day and whether it's cloudy or sunny. The important thing to realize about using color in knitting is that there are no right or wrong combinations; there are just color groupings, or colorways, that have different effects.

{Describing Color}

Because people see and respond to color in such different ways, color can be extremely difficult to describe. This is not a color theory book, but we do need to be able to talk about color, so, for discussion purposes, I'm going to define three characteristics of color:

» **Hue** describes the color itself, like red, green, or blue.
» **Value** describes how dark or light the color is.
» **Saturation** describes how much of the pure hue is included in the color.

If you're like me, you understand what hue is with no problem. Value also makes sense, but it's difficult to determine value just by looking at an individual color. Saturation? This is where my eyes used to glaze over in formal discussions of color theory. But don't worry: the examples below will give you a working understanding of all three of these concepts, especially as they relate to yarn and knitting.

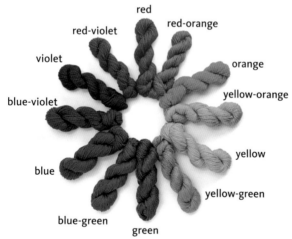

Discovering Hues

Hue is what we think of most often as color. When you ask: "What color is it?" and the answer is "Red," *red* is the hue. Hues are divided up into groups called *primary, secondary,* and *tertiary* colors. Color wheels make it easy to understand the relationships between colors.

▲ *Primary colors.* Red, yellow, and blue are the standard primary colors. They are called primary because they are the first colors, the ones mixed together to make all other colors.

▲ *Secondary colors.* You get secondary colors when you mix any of the primaries equally with another primary. Orange is made of red and yellow, green of yellow and blue, and purple (or violet) of blue and red.

▲ *Tertiary colors.* Mix any primary color with a secondary color next to it to create a tertiary color. There are, of course, almost infinite gradations in hue between the hues. For example, this swatch shows gradations between blue-green and blue.

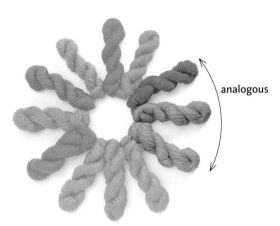

▲ *Analogous colors.* Any group of three colors next to each other in the 12-color wheel are known as analogous colors. For example, orange, yellow-orange, and yellow are analogous colors. Any group of three neighboring colors, such as this one, can be used together to good effect.

COLOR TEMPERATURE

You've probably heard colors referred to as warm or cool. This is just another way to group hues. Blues, greens, and mixtures of these are cool colors. Yellows, oranges, and reds are warm.

Context affects color temperature. Yellow-green and red-violet, mixtures of warm and cool colors, can appear either warm or cool, depending on context. For example, study the three twists of yarn above: Cover the blue twist at the top and notice that the purple in the middle seems cooler than the reddish purple at the bottom. Now cover the yarn at the bottom and note that the middle purple seems warm compared with the blue at the top. In a design, cool colors tend to recede, while warm colors seem to come forward toward the viewer.

▲ *Complementary colors.* Colors that are directly across from each other on the color wheel are known as complementary colors. The arrow indicates the complementary colors red and green. Note that the tertiary colors on either side of each of these are also complements: red-violet is the complement of yellow-green, and red-orange is the complement of blue-green.

▲ *Context affects hue.* Because of the way the human eye works, each color seems to impose its complement on any colors adjacent to it. For example, if you place green next to gray, it makes the gray look redder. On the other hand, if you place red next to gray, the gray looks greener. Blue yarn (B) twisted with yellow or orange still looks blue (C), but when twisted with turquoise it looks purple (A). Red-violet (E) looks burgundy when twisted with olive (F), but when twisted with violet it looks brown (D). This shift is far more noticeable in some lights (under a halogen lamp for example) than others, and it is why colors look one hue by themselves but may look completely different when combined with other colors.

▶ *Complementaries energize one another.* When you use complementary colors together, they enhance each other: when green and red are next to each other, the red looks redder and the green looks greener. If the areas of each color are large, this effect may not be so noticeable, but if they are small, the colors really pop.

▲ *Complementaries provide accents.* You can use this property to good effect — if you want a particular color to be more noticeable, include a bit of its complement. Compare the different parts of the swatch above. Where dark purple is used on the lighter purple background at the bottom the design is called *monochrome*, because it uses just one hue. It looks fine as is, but the colors become more exciting where a highlight of yellow, the complement of purple, was added. Depending on the yellow, it emphasizes either the dark or the light purple. Choose your color based on your personal preference and on the yarns you have available.

All of the hues I've used as examples so far are made by blending just two primaries together. The analogous colors yellow, yellow-orange, and orange, for instance, are made up of just yellow and red. You can, of course, create other colors not adjacent on the color wheel. When you do this, all three primary colors are included in the mix, which causes the resulting hue to be duller or muddier.

Color Harmonies

Besides helping us identify temperature, complements, and analogous colors, the 12-color wheel allows us to easily identify *color harmonies,* which are simply relationships between hues. They define groups of colors that work well together. There are seven color harmonies:

SPLIT COMPLEMENTARY. A hue, plus one hue on either side of its complement

DOUBLE-SPLIT COMPLEMENTARY. A hue, plus two hues on either side of its complement

TRIAD. Three hues equidistant on the wheel (Primaries are the most obvious example.)

DOUBLE TRIAD. Two trios of hues equidistant on the wheel

TETRAD. Two pairs of complements that form a rectangle on the wheel

SQUARE TETRAD. Two pairs of complements that form a square on the wheel

HEXAD. Three pairs of complements equidistant on the wheel (Note that there are only two possible hexads; all the primary and secondary colors make up one hexad and all the tertiary colors make up the second.)

Whether you are choosing colors from scratch or you already have one color of yarn and want to choose others to go with it, the color harmonies provide you with balanced groups that you know work together. If you can't find a specific hue, look for something in its general neighborhood. For example, if you can't locate a particular blue, try other blues to see if they work for you. Use the harmonies described here as a starting point when you don't already know what you want. If you need to select additional colors, experiment to see what works best.

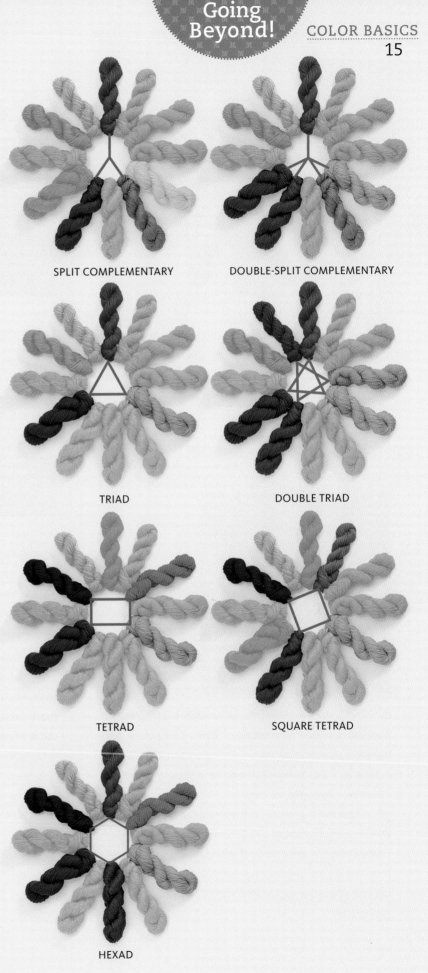

SPLIT COMPLEMENTARY

DOUBLE-SPLIT COMPLEMENTARY

TRIAD

DOUBLE TRIAD

TETRAD

SQUARE TETRAD

HEXAD

Discovering Value

Value is perhaps the hardest color attribute to identify visually, but it simply refers to the amount of contrast between colors. If you look at a black and white picture of the color wheel, you can see that there is very little contrast between the reds and purples but a great deal between yellow and its neighbors.

A. RELATIVE VALUES, color

B. RELATIVE VALUES, black and white

▲ *Using background color to change relative value.*
Relative values of colors used together can make them appear lighter or darker. Blue, green, red, and yellow are each shown on progressively darker backgrounds (A). All the colors appear darker than the white background, and all appear lighter than black, but the amount of contrast varies depending on the value of the gray background. The relative values of these colors are far more apparent in dim light or in a black and white photo (B), where blue, green, and red merge with the middle gray, and yellow vanishes into the light-gray background.

▲ *Using value to define pattern.* Value is important because it affects how subtle or how intelligible a pattern will be. A Fair Isle pattern in yellow on a blue background is far more noticeable than a pattern in purple on the same blue background. You can make both patterns intelligible, however, by using a paler blue for the background or by changing the foreground to a lighter purple. Remember that contrast is important: If you want colors to stand out, they should be darker or lighter than the colors around them. For a more subtle effect, choose colors that have a similar value.

TESTING YARN VALUES

It can be difficult to tell the relative values of balls of yarn just by looking at them, because we tend to notice the hues first. Luckily, there are several ways to test the relative values:

» Twist together strands of the yarns you want to use. View them at an arm's length in dim light and see if the yarns blend together or if the two strands are still clearly defined. You may be able to get the same effect by holding them at an arm's length and squinting.

» If you have a computer and a scanner or digital camera, make color and grayscale images of the yarns to help determine their values. Here, the grayscale photo shows that yellow is the lightest in value, green and red are both medium (the green is slightly lighter), blue is very dark, and purple is darkest.

Discovering Color Saturation

Saturation refers to the amount of pure hue that a color contains. For example, primary red is 100 percent saturated. Pink is just red mixed with white, so it's a less saturated version of red, called a *tint*. Hues can be mixed with any other color, but when they are mixed with white, gray, or black, they are known as *tints, tones,* or *shades,* respectively. Each of the swatches below is green at one end and white, gray, or black at the other; in between, the stripes contain varying mixtures of both. You can achieve many variations even if you restrict yourself to just one hue — green.

TINT. Mixing a hue with white results in a *tint*.

TONE. Mixing a color with gray produces a *tone*.

SHADE. Mixing a hue with black produces a shade.

    Saturation influences the value of a color, so it affects the amount of contrast. A color gets lighter when you mix it with white. When you mix it with black, it gets darker. But, if the gray you mix with a color has the same value the color had to begin with, its value stays the same, no matter how much gray you add.

{Putting Color to Work}

If you don't spin or dye your own yarn, you can't completely control the hue, value, and saturation. However, you *can* collect colors at your local yarn store and at shows, as well as purchasing over the Internet and through catalogs. Unfortunately, it's very difficult to choose colors on the Internet or from a catalog. This might be a good excuse for purchasing a skein or ball of every possible color in every yarn you can find, so that you have a wide palette to experiment with. Or you may find it more practical to collect yarn sample cards for lines of yarn that come in many colors.

Experimenting with Colorways

If you're an intrepid adventurer who prefers to leave yourself open to serendipity and thrives on experimentation, pick some colors and start playing with them. Keep concepts of complementary relationships, value, and saturation in mind as you experiment. Vary the amount of each color you use until you get an effect you like.

If you prefer to exercise more control over your results and spend less time experimenting, you can put the color wheel and your knowledge of color harmonies to work. If you've got an idea for a project but no yarn, start from scratch with the color wheel and pick a color harmony you like, then look for yarn to match it. You'll probably face situations where you've already got one or two colors and you want to add to your palette, especially if the two don't look great together by themselves. You can use color harmonies to help select additional colors. See Do the Twist, facing page, for examples.

FIND COLORS TO PLAY WITH EVERYWHERE

Use paint samples from paint or hardware stores or a large collection of colored pencils, crayons, or markers to document the colors you've selected. Refer to your reference collection of yarn sample cards to get an idea of what's available in the marketplace, then sally forth to your yarn shop to gather just the right materials for your project.

DO THE TWIST

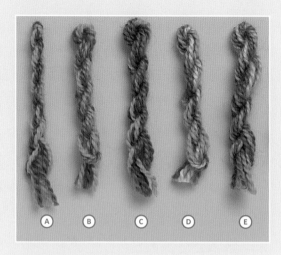

STARTING WITH GOLD AND SALMON. Let's say you've got orange and salmon (A), which don't really inspire you, but you need to use the yarn. First, match them as closely as possible to the 12-color wheel. Gold matches best with yellow-orange and salmon with red-orange. Now let's look at the possibilities. You can add orange, which falls between them, to make a group of analogous colors (B).

Twisting the yarns together helps you to see how the colors look when intimately combined, as well as to get a sense of their relative values. The orange and salmon in (A) are very close in value as well as in hue, so they tend to blend together. The gold in (B) is darker and stands out just a bit from the other two colors. It could effectively be used as a foreground against a salmon and orange background, or vice versa. If the salmon and orange are used alone, they tend to blend, and any color patterns will be difficult to see. *Add blue.* You could add blue to make a split complementary color harmony. In this case, the gold and salmon are closer in value and hue, so they seem to blend while the blue stands out (C). Substitute a lighter tint of blue for a completely different effect (D).

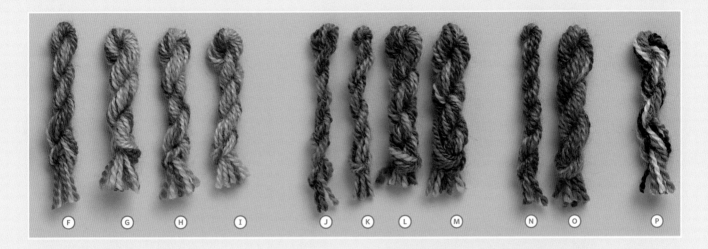

F   G   H   I   J   K   L   M   N   O   P

Use both blues. This gives you a wide range of values to work with: light (light blue), medium (gold and salmon), and dark (dark blue) (E).

Add more colors. If you want to work with more colors, adding yellow and red as well as blue will give you a double-split complementary harmony. Once again, you end up with a range of values: yellow is light; salmon, and gold fall into the middle; and red and blue are dark (F).

For more complexity. If you have a selection of shades, tints, or tones, you can substitute lighter and darker versions of a color to achieve more variation in value, or you can include all the variations available. Adding light blue, apricot (which is a tint of gold), and pink (a tint of salmon) helps to provide more balance. There are now three light colors (blue, apricot, and yellow), two medium colors (gold and salmon), and two dark colors (red and blue). The extra strand of blue also helps balance the warm/cool color mix (G).

For greater simplicity. If including so many different yarns makes this colorway too busy for your taste, you can simplify it by sticking to shades of the two original colors and adding a single blue, a return to the split-complementary harmony. Dark blue makes a brighter combo, emphasizing the contrasts because of its dark value (H). Light blue creates a more pastel effect, with less contrast (I).

STARTING WITH GREEN AND BLUE. Using just these two colors makes a striking statement (J).

Adding analogous colors. What if you want something a bit more subtle? Since blue and green are close to each other on the color wheel, you can add blue-green to make a group of analogous colors (K). Don't be afraid to add any color that falls within the analogous group: they all go together beautifully (L).

Adding a complement. As a highlight, you can always add a bit of one of the complements to these colors from the opposite side of the wheel (M).

DEALING WITH CLASHES. Sometimes you'll have two colors close to each other in the color wheel that don't look good together on their own; instead, they seem to clash. Red, red-violet, and violet are analogous colors, but they don't always cooperate when in close proximity (N). One solution to this problem is to add as many shades, tints, tones, and blends of these colors as you can (O). Where two or three colors just look wrong, combining many variations looks much more acceptable.

SHADES, TINTS, AND TONES OF A HUE, PLUS NEUTRALS.
Of course, you can always use shades, tints, and tones of any one hue together, and you can combine any color with white, gray, and black (P).

Color: It's in the Cards

Once you've selected your colors, you need to decide what proportion to use them in. It can be very time consuming to swatch all the possibilities, so you may want to try a quicker method — wrapping cards. Wrapping at least twice with each color gives you an idea of how a stitch or a row will look. Play with the order of the colors and how much of each is used in proportion to the rest. To get an idea of how small amounts of highlight colors will look, weave them in with a yarn needle.

Wrapping cards to test color combinations.

Problem-Solving Color Choices

Having trouble achieving what you want in a design? Here are some hints on how to make adjustments.

The pattern just isn't visible. You need more contrast. Look for a paler tint or a darker shade of one or two of your colors.

So many colors, you don't know what to do! If you have a large number of colors to deal with, organize them into groups to simplify the task. For example, put all the warm purples, reds, oranges, and yellows in one group and all the cool purples, blues, and greens in a second group. You might put very dark colors, regardless of hue, in one group and very light colors and neutrals in another. Develop your design based on the groups you've chosen, then, as you work, use colors at random from within each.

▲ *Toning things down.* It's too vibrant and you want something subtler. Knitting a fine strand of black, gray, or white along with your main yarn produces a flecked fabric (see above), which changes the effect through optical color blending. Color blending is most effective in simple pattern stitches that combine knits and purls, such as seed stitch. Knitting two strands of yarn, even if one of them is very thin, is like knitting with a thicker yarn — it can change your gauge or make the fabric too thick and stiff. To prevent this, you might substitute two strands of finer yarn. Adding a strand of woolly nylon (a thread used for serger sewing machines, available at fabric stores) will also modify the color with little effect on the gauge.

Livening things up. If your selection of colors seems dull and uninteresting, decide which color you'd like to emphasize and add its complement. If this doesn't work, try removing the other colors one at a time to see if one is having a deadening effect or use a black or dark gray background to make the other colors seem brighter.

▶ *Need inspiration?* Use the colors you find together in nature, photos, a piece of fabric, or any other object you like and develop your own colorways.

FABRIC DESIGN CASE STUDY

I designed fabric for a vest by pulling together many colors and organizing them in groups. The yarns were contributed by a group of hand spinners. The design challenge was to use some of each ball of yarn in a vest to be given as a birthday gift to the organizer of the group's semiannual retreats. The donors' only guideline was that the yarn should be purple. As you can see in the photo at the left, many of the donors ignored this restriction. The colors vary from almost black through pink, turquoise, and purple to grays and rusts. The yarns also varied in thickness from bulky to a fine strand of glittering purple Mylar.

After living with the yarn for a few weeks, I arranged it in piles on my sofa, contemplating and rearranging them over a period of days. I finally grouped it into what I mentally thought of as "brights" (pinks, light to medium purples, and some green and teal), "browns" (rusts, browns, and dark pinks), "pastels" (grays, pastel pinks, and some of the duller dark colors), and "darks" (black, dark purples, and dark grays). I created a fabric that used these groups in a specific order. Garter stitch ridges in the darks separate stripes of the other groups. Between the ridges, in seed stitch stripes, I used pastels, then brights, then browns, changing colors at random within each group every two rows. If I pulled a thinner yarn from the group, I either doubled it or knitted it along with a second color to provide consistency in thickness and more variation in appearance. The amount of each yarn I had available dictated the proportion of each color in the fabric.

{Yarn Practicalities}

Because you are working with yarn, you also need to take into account the properties of this material and its effect on color. A smooth yarn appears more color-saturated than a fuzzy yarn. Shiny yarns, whether silk, rayon, or metallic, seem lighter because of reflected highlights. Handpainted or space-dyed yarns change color along their length. They can be both a joy and a challenge to work with, so I've dedicated a large part of chapter 4 to them. Some yarns are made of different colors blended together before spinning, and others are made of solid colors plied together. Still others have individual plies in different colors that may change throughout a skein.

Marled yarn

▲ *The effect of yarn structure.* The complexity of the yarn affects the way the colors appear in the knitted fabric. For example, marled yarns (those twisted from plies of different colors) appear flecked when knitted up. The smaller the dots of color in the yarn, the more the colors blend in the finished fabric. The larger the spots or lengths of color, the less the colors blend in the fabric. Your gauge also has an effect on the appearance. The larger your stitches, the more noticeable the structure of the yarn and any flecks of color will be.

With so many factors affecting the final results, it's very important to experiment with your yarn, your needle size, and any color or stitch patterns you're considering, until you get the result you want. When you compose a colorway, there are a few practical considerations to keep in mind.

Combining fibers. As long as the yarns can all be cleaned the same way, you can certainly combine fibers. If you use one yarn that must be dry-cleaned and another that will dissolve in dry-cleaning chemicals, you've got an insoluble cleaning problem to cope with.

Combining thicknesses. If you have a variety of yarns of different thicknesses, choose your needle size based on the thickest of the yarns. This prevents the thicker sections from being too tight. Double your thin yarns or knit them along with other thin yarns so their size is more consistent with the thicker yarns. Wool sock yarn is available in many colors and works extremely well as an add-in for wool. Crochet cotton and embroidery floss are great carryalongs with cotton or silk. But whatever varied yarns you choose, spread them throughout the fabric so that it has consistent stretch, weight, and thickness. On the other hand, you can also achieve a good effect by making the borders or the shoulder yokes of a garment from entirely different material than the rest, even knitting them at a different gauge on different-sized needles.

Using multiple strands. If you are using multiple strands of yarn to blend colors together throughout your garment, choose your needle size based on the thickness of the combined yarns. To find the suggested needle size, take all the yarns you plan to knit together, twist them lightly, then fold this twisted bundle in half and stretch it out flat across a knitting needle gauge. Your doubled twisted strand should just barely cover the hole of the suggested needle size. Use this size as a starting point when you knit a test swatch, and adjust to a larger or smaller needle until you like the feel and look of the fabric you're creating.

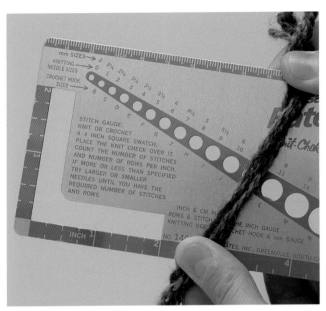

Find needle size by twisting, doubling, and stretching yarns over needle gauge.

Confirming dye lots. When you purchase yarn, check the labels on all the balls of the same color to make sure they are from the same dye lot. Even the best-quality yarns can vary in color from one batch to another, and you might not notice the slight difference in dye lots until after you've finished knitting. Also, the color in hand-painted yarns may change within the same dye lot, and even within the same skein. If you must use more than one dye lot or a skein where the color varies significantly, use the yarn in separate sections of the garment, where the colors won't be placed against each other. Or blend the transitions by working alternate rows from the two balls of yarn. You can do this easily in circular knitting by simply working alternate rounds with each ball. In flat knitting, you can accomplish the same thing by using a circular needle and knitting one row with one yarn, then returning to the beginning of the row and knitting across again with the second yarn. Assuming you are working in stockinette, you would then turn your work, purl back with the first yarn, and then purl back with the second yarn. This may not be a practical solution if you are working a complicated pattern stitch, in which case you may want to work two rows of each color to simplify the process.

Avoiding the risk of running. Whenever you use two different colors of yarn in the same piece of knitting, you take the risk that the dye in one or both will run when they are washed, and the knitting may be stained beyond repair. It's best to discover this problem before you start knitting, so test your yarn. If you've already knitted a swatch, wash it exactly the way you'll wash the finished piece. Notice whether any of the dye bleeds into the water and whether any of it is absorbed into the other colors in the fabric. Roll it in a white paper towel and observe whether any dye transfers to the towel.

You can also test the yarn before knitting. Cut between a foot and a yard of each color and immerse the pieces, one at a time, in a small bowl of hot water; if the bowl is white, you can easily see whether the color of the water changes. Roll the yarn up in a white paper towel, or rub it against the towel to see if any dye transfers. If you see no sign of running, there should be no problem using the yarns together. If there is some running, you can wash the skeins of yarn before knitting.

If the yarn is already put up in balls, you'll need to wind it into skeins and tie it in several places to prevent tangling before washing. Washing in hot water removes the dye more efficiently, but it may shrink the yarn (not a problem if you have plenty of yarn) or be harmful to some fibers. To prevent felting, be sure not to agitate animal fibers and to keep the water temperature consistent while washing and rinsing. To remove all of the excess dye, continue rinsing until the water is clear. Several products are available to help eliminate this excess dye, among them Synthrapol, a surfactant you can add to the wash water to remove excess dye, and Retayne, a fixative that helps set colors and prevent running. Both are available where quilting, dyeing, and art supplies are sold. Another option, Shout Color Catcher dye-trapping cloths (available at grocery and discount stores), are put in the washing machine to prevent red socks from turning the rest of your laundry pink, but you can also use them when hand-washing to absorb dye that bleeds into the water.

2 STRIPES

Stripes are just about the easiest thing you can do with color in knitting: Start with a different ball of yarn at the beginning of a row or round, and you get a horizontal stripe. You can make vertical stripes simply by knitting your project from side to side instead of from bottom to top (or top to bottom). Diagonal stripes take a bit of shaping at the edges, but are worth the effort.

Stripes can be exciting or reserved; their colors can be bold and vibrant or subtly blended. Use just two colors or collect as many as you can get your hands on. You can knit stripes in a completely consistent pattern, introduce random widths and color changes, follow arithmetic rules, or knit a code. To accomplish all of this, you just need to know how to start knitting with a different ball of yarn. Isn't it amazing that the possibilities are limitless?

Techniques for working stripes vary depending on whether you are knitting flat or circularly. We'll look at these first, then move on to the real fun — designing stripes.

{Flat Knitting}

When you work back and forth in rows, it's easy to develop stripes of any width. Your main challenges will be planning when to change colors and whether or not to cut the yarn each time you begin a new stripe. Let's take a look at how the width of your stripes, the number of colors, and textured patterns affect your knitting.

Beginning a New Stripe

There are a number of simple ways to handle your yarn when you start a stripe in a new color. At the beginning of a row, stop knitting with the old yarn, pick up a new color, and start knitting with it. When the distance between stripes is too long, you must cut the yarn between uses, or the edge won't stretch. If, however, you have main color and narrow stripes of contrasting colors, you may be able to leave the main color attached while cutting the other yarns.

▲ *Carry it along.* If you plan to use the same yarn every few rows, you don't need to cut it between stripes. Just carry it along the side of the knitting between uses, leaving it loose enough that the knitting can stretch naturally.

▲ *Starting a stripe.* Leave the ends of both yarns hanging down to be dealt with later. Keep working until the new stripe is as wide as you like.

▲ *Give it a twist.* If you think carried yarn looks bad, and the edge will be visible, you can secure the yarn by twisting it every two rows with the working yarn or cut the yarn between stripes.

DEALING WITH YARN ENDS

As you knit, plan ahead and cut your tails accordingly. If you intend to weave the ends in on the back of the knitting, 4"–6" (10–15 cm) tails work perfectly. For fringe or braids, you may need longer tails. But if weaving in all those ends seems like too much work, you have quite a few options.

» Don't leave them to the end — stop every so often and weave them in (see page 183).

» Weave them in as you knit.

» Incorporate the ends into fringe at the edge (see pages 260–262).

» If the ends are along an edge that won't show (for example, a side seam), French-braid them together (see page 241).

» Use the ends to make numerous tiny braids on the outside. Embellish these with beads or bells if you like (see page 241).

» Enclose the edge with the loose ends in some way, such as a binding or a knitted facing (see page 242).

Working Pairs of Rows

When you're making striped fabrics, there are a few tricks that will make the process more efficient and minimize the need to cut your yarn so there won't be so many tails to weave in later. The best approach will vary depending on your choice of pattern stitch, the width of your stripes, and the number of colors of yarn.

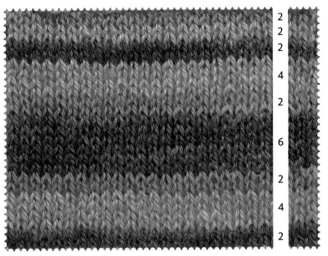

STOCKINETTE. If you always begin a new color stripe after completing a pair of knit-purl rows, all of the ends will be at the same edge of the fabric. This allows you to bring the yarn up along the edge rather than cutting it, as long as the stripes are not too wide. Stripes of 2, 4, and 6 rows easily allow the knitter to carry the yarn along.

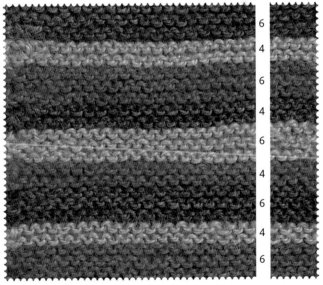

GARTER STITCH. An even number of garter-stitch rows creates neat ridges between color changes on the right side. You can make the stripes as wide as you like, as long as you use each color for an even number of rows.

Single-Row Stripes

When you're knitting flat and you want single-row stripes with just two colors, you can use a circular needle and work from either end, enabling you to avoid cutting your yarn at each color change. Alternate colors, sliding your knitting to the opposite end of the needle when necessary so that you can knit across twice on the right side, then purl across twice on the wrong side. This technique can be used whenever you want to work single-row stripes with an even number of colors.

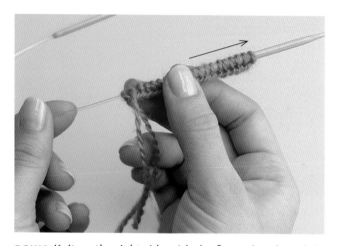

ROW 1: Knit on the right side with the first color, then slide the knitting back to the other end of the needle.

ROW 2: Knit again on the right side with the second color, then turn your work.

ROW 3: Purl on the wrong side with the first color, then slide the stitches back to the other end of the needle.

ROW 4: Purl again on the wrong side with the second color.

Single-Row Stripes in an Odd Number of Colors

If you have an odd number of colors, it's also very simple to work single-row stripes. For example, with three colors, work stockinette stitch, making a single row with each color, turning at the end of each row. After the first three rows, each time you reach the end of the row, pick up the yarn already attached at that edge and work with it. You will always use your colors in the same sequence. This technique works with as many colors as you like, so long as there is an odd number. Just pick up the lowest yarn at the beginning of each row. This is how swatch A (facing page) was made.

ROW 1: Knit with color 1.

ROW 2: Purl with color 2.

ROW 3: Knit with color 3.

ROW 4: Purl with color 1.

ROW 5: Knit with color 2.

ROW 6: Purl with color 3.

MANY-COLORED PROJECTS

When you're working with more than a few colors, whether in odd or even numbers, the strands of yarn will travel too far up the side of the knitting between stripes, so you'll probably have to cut them anyway. And, if you're cutting your yarn, you can use any number of colors to make single-row stripes.

Working Stripes in Stockinette Stitch

Stockinette stitch has a definite right and wrong side. When you change colors, the stripe has a smooth, solid edge on the knit side (A). On the purl side, you see a broken, speckled edge (B). If you like it better, the purl side can be the "right" side of your fabric, in which case it's called *reverse stockinette*.

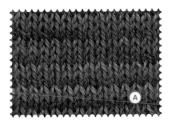 

Working Stripes in Garter Stitch

Like stockinette stitch, garter stitch lends itself most easily to changing colors every two rows, because you can be sure the yarn will be attached at the edge where you need it. When you work two rows in garter stitch, you make one single-color ridge (C). The reverse side of the fabric is noticeably different (D).

RIGHT SIDE   WRONG SIDE

CREATING DIAGONAL STRIPES

Diagonal stripes take a bit of shaping, working increases at one end of a row and decreases at the other, but they are definitely worth the effort. Here's how to do it:

Start with just two stitches and work in garter stitch, increasing one stitch at the beginning of every row until one side of the triangle you've made is as wide as you want your knitting to be. From this point on, continue to increase at the beginning of each row at one side, but decrease at the beginning of each row on the other side. This makes the two edges of your knitting parallel, while the grain of the knitting continues on the diagonal. When your knitting is long enough, shape the final corner by decreasing one stitch at the beginning of every row until three stitches remain. K3tog, cut the yarn, and pull through the one remaining stitch. Note: Work your increases and decreases at least one stitch in from the edge to prevent the edges from being too tight.

Going
Beyond!

Striping Subtleties

Sometimes you want additional control over the way the colors appear at the beginning and end of your stripes, for example, when making a reversible fabric in garter stitch or a neat striped ribbing.

NEATENING STRIPED RIBS

Color changes in ribbing look messy on the purled ribs, where the color change is broken (A, top). This is not so noticeable in K1, P1 ribbing, especially in fine yarn, but it is very apparent in wider ribs. When you change colors on every row, you can't do much about this. If you are making wider stripes, though, it's easy to disguise the color change. On the right side, just knit the first row with the new color (A, bottom). Or, if the first row is on the wrong side, purl. On the following row, return to your ribbing pattern. The more rows there are between color changes, the more successful this will be.

CREATING A REVERSIBLE FABRIC

If you're making a scarf, you'll want both sides of your garter stitch to look the same. To put half of the color changes on each side of the fabric, work an odd number of rows in each stripe (one, three, five, and so on) (B). Or, on the first row of a new color, instead of knitting, work K1, P1 all the way across, then knit all the other rows of that color (C). This works best for wider stripes because it affects the overall texture of the fabric; if you do it every other row, you won't have garter stitch.

HALF THE COLOR changes were made on each side of the fabric.

THE FIRST ROW of each color change was worked K1, P1.

THE TOP FOUR STRIPES of this swatch were worked K2, P2; in the bottom stripes, the first whole row of each new color change was knit.

{Circular Knitting}

Stripes are just as straightforward in circular knitting as in flat knitting. In fact, it's easier to make single-row stripes when working circularly because the yarn from earlier stripes is waiting for you at the beginning of every round. But if you're a perfectionist, you probably dislike the way the stripes shift at the beginning and end of each round, and the way the stitches are distorted when you carry the yarn up across contrasting stripes (see below). There are several techniques you can employ to overcome this problem, either while or after you knit.

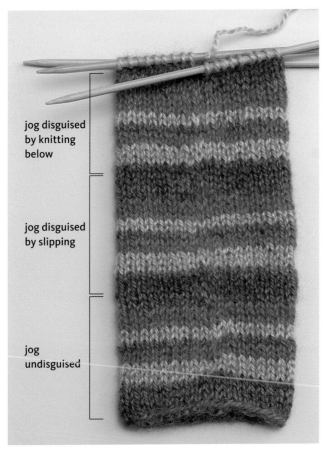

THE UNWANTED JOG. Working stripes circularly results in a jog and distorted stitches at the start of each new round. These can be hidden very successfully using slipped stitches, knitting below, and duplicate stitch.

Hiding the Jog in Multiround Stripes

While knitting stripes wider than one round, it's possible to disguise the jog by making some adjustments while you knit and then using duplicate stitch to weave in the ends. Knit the first round in the new color. When you come to the first stitch of the next round, use one of the following techniques.

SLIP THE FIRST STITCH of the second round purlwise, and then continue knitting the rest of the stripe as usual.

SLIPPING STITCHES tends to make the knitting tighter. If you knit tightly to begin with, knit into the stitch below instead (see Knit Below, page 70), then continue knitting the rest of the stripe.

Each time you start a new stripe, use one of these techniques on the first stitch of the second round. You may do this on stripes as narrow as two rounds, but it works best when they are at least three-rounds wide. When you weave in the ends, use the duplicate stitch on the purl side to align the colors at the beginning and end of each stripe. (See Fixing the Jog with Duplicate Stitch, page 32.)

Fixing the Jog with Duplicate Stitch

This technique eliminates the jog in single-round stripes and helps to disguise it in multiround stripes. You must plan ahead and cut the yarn at the end of each stripe, leaving a 4–6" (10–15 cm) tail. When you are finished, turn the piece inside out and duplicate stitch the yarn ends across the end of the round and directly behind the stitches of the same color. As you work, be careful to adjust the tension of the last stitch attached to the tail so it is the same size as its neighbors. Duplicate stitch can be time-consuming and can make the fabric thick. Speed it up by working just a couple of stitches in duplicate stitch, then quickly weave in the rest of the tail using any other method.

3] Duplicate stitch *main color* right to left.

1] Duplicate stitch *contrast color* right to left.

4] Duplicate stitch *main color* left to right.

2] Duplicate stitch *contrast color* left to right.

5] Weave in the tails.

Adding Texture to Circular Stripes

Simple textured patterns, those with just a one- or two-row repeat, work well in combination with circular stripes. Pick a pattern stitch you know by heart, though, so it's easy to continue working it while changing colors. If you're unsure of yourself, work the pattern circularly with just one color until you could do it in your sleep, and then begin changing colors.

SEED STITCH. Standard Seed Stitch is shown in the lower half of this swatch. If this looks too busy to you, try an exploded version, as shown in the upper half: knit a plain round between each knit and purl round.

RIBBED STRIPES.

Combining Stripes and Pattern Stitches

Stripes are the most straightforward of the knitted color-work techniques, but there are endless variations. It can be great fun to incorporate stripes into other pattern stitches. It may require experimentation to find the best place to change colors in a more complicated pattern stitch, such as the cable pattern shown (facing page, right). Look for a row that is plain knitting or plain purling, which frequently forms a visual break between sections of the pattern. For projects using various stripe techniques, see pages 38–41.

Color Change Variations

You can do several simple things to make stripes more interesting. Instead of using your colors repeatedly in the same order, making stripes all the same size, vary the width of the stripes and use the colors at random.

ADD TEXTURE by making your stripes in simple pattern stitches. Change the pattern each time the color changes. The wide stripes above are worked in Seed Stitch and rib patterns, while the narrow stripes are worked in garter stitch.

USE VARIEGATED OR SELF-STRIPING YARNS with solid yarns for complex-looking results. Or try two multicolor yarns together (see chapter 4 for some examples). If you're planning to use lots of colors but aren't sure how to manage them, take a look at chapter 1 for suggestions.

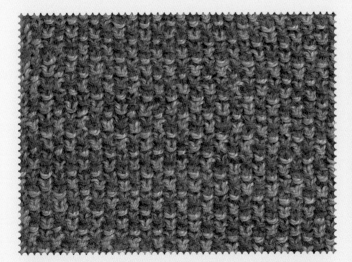

SEED STITCH SPECKLES. Changing color every row or two in Seed Stitch produces a speckled effect, especially when the colors are subtly different.

CABLE OR TWISTED-STITCH PATTERNS may actually look best if you start your new color on the row where the cable is crossed or the twist is made. The swatch shows the difference in appearance when the color is changed halfway between the cable crossings (top) and on the same row as the cable crossing (bottom).

BASKET WEAVE STITCHES lend themselves to changes after each half of the pattern repeat. Changing on a plain knit or purl row will produce a fabric with a definite right and wrong side (right side shown in top half of the swatch). Changing on the rows that combine knits and purls will make a reversible fabric (bottom half of swatch). Choose the effect you like best.

SLIPPED-STITCH PATTERNS can make it look like you're doing complicated color changes. These are so versatile that I explore them extensively in chapter 3.

A Matter of Chance

Just for fun, randomize your stripes using a pair of dice, which will need to be two different colors so you can tell them apart. Before you start, decide which die will determine the yarn and which the number of rows. Collect six yarns you like together and number them 1 to 6. Roll the dice. The number on the "yarn" die indicates which yarn, and the number on the "rows" die indicates the number of rows to work with it. Cast on with the yarn whose number matches your die and work the number of rows indicated. Don't cut the yarn yet! Roll the dice again. If the yarn number is the same, continue with the current yarn for the number of rows on the "rows" die. If the yarn number is different, cut the yarn, change to the new yarn, and work the correct number of rows. Continue until the piece is as long as you need. It's best to have lots of extra yarn in each color, just in case that color's number comes up more frequently than the others. If you do run out, just continue with the other five yarns or substitute a new ball in a similar color.

You can also collect lots of different yarns and arrange them in six groups, based on color, texture, contrast value, or any criteria you like. Put all the yarns in each group into a bag labeled with the number. Start with a set of six empty bags, also labeled 1 to 6. Each time you roll the dice, pull a ball at random from the correct bag. When you're done with it, put it into the empty bag with the same number. Whenever you empty one of the bags, trade it for the full bag with the same number, and use those yarns over again at random.

Top-Secret Ciphers

Base repeating stripe patterns on a name or a code word, with the width of each stripe determined by the letter. This is especially appropriate when you're making a gift — use the recipient's name: for example, Amanda. Assign a number based on each letter's position in the alphabet. A=1, M=13, N=14, D=4, which tells you how many rows will be in each stripe. If you are using only two colors, just alternate between them (below). Since there is an even number of letters, begin again with the first stripe and repeat this pattern until the piece is as long as you need. If you have an odd number of letters, reverse the colors the second time through.

A	=	1 row burgundy
D	=	4 rows pink
N	=	14 rows burgundy
A	=	1 row pink
M	=	13 rows burgundy
A	=	1 row pink

"AMANDA" coded in two colors. Note that you "read" this from bottom to top (the order in which it was knit).

You can also choose one color for each letter of the alphabet. Amanda would require 4 colors. A=pink, M=burgundy, N=purple, and D=lavender. Note that the first and last A stripes fall together to make a two-row stripe. Avoid this by using six colors and assigning different colors to each occurrence of each letter: you'll have colors A1, M, A2, N, D, and A3.

A	=	1 row pink
D	=	4 rows lavender
N	=	14 rows purple
A	=	1 row pink
M	=	13 rows burgundy
A	=	1 row pink

"AMANDA" coded in four colors.

Paint by Numbers: Fibonacci

Put arithmetic to work to design a pleasing progression of stripes. Many designers use the Fibonacci progression, where each number is added to the number before it to get the next number in the series. Use the numbers produced by this progression to dictate the number of rows in each stripe. Start with the number 1: make the first stripe just one row wide. After that, the width of the next stripe is determined by adding the widths of the two previous stripes, like this:

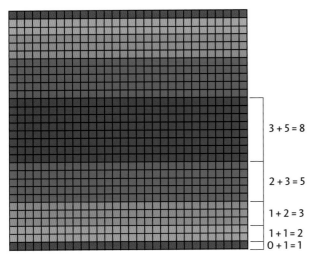

$3 + 5 = 8$

$2 + 3 = 5$

$1 + 2 = 3$

$1 + 1 = 2$
$0 + 1 = 1$

FIBONACCI SERIES. **Read from bottom to top.**

Depending on how big your piece of knitting will be, you may want to stop before the stripes become too wide. You can also start the sequence over with a one-row stripe or reverse it, as shown in the chart (below left).

Or, use just part of the sequence, starting with a three-row stripe, for example, instead of the narrower ones. Depending on how many colors you're using, it may not be at all obvious that you're repeating the same sequence over and over.

▲ *A four-stripe progression for a vest.* The progression in this segment of a vest is just four stripes, from a one-row to a five-row stripe, but five different colors are used repeatedly in the same order. Each time the progression begins again, it is with a different color. The result is that equal amounts of each color are used overall, and each color is emphasized in succession in the widest stripe of subsequent progressions.

REVERSIBLE SCARVES

These scarves are knit with lengthwise stripes, leaving the ends behind, so that you can tie them off and incorporate them in a colorful, luxurious fringe. No ends to weave in when the knitting is complete!

Measurements
Scarf A   6" (15.25 cm) wide × 60" (1.5 m) long (not including fringe)
Scarf B   6½" (16.5 cm) wide × 60" (1.5 m) long (not including fringe)
Scarf C   6½" (16.5 cm) wide × 60" (1.5 m) long (not including fringe)
Yarn   Kid Hollow semi-worsted, 50% wool/50% mohair, 4 oz (113 g)/180 yd (164.5 m)
(For colors and amounts, see individual scarves, below.)
Needles   One US #6 (4.5 mm) circular needle, 29"–32" (74–81 cm) long, *or size needed to achieve correct gauge*
Gauge   16 stitches = 4" (10 cm) in garter stitch

Preparing for Fringe

For each of these scarves, when you begin a new color, leave 7" (18 cm) tails of both the working and the new-color yarns. Loosely tie these tails together in an overhand knot, sliding the knot as close as possible to the edge of the fabric. When the scarf is complete, you can use additional lengths of yarn to create thicker fringe. (See page 260 for additional information.)

Scarf A

Yarn   One skein of each of the following: C1: Aubergine Heather; C2: Raspberries

NOTE   See Preparing for Fringe (above) for technique for changing colors. Although this scarf is knit almost entirely in garter stitch, the color-change rows are worked K1, P1, which makes the scarf reversible.

SETUP ROW: Using C1, loosely cast on 240 stitches.

ROWS 1–4:   Knit.

ROW 5 (RIGHT SIDE):   Leaving a 7" (18 cm) tail of both colors, change to C2. Loosely tie these tails together as described in Preparing for Fringe. *K1, P1; repeat from * to end of row.

ROWS 6–8:   Knit.

ROW 9:   Leaving a 7" (18 cm) tail of both colors change to C1. *K1, P1; repeat from * to end of row.

ROWS 10–12:   Knit.

NEXT ROWS: Repeat Rows 5–12 until piece measures about 6" wide (15 cm). End with Row 12, having just finished 3 rows with C1.

Using C1, bind off loosely. Add more fringe to fill out both ends of the scarf evenly, as shown in the photo on facing page.

Scarf B

| YARN | One skein of each of the following: C1: Violet; C2: Late Summer; C3: Bright Milling Blue |

NOTE: See Preparing for Fringe (page 38) for technique for changing colors. The technique for making this scarf reversible is to make the color changes on alternating sides of the piece — the first color change is done on the "right" side, the second on the "wrong" side, and so on.

SETUP ROW: Using C1, loosely cast on 240 stitches.

ROWS 1–3:   Knit.

ROW 4:   Leaving a 7" (18 cm) tail of both colors, change to C2, and knit to end of row.

ROWS 5 AND 6:   Knit.

ROW 7:   Leaving a 7" (18 cm) tail of both colors, change to C3, and knit to end of row.

ROWS 8 AND 9:   With C3, knit.

ROWS 10–12:   Repeat Rows 4–6.

Continue in this manner, knitting three rows of each color in the same order (C1, C2, C3) until the piece measures about 6" (15 cm) wide. End having just finished 3 rows with C1.

Bind off using C1. Add more fringe to fill out both ends of the scarf evenly, as shown in the photo on page 39.

Scarf C

YARN	One skein of each of the following: C1: Wild Iris; C2: Kiwi; C3: Violet Heather

NOTE: See Preparing for Fringe (page 38) for technique for changing colors. This scarf gets its textural bang with wide, alternating stripes of Seed and Moss Stitch, separated by narrow ridges of garter stitch. This scarf is not truly reversible.

SETUP ROW: Using C1, cast on 240 stitches.

ROWS 1 AND 2:   Using C1, knit to end of row.

ROWS 3 AND 4:   Using C2, *K2, P2; repeat from * to end of row.

ROWS 5 AND 6:   *P2, K2; repeat from * to end of row.

ROWS 7–10:   Repeat Rows 3–6 (Moss Stitch).

ROWS 11 AND 12:   Using C1, knit to end of row.

ROW 13:   Using C3, *K1, P1; repeat from * to end of row.

ROW 14:   *P1, K1; repeat from * to end of row.

ROWS 15–20:   Repeat Rows 13 and 14 (Seed Stitch).

ROWS 21 AND 22:   Using C1, knit to end of row.

ROWS 23–42:   Repeat Rows 3–22 one more time, continuing with the same color sequence.

ROWS 43–52:   Repeat Rows 3–12.

Bind off loosely using C1. Add more fringe to fill out both ends of the scarf evenly, as shown in the photo on page 39.

3 PATTERN STITCHES

This chapter offers a selection of stitches that produce a wide range of effects, both in the way the colors appear and in the fabric created. It also introduces a variety of techniques for stitch manipulation. You'll find sections on slipped stitches, extra wraps, outlined blocks of color, swapping stitches and twists, working into previous rows, manipulating strands, chevrons and ripples, picots, and bobbles. Once you are familiar with these techniques, you can experiment and create your own pattern stitches by changing their placement on the fabric (make them closer together or farther apart) and in relation to the color changes (on the same row as the new color or at another point). If you want them larger, try expanding them over more stitches or rows; if you want them smaller, do the opposite. Like everything in knitting, pattern stitches are open to many variations. (For additional stitch resources, see page 309.)

{Slip Stitch Patterns}

Slipping stitches is one of the simplest knitting techniques, but it offers so many variations that it was difficult to decide what to include in this chapter. I've selected slip stitch patterns that showcase many possible uses and results. You'll find a range of smaller and larger patterns, so you can choose the scale you want for whatever you're making and achieve a variety of effects.

More than a few slipped stitches in the knitted fabric tend to make it tighter and less stretchy. The thicker and denser the fabric, the more yarn it takes to complete your project. Some slipped-stitch fabrics are so tight and have so little stretch that they aren't appropriate for sweaters, but they may be perfect for potholders and placemats. You can control these properties using your needle size. For a stretchy, less dense fabric, use bigger needles; for a tighter, inelastic fabric, use smaller ones. Beware of using too-small needles, however, because you may find it impossible to work the pattern so tightly. As always, it makes sense to experiment to find the best needle size for your project.

Positioning Your Yarn and Needles for Slipping

There are two completely separate elements to slipping stitches: how you insert your needle and where you hold your yarn while you do it. Stitches can be slipped purlwise or knitwise. In some instructions you'll see the phrases "as if to purl" or "as if to knit," which mean exactly the same as "purlwise" and "knitwise."

▲ *Slipping purlwise.* If the instructions don't specify which way to insert your needle, do it purlwise. After working the stitch on the next row, take a look at the results to see if it looks the way you intended. If the stitch has been manipulated so it's now twisted but it shouldn't be, then you'll know it should have been slipped knitwise instead of purlwise. In all the instructions in this chapter, the stitches are slipped purlwise. To slip purlwise, insert your needle through the back of the stitch, just as if you were about to purl it, but rather than purl the stitch, slip it from the left needle onto the right one.

▲ *Slipping knitwise.* Needles can also be inserted knitwise into the front of the stitch, just as if you were about to knit it. Slipping the stitch knitwise rotates it a half-turn, so it ends up on the right needle facing the opposite direction. If this stitch is knit or purled normally on the next row, it will be twisted. There are occasions in which you might twist a stitch intentionally, but when following pattern instructions, don't do it — in other words, don't slip knitwise unless explicitly told to do so. To slip knitwise, insert your needle in the stitch as if you were about to knit, then slip it from the left needle to the right needle.

Positioning your yarn. Yarn can be held either in front of or in back of your work. The yarn is held in back when you knit and in front when you purl, but when you slip a stitch, it may be in either position. Knitting instructions frequently use the abbreviations *wyif* and *wyib,* which stand for "with yarn in front" and "with yarn in back." What does this mean? "Front" is the side facing you on this particular row, and "back" is away from you. These are different from the right side and wrong side of the fabric.

Make sure your yarn is in the correct position before and after you slip the stitch. Keep in mind that you may not need to move it at all. For example, if you're purling the stitch before and after, and the instructions say to slip wyif, the yarn is already in front of your work when you finish the preceding stitch, and it's already in the correct position to purl the following stitch. But if you are knitting the stitch before and after and are told to slip wyif, you knit the preceding stitch, bring the yarn to the front between the two needles, slip the next stitch, bring the yarn to the back between the two needles, then knit the third stitch.

Some instructions use the abbreviations yb and yf. These mean "yarn back" and "yarn front." Instead of telling you the position of the yarn while the stitch is slipped and forcing you to use your wits to move it as necessary, these instructions tell you exactly how and when to move it. For example, the following abbreviations actually mean the same thing:

K1, slip 1 wyif, K1

K1, yf, slip 1, yb, K1

A NOTE ON KNITTING STYLES

The instructions in this book assume that you knit the "standard" way, which means that your stitches are on the knitting needle with the leading leg (the one attached to the strand that travels from the left needle point to the right needle point) in front of the needle. If your stitches are on the needle the opposite way, either all the time or only after purling, then you may need to adjust the directions to achieve the desired results.

When slipping and working decreases, be particularly careful that the stitches face the correct direction and the decreases slant in the correct direction. If you work from left to right across the row, rather than from right to left, you'll need to reverse all the directions that refer to left and right.

STANDARD STYLE. The leading leg (circled) is normally in front on the left-hand needle.

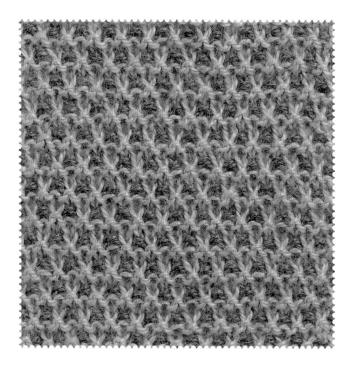

Waffle Check

Tiny purl bumps of the contrasting color nestle in diamonds of the main color. Even though a high proportion of stitches are slipped, Waffle Check is still surprisingly light, stretchy, and fluffy. It doesn't curl since it's based on garter stitch, which is knit on every row, so it's a good choice for sweaters, hats, scarves, or household items like placemats.

Stitches: Odd number

Colors: 2

IN C1, CAST ON.

ROW 1 (WS): In C1, knit.

ROW 2: In C2, K1, * Sl1 wyib, K1; repeat from *.

ROW 3: In C2, *K1, Sl1 wyif; repeat from *, end K1.

ROW 4: In C1, knit.

ROW 5: In C1, knit.

ROW 6: In C2, K1, *K1, Sl1 wyib; repeat from *, end K2.

ROW 7: In C2, K2, *Sl1 wyif, K1; repeat from *, end K1.

ROW 8: In C1, knit.

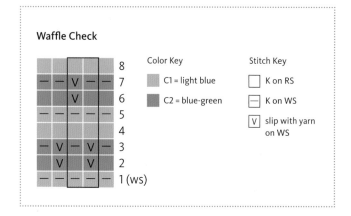

Waffle Check

Color Key
C1 = light blue
C2 = blue-green

Stitch Key
K on RS
K on WS
slip with yarn on WS

CONVERTING PATTERN STITCHES FOR CIRCULAR KNITTING

All of the instructions in this chapter assume you are working back and forth in flat knitting. To work in circular knitting, convert the wrong-side rows into right-side rows. When you do this, all knits become purls and vice versa. Slip stitches purlwise or knitwise as in the original pattern, but hold the yarn in the opposite position on the rows that were originally wrong-side rows. If there are edge stitches that center the pattern on flat knitting, delete them so the pattern repeats seamlessly around. You may find it easier to just read from the charts without rewriting the instructions for the wrong-side rows, but remember to work these rows from right to left. Circular Waffle Check is an example of a converted pattern.

Some pattern stitches are not easily converted from flat to circular knitting. For example, when there is a psso instruction on a wrong-side row, the stitch passed over travels from left to right on the right side of the fabric. If this is done on a wrong-side row, it will travel in the opposite direction. The result may still be acceptable, but it will not be identical to the original and, if some sections of a garment are worked flat and others circularly, the difference will be quite noticeable.

Circular Waffle Check

The chart and directions below have been rewritten for circular knitting.

Stitches: Even number

Colors: 2

IN C1, CAST ON.

ROUND 1: In C1, purl.

ROUND 2: In C2, *Sl1 wyib, K1; repeat from *.

ROUND 3: In C2, *Sl1 wyib, P1; repeat from *.

ROUND 4: In C1, knit.

ROUND 5: In C1, purl.

ROUND 6: In C2, *K1, Sl1 wyib; repeat from *.

ROUND 7: In C2, *P1, Sl1 wyib; repeat from *.

ROUND 8: In C1, knit.

Circular Waffle Check

Color Key

C1 = light blue

C2 = blue-green

Stitch Key

knit

purl

V slip with yarn on WS

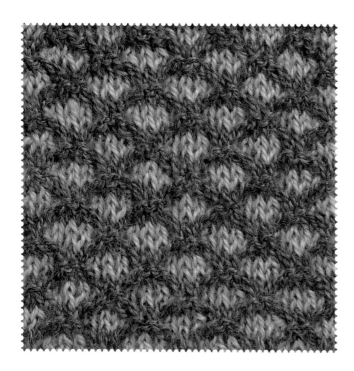

Two-Tone Lattice

This pattern looks quilted, but it's actually formed by cleverly slipping first the contrast color to form the lattice, then the main color to form the diamonds. Two-Tone Lattice has good definition even when knitted loosely, so it is an excellent choice when you want a soft stretchy fabric but a well-defined pattern.

Stitches: Multiple of 6, plus 2
Colors: 2

IN C1, CAST ON.
SETUP ROW (WS): In C1, knit.
ROW 1 (RS): In C2, K1, Sl1 wyib, *K4, Sl2 wyib; repeat from *, end K4, Sl1, K1.
ROW 2: In C2, P1, Sl1 wyif, P4, *Sl2 wyif, P4; repeat from *, end Sl1, P1.
ROW 3: In C1, repeat Row 1.
ROW 4: In C1, K1, Sl1 wyif, K4, *Sl2 wyif, K4; repeat from *, end Sl1, K1.
ROW 5: In C2, K3, *Sl2 wyib, K4; repeat from *, end Sl2, K3.
ROW 6: In C2, P3, *Sl2 wyif, P4; repeat from *, end Sl2, P3.
ROW 7: In C1, repeat Row 5.
ROW 8: In C1, K3, *Sl2 wyif, K4; * repeat from *, end Sl2, K3.

VARIATION

» Use a third color for Rows 5–6.

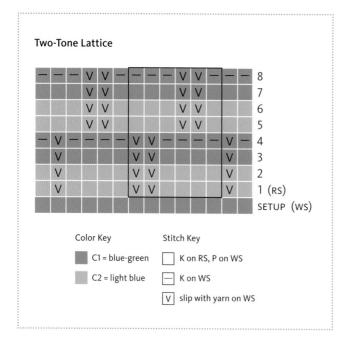

Two-Tone Lattice

Color Key

C1 = blue-green

C2 = light blue

Stitch Key

K on RS, P on WS

— K on WS

V slip with yarn on WS

Three-and-One Stitch

Knit with just two colors, Three-and-One Stitch produces nubbly ribs. It can be confusing until you realize you're working garter stitch, so every row is knitted, but you are always holding the yarn on the wrong side of the fabric while slipping. Each color is used alternately for two rows. Worked in a fine yarn with colors that are close in value, it will produce more blending. It doesn't curl at all, even at the corners. Worked tightly, it's perfect for collars or placemats because it will hold its shape.

Stitches: Multiple of 4, plus 3

Colors: 2

IN C1, CAST ON.

ROW 1 (RS): In C2, K3, *Sl1 wyib, K3; repeat from *.

ROW 2: In C2, *K3, Sl1 wyif; repeat from *, end K3.

ROW 3: In C1, K1, *Sl1 wyib, K3; repeat from *, end Sl1, K1.

ROW 4: In C1, K1, *Sl1 wyif, K3; repeat from *, end, Sl1, K1.

VARIATIONS

» Work in a single color using a variegated yarn.

» Work three colors (or any odd number of colors) repeatedly in the same order to make a check, starting each color on an odd-numbered row and working it for two rows.

» Use three colors, working the first on Rows 1–2 and alternately using the other two for Rows 3–4.

» Use four colors, working each for 2 rows, then repeat.

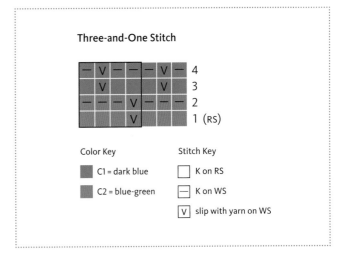

Three-and-One Stitch

Color Key

■ C1 = dark blue

■ C2 = blue-green

Stitch Key

☐ K on RS

⊟ K on WS

Ⅴ slip with yarn on WS

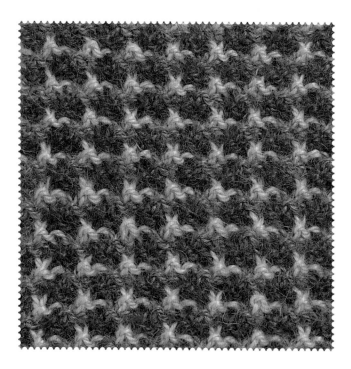

Triple-L Tweed

A nubbly tweed fabric with L-shaped spots of each color, Triple-L Tweed will vary in appearance, depending on the values of the three colors you choose. So that the pattern stitch itself will be noticeable, choose a very light, a medium, and a very dark color. For a more subtle effect, choose colors closer in value. When changing colors, work the new one firmly to prevent flaring along the right edge.

Stitches: Multiple of 3, plus 1
Colors: 3

IN C1, CAST ON.
SETUP ROW (WS): In C1, knit.
ROW 1 (RS): In C2, K3, *Sl1 wyib, K2; repeat from *, end K1.
ROW 2: In C2, K3, *Sl1 wyif, K2; repeat from *, end K1.
ROW 3: In C3, *K2, Sl1 wyib; repeat from *, end K1.
ROW 4: In C3, K1, *Sl1 wyif, K2; repeat from *.
ROW 5: In C1, K1, *Sl1 wyib, K2; repeat from *.
ROW 6: In C1, *K2, Sl1 wyif; repeat from *, end K1.

VARIATIONS
» Use one color for C1 and C2, and a second color for C3, which will set off C3.
» Try variegated yarns for some or all of the colors.

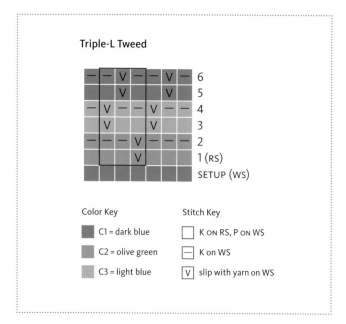

Triple-L Tweed

Color Key
C1 = dark blue
C2 = olive green
C3 = light blue

Stitch Key
K ON RS, P ON WS
K on WS
slip with yarn on WS

Tricolor Fabric Stitch

This is simply Linen Stitch worked in three colors, using each for just one row at a time. Improbably, the slipped stitches line up with the strands that cross the face of the fabric three rows later, to form tiny triangular dots. For all of the colors to be equally visible, it's important to choose a dark, a medium, and a light color to ensure good contrast. The fabric produced behaves like a true woven fabric, is extremely flat, and doesn't curl. Here are some tips to make this more pleasant to knit:

» *Avoiding tight fabric.* The high percentage of slipped stitches may make the fabric tight. If it's difficult to work, change to a larger needle, or adjust by spreading your knitting out on the needles more as you work. Knit a swatch big enough that your tension becomes consistent.

» *Identifying the right side.* When starting this pattern stitch, it can be difficult to tell the right side from the wrong side. Attach a safety pin or marker to the right side of the fabric and work the odd-numbered rows when the side with the safety pin or marker is facing you. You'll discover that there are only two pattern rows: a right side and a wrong side. These are alternated while working one row of each of the three colors.

» *Identifying what row you're on.* If you put your work down and aren't sure where to begin, pick up the color hanging at the beginning of the needle, two rows below the live stitches.

***

Stitches: Odd number

Colors: 3

***

IN C1, CAST ON.

SETUP ROW (WS): In C1, purl.

ROW 1 (RS): In C2, K1, *Sl1 wyif, K1* repeat from *.

ROW 2: In C3, K1, P1, *Sl1 wyib, P1* repeat from *, end K1.

ROW 3: In C1, repeat Row 1.

ROW 4: In C2, repeat Row 2.

ROW 5: In C3, repeat Row 1.

ROW 6: In C1, repeat Row 2.

VARIATION

» Use two balls of the same color and one ball of a contrasting color, which will produce dots of the contrast color on a solid background.

Note: For project using this stitch pattern, see pages 90–93.

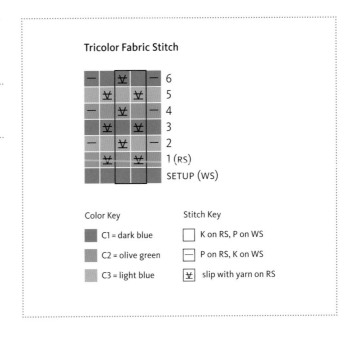

Tricolor Fabric Stitch

Color Key

■ C1 = dark blue

■ C2 = olive green

■ C3 = light blue

Stitch Key

☐ K on RS, P on WS

— P on RS, K on WS

⊻ slip with yarn on RS

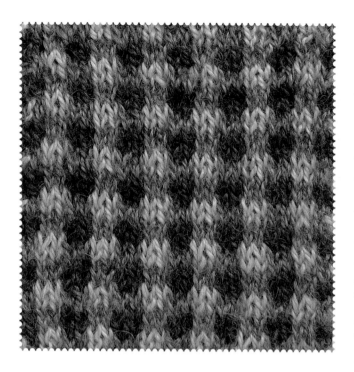

Dice Check

Worked in three shades of one color, using the medium shade as C1, it produces the effect of gingham. Notice that this color is used only one row at a time, first purling across on the wrong side, then, after two rows of another color, knitting across on the right side.

Stitches: Multiple of 4, plus 2
Colors: 3

IN C1, CAST ON.

ROW 1 (WS): In C1, purl.

ROW 2: In C2, K1, Sl1 wyib, *K2, Sl2 wyib; repeat from *, end K2, Sl1, K1.

ROW 3: In C2, P1, Sl1 wyif, P2, *Sl2 wyif, P2; repeat from *, end Sl1, P1.

ROW 4: In C1, knit.

ROW 5: In C3, P2, Sl2 wyif, *P2, Sl2 wyif; repeat from *, end P2.

ROW 6: In C3, K2, *Sl2 wyib, K2; repeat from *.

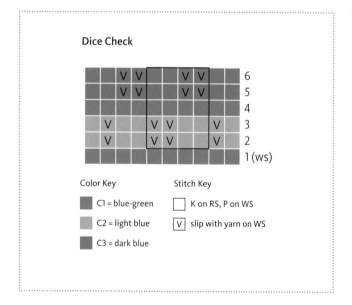

Dice Check

Color Key

■ C1 = blue-green
■ C2 = light blue
■ C3 = dark blue

Stitch Key

□ K on RS, P on WS
V slip with yarn on WS

Thorn Pattern

This pattern stitch looks like little flowers. For the flowers to be visible, use colors very different in value and use the dark color as the background (C2). Notice that the stitches increase on Rows 1 and 5, then return to their original number on Rows 3 and 7. When blocking, do not stretch horizontally, or the foreground pattern will be broken up.

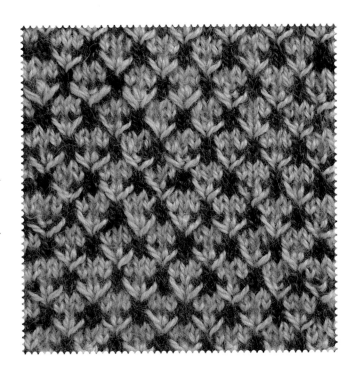

Stitches: Multiple of 4, plus 1
Colors: 2

IN C1, CAST ON.

ROW 1 (RS): In C1, K2, *[K1, yo, K1] in next stitch, K3; repeat from *, end last repeat K2 instead of K3.

ROW 2: In C2, P2, *Sl3 wyif, P3; repeat from *, end last repeat P2 instead of P3.

ROW 3: In C2, K1, *K2tog, Sl1 wyib, ssk, K1; repeat from *.

ROW 4: In C1, P4, *Sl1 wyif, P3; repeat from *, end P1.

ROW 5: In C1, K4, *[K1, yo, K1] in next stitch, K3; repeat from *, end K1.

ROW 6: In C2, P4, *Sl3 wyif, P3; repeat from *, end P1.

ROW 7: In C2, K3, *K2tog, Sl1 wyib, ssk, K1; repeat from *, end K2.

ROW 8: In C1, P2, *Sl1 wyif, P3; repeat from *, end last repeat P2 instead of P3.

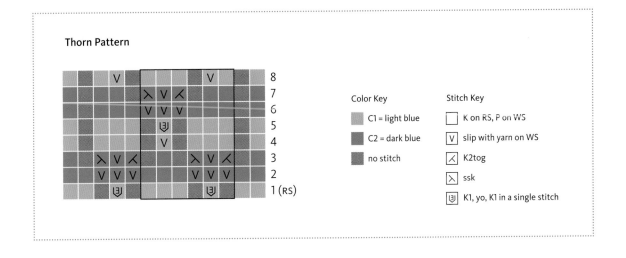

Thorn Pattern

Color Key

- C1 = light blue
- C2 = dark blue
- no stitch

Stitch Key

- K on RS, P on WS
- V slip with yarn on WS
- K2tog
- ssk
- K1, yo, K1 in a single stitch

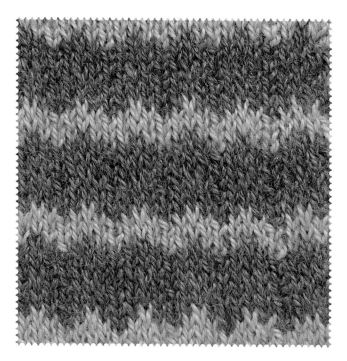

Tricolor Wave Stripes

Slipped stitches create a slightly rippled fabric, carrying each color up into the next stripe. They also make the fabric narrower and less stretchy horizontally than stockinette worked on the same number of stitches.

Stitches: Multiple of 4, plus 1

Colors: 3

IN C1, CAST ON.

SETUP ROW (WS): In C1, purl.

ROW 1 (RS): In C1, K1, *Sl3 wyib, K1; repeat from *.

ROW 2: In C1, P2, *Sl1 wyif, P3; repeat from *, end Sl1, P2.

ROW 3: In C1, knit.

ROW 4: In C1, purl.

ROWS 5–8: In C2, repeat Rows 1–4.

ROWS 9–12: In C3, repeat Rows 1–4.

VARIATION

» Use any number of colors, in any order you please.

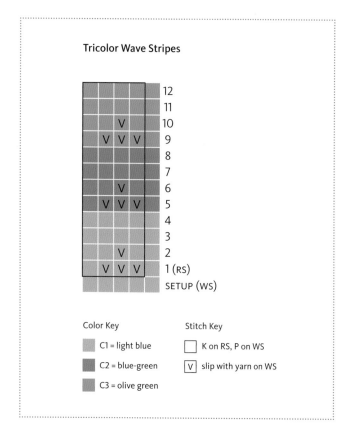

Tricolor Wave Stripes

Color Key

- C1 = light blue
- C2 = blue-green
- C3 = olive green

Stitch Key

- K on RS, P on WS
- V slip with yarn on WS

Windowpane Stripes

This pleasant pattern is a striped garter stitch, broken up by a slipped-stitch pattern. As with garter stitch, it doesn't curl and the fabric is thicker and wider than stockinette. It must be stretched during blocking so that the dots within the windowpanes are visible.

Stitches: Odd number

Colors: 2

IN C1, CAST ON.

ROW 1 (RS): In C2, K1, *Sl1 wyib, K1; repeat from *.

ROW 2: In C2, *P1, Sl1 wyif; repeat from *, end P1.

ROWS 3–4: In C1, knit.

ROWS 5–6: In C2, knit.

ROWS 7–8: In C1, knit.

VARIATION

» Work Rows 5–6 in a third color.

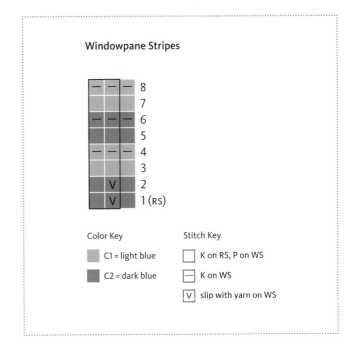

Windowpane Stripes

Color Key

■ C1 = light blue

■ C2 = dark blue

Stitch Key

☐ K on RS, P on WS

— K on WS

V slip with yarn on WS

Ridge Check Pattern

Simple stockinette stripes are broken up by a slipped stitch of the previous color pulled up across the next 4-row stripe. Like stockinette stitch, this pattern curls and requires a border.

Stitches: Multiple of 4, plus 3

Colors: 2

IN C1, CAST ON.

ROW 1 (WS): In C1, purl.

ROW 2: In C2, K3, *Sl1 wyib, K3; repeat from *.

ROW 3: In C2, *P3, Sl1 wyif; repeat from *, end P3.

ROW 4: Repeat Row 2.

ROW 5: In C2, purl.

ROWS 6–8: In C1, repeat Rows 2–4.

VARIATIONS

» Use more colors by changing to a new color on Row 2 and on Row 6.

» Reduce the width of the stripes to 2 rows or expand to 6 rows.

» Rather than slipping the stitch in the same position every time, on each successive stripe slip the stitch halfway between. That is, on Rows 2–4, knit or purl 3 stitches before slipping the next stitch, and on Rows 6–8, knit or purl only 1 stitch before slipping.

» Work the slipped stitches farther apart.

» Work the slipped stitches in different positions so they don't line up on subsequent rows. Swap stitches to make diagonal lines of slipped stitches. *See also* variations at end of chapter (page 87).

Ridge Check Pattern

				V				8
				V				7
				V				6
								5
				V				4
				V				3
				V				2
								1 (ws)

Color Key

■ C1 = dark blue

■ C2 = olive green

Stitch Key

☐ K on RS, P on WS

Ⅴ slip with yarn on WS

Slipped Honeycomb Stripes

Slipping stitches on the wrong-side rows forms longer strands of the yarn on the right side, and changing colors every two rows produces clear stripes, in spite of the texture of the pattern stitch. Since this pattern is based on garter stitch, it produces a thick fabric that doesn't curl. It's not even necessary to block it.

Stitches: Odd number

Colors: 4

IN C1, CAST ON.

ROW 1 (RS): In C1, knit.

ROW 2: In C1, K1, *Sl1 wyib, K1; repeat from *.

ROW 3: In C2, knit.

ROW 4: In C2, K2, *Sl1 wyib, K1; repeat from *, end last repeat K2.

ROW 5: In C1, knit.

ROW 6: In C1, K1, *Sl1 wyib, K1; repeat from *.

ROW 7: In C3, knit.

ROW 8: In C3, K2, *Sl1 wyib, K1; repeat from *, end last repeat K2.

ROW 9: In C4, knit.

ROW 10: In C4, K1, *Sl1 wyib, K1; repeat from *.

ROW 11: In C3, knit.

ROW 12: In C3, K2, *Sl1 wyib, K1; repeat from *, end last repeat K2.

VARIATION

» Use as many or as few colors as you like, starting each one on a right-side row and working two rows of each.

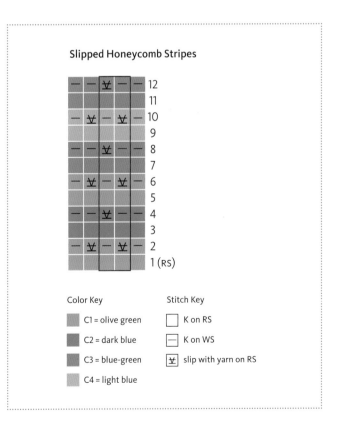

Slipped Honeycomb Stripes

Color Key

C1 = olive green

C2 = dark blue

C3 = blue-green

C4 = light blue

Stitch Key

K on RS

K on WS

slip with yarn on RS

Dotted Ladders

This looks like a vertical cousin of Windowpane Stripes, but since it's based on stockinette stitch, it will curl unless provided with borders. To make the stripes neater, stretch it vertically while blocking.

Stitches: Multiple of 6, plus 5
Colors: 2

IN C1, CAST ON.

SETUP ROW (WS): In C1, purl.

ROW 1 (RS): In C2, K1 *Sl1 wyib, K1, Sl1 wyib, K3; repeat from *, end last repeat with K1.

ROW 2: In C2, K1, *Sl1 wyif, K1, Sl1 wyif, P3; repeat from *, end [Sl1 wyif, K1] twice.

ROW 3: In C1, K1, *K3, Sl1 wyib, K1, Sl1 wyib; repeat from *, end K4.

ROW 4: In C1, K1, *P3, Sl1 wyif, K1, Sl1 wyif; repeat from *, end P3, K1.

Dotted Ladders

−				V	−	V				−	4
				V		V					3
−	V	−	V				V	−	V	−	2
	V		V				V		V		1 (RS)
											SETUP (WS)

Color Key

■ C1 = blue-green
▨ C2 = light blue

Stitch Key

□ K on RS, P on WS
− K on WS
V slip with yarn on WS

{Outlined Patterns}

Outlined blocks of color can be a challenge in knitting, but simple slipped-stitch techniques make it easy to draw shapes in one or more colors against a solid background.

Bricks

In this very satisfying but easy to execute pattern, C1, the mortar, outlines C2, the bricks. If your bricks aren't rectangular, you may need to gently block them horizontally to whip them into shape.

Stitches: Multiple of 4, plus 3
Colors: 2

IN C1, CAST ON.
ROW 1 (RS): In C1, knit.
ROW 2: In C1, knit.
ROW 3: In C2, K1, *Sl1 wyib, K3; repeat from *, end Sl1, K1.
ROW 4: In C2, P1, *Sl1 wyif, P3; repeat from *, end Sl1, P1.
ROWS 5–6: In C1, knit.
ROW 7: In C2, K3, *Sl1 wyib, K3; repeat from *.
ROW 8: In C2, P3, *Sl1 wyif, P3; repeat from *.

VARIATIONS

» Use a different color for C2 on Rows 7–8 than on Rows 3–4. Use as many different colors as you like.
» Use a variegated yarn for C2.
» Make the pattern wider by slipping more stitches between worked stitches.

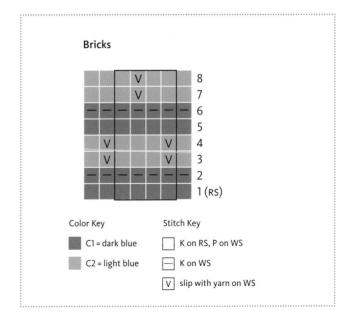

Bricks

Color Key
C1 = dark blue
C2 = light blue

Stitch Key
K on RS, P on WS
K on WS
slip with yarn on WS

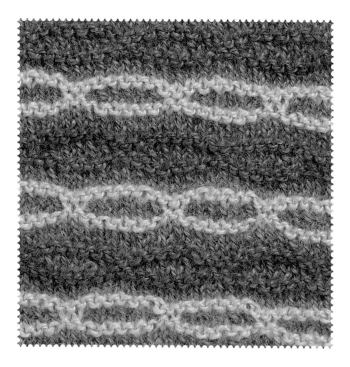

Chain Stripes

Garter stitch chains of the contrast colors snake across the smooth main-color background. This is a great way to showcase a small amount of a cherished yarn or set off a heavily textured yarn. For a more subtle effect, use yarns that are similar in color.

Stitches: Multiple of 8, plus 6

Colors: 3

IN C1, CAST ON.

ROW 1 (RS): In C1, knit.

ROW 2: In C1, purl.

ROWS 3–4: In C2, knit.

ROW 5: In C1, K6, *Sl2 wyib, K6; repeat from *.

ROW 6: In C1, P6, *Sl2 wyif, P6; repeat from *.

ROW 7: In C2; repeat Row 5.

ROW 8: In C2, knit.

ROWS 9–10: In C1; repeat Rows 1–2.

ROWS 11–12: In C3, knit.

ROW 13: In C1, K2, *Sl2 wyib, K6; repeat from *, end Sl2, K2.

ROW 14: In C1, P2, *Sl2 wyif, P6; repeat from *, end Sl2, P2.

ROW 15: In C3; repeat Row 13.

ROW 16: In C3, knit.

VARIATIONS

» Repeating Rows 1–8, whether the contrast color changes or not, will line up the links of the chains rather than stagger them.

» Use as many or as few colors as you like for C2 and C3.

» Change the background color.

» Add garter ridges in the contrast color or colors between Rows 1 and 2 and again between Rows 9 and 10.

» See photos on page 88 for some of these variations.

Chain Stripes

Color Key

■ C1 = olive green

■ C2 = light blue

■ C3 = dark blue

Stitch Key

☐ K on RS, P on WS

— K on WS

V̄ slip with yarn on WS

Hexagon Pattern

If you've ever wanted to knit chicken wire, this is the way to do it! Garter stitch hexagons outline the background color. You'll notice that this is really a variation of Chain Stripes, except that the garter-stitch chains are all the same color and, because there's no background separating them, the chains are thicker. To turn the naturally occurring rectangles into hexagons, block and stretch the fabric.

Stitches: Multiple of 8, plus 6
Colors: 2

IN C1, CAST ON.

ROW 1 (RS): In C1, knit.

ROW 2: In C1, knit.

ROW 3: In C2, K2, *Sl2 wyib, K6; repeat from *, end Sl2, K2.

ROW 4: In C2, P2, *Sl2 wyif, P6; repeat from *, end Sl2, P2.

ROWS 5–8: Repeat Rows 3–4 twice.

ROWS 9–12: In C1, knit.

ROW 13: In C2, K6, *Sl2 wyib, K6; repeat from *.

ROW 14: In C2, P6, *Sl2 wyif, P6; repeat from *.

ROWS 15–18: Repeat Rows 13–14 twice.

ROWS 19–20: In C1, knit.

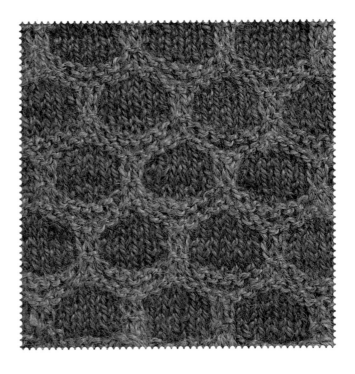

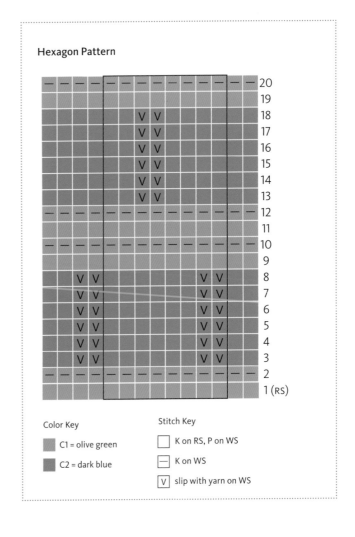

Hexagon Pattern

Color Key

■ C1 = olive green

■ C2 = dark blue

Stitch Key

☐ K on RS, P on WS

— K on WS

[V] slip with yarn on WS

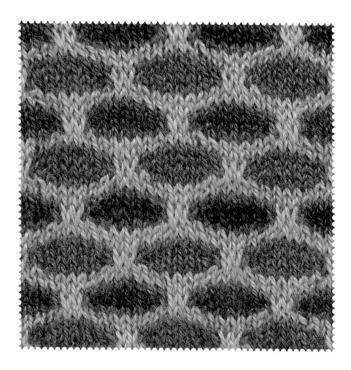

Outlined Check

Two different-colored lozenges, outlined by a third color, float on a contrasting background. Slipping stitches and working only one color at a time is much easier than achieving the same effect in intarsia.

The background color (C1) is used two rows at a time, starting from the right edge (right side, then wrong side). The two contrasting colors (C3 and C4) are worked from the left edge, two rows at a time (wrong side, then right side). The outline color (C2) is worked only one row at a time, back and forth between the other yarns.

Stitches: Multiple of 10, plus 4
Colors: 4

IN C1, CAST ON.

ROW 1 (RS): In C1, knit.

ROW 2: In C1, purl.

ROW 3: In C2, K1, *Sl2 wyib, K8; repeat from *, end Sl2, K1.

ROW 4: In C3, P1, Sl3 wyif, *P6, Sl4 wyif; repeat from *, end P6, Sl3, P1.

ROW 5: In C3, K1, Sl3 wyib, *K6, Sl4 wyib; repeat from *, end K6, Sl3, K1.

ROW 6: In C2, P1, *Sl2 wyif, P8; repeat from *, end Sl2, P1.

ROW 7: In C1, knit.

ROW 8: In C1, purl.

ROW 9: In C2, K6, *Sl2 wyib, K8; repeat from *, end Sl2, K6.

ROW 10: In C4, P5, *Sl4 wyif, P6; repeat from *, end Sl4, P5.

ROW 11: In C4, K5, *Sl4 wyib, K6; repeat from *, end Sl4, K5.

ROW 12: In C2, P6, *Sl2 wyif, P8; repeat from *, end Sl2, P6.

VARIATION

» Change to a new outline color (C2) or inner color (C3 or C4) on the first row of each pair; if you want to change the background, introduce a new C1 on either Row 2 or Row 8, then work the next row of C1 (Row 7 or Row 1) in the same color. (See photos on page 89.)

Outlined Check

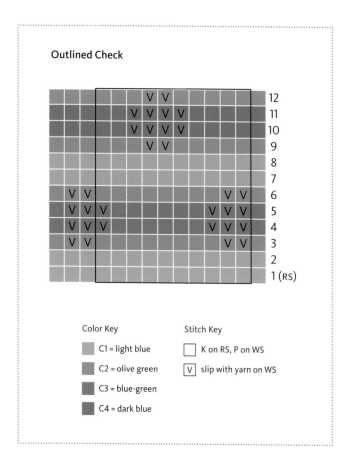

Color Key

■ C1 = light blue

■ C2 = olive green

■ C3 = blue-green

■ C4 = dark blue

Stitch Key

□ K on RS, P on WS

Ⅴ slip with yarn on WS

{Extra Wraps}

Extra wraps around the needle when knitting or purling add extra yarn to selected stitches. On following rows, the extra wraps can be dropped to make taller stitches, which are sometimes left loose and sometimes pulled up vertically or horizontally across the face of the fabric. The extra height of these stitches allows them to stretch and other stitches to be slipped without distorting the fabric and making it denser. You'll need to know the following basic techniques to work these stitches.

Yarn over. Extra wraps are sometimes made between stitches, simply by working several yarn overs. Wrap the yarn around the needle once for each yarn over.

▲ *Dropping the extra wraps.* A stitch with extra wraps is connected to the stitch below it by a vertical strand at its beginning and end, just like a normal stitch. In between, the extra wraps hug the needle tightly. To drop the extra wraps when knitting, purling, or slipping a stitch, insert the needle between the two vertical strands and work it as you normally would (C). When you slide the stitch off the needle, the extra wraps drop naturally, without any extra effort on your part.

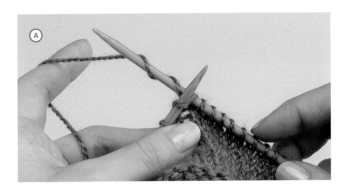

▲ *Wrapping the yarn twice around the needle.* You'll see this instruction for both knit and purl stitches. Instructions may call for wrapping the yarn three or even four times around the needle. Insert your needle into the stitch as usual, wrap (or pick) the yarn once as usual, wrap (or pick) it a second time (A). Draw the double wrap through the old stitch to form a new one, then slide the old stitch off the left needle (B).

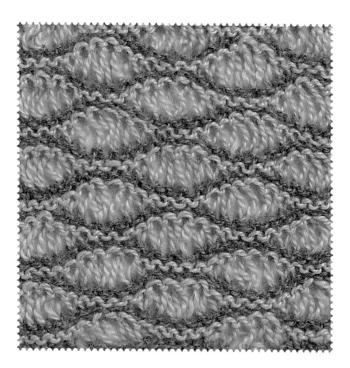

stretch the loops to their fullest extent during blocking to even out the waves and flatten the fabric.

Stitches: Multiple of 10, plus 6
Colors: 2

IN C1, CAST ON.
ROW 1 (RS): In C1, knit.
ROW 2: In C1, knit.
ROW 3: In C2, K6, *yo twice, K1, yo 3 times, K1, yo 4 times, K1, yo 3 times, K1, yo twice, K6; repeat from *.
ROW 4: In C2, knit, dropping all yarn overs.
ROWS 5–6: In C1, knit.
ROW 7: In C2, K1, *yo twice, K1, yo 3 times, K1, yo 4 times, K1, yo 3 times, K1, yo twice, K6; repeat from *, end last repeat K1 instead of K6.
ROW 8: In C2, knit, dropping all yarn overs.

Seafoam Stripes

Dropped yarn overs alone, in a sea of garter stitch, form this lacy wave pattern. Yarn overs on Rows 3 and 7 increase the number of stitches dramatically, but all of these are dropped on the following row, returning to the original stitch count. C1 forms the ridges between the waves of C2. Since it's based on garter stitch, the fabric won't curl, so it's wonderful for lacy scarves and shawls.

Use a needle small enough to knit the garter stitch ridges at a normal gauge; resist the urge to use a larger needle, or the waves will be ill-defined. You'll need to

VARIATIONS

» Use a textured yarn for C1.
» To make very open lace, use a fine yarn for C2.
» Rather than using C1 for the garter-stitch ridge between waves of C2, work Rows 1–4 in one color and Rows 5–8 in a second color, creating interlocking waves of color.
» Use a different color for C2 in Rows 7–8 than you did in Rows 3–4 — alternate just two colors or keep changing colors throughout.

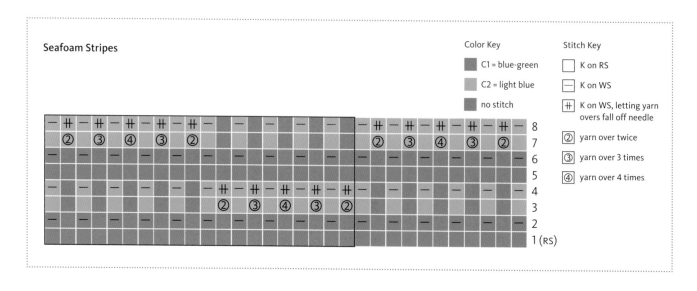

Seafoam Stripes

Color Key
■ C1 = blue-green
■ C2 = light blue
■ no stitch

Stitch Key
☐ K on RS
⊟ K on WS
⊞ K on WS, letting yarn overs fall off needle
② yarn over twice
③ yarn over 3 times
④ yarn over 4 times

Shadow-Box Pattern

Contrast and texture work together to create depth in the pattern stitch. You'll need three colors with distinct contrast: a light, a medium, and a dark. Use the light color for the C1 frames, the dark color for C2 to create the shadow that lines two sides of the frame, and the medium color for C3.

As you work, notice that the yarn is always held on the wrong side of the fabric while slipping stitches and that, while the rest is worked in garter stitch, the second row of C3, with the exception of the first and last stitches, is purled on the wrong side to create stockinette stitch. The large proportion of garter stitch prevents curling, however blocking and stretching slightly will open up the boxes to show off C3.

Stitches: Multiple of 4, plus 3
Colors: 3

IN C1, CAST ON.
ROW 1 (RS): In C1, knit.
ROW 2: In C1, K1, *K1, wrapping the yarn twice around the needle, K3; repeat from *, end last repeat K1 instead of K3.
ROW 3: In C2, K1, *Sl1 wyib, dropping the extra wrap, K3; repeat from *, end last repeat K1 instead of K3.
ROW 4: In C2, K1, *Sl1 wyif, K3; repeat from *, end Sl1, K1.
ROW 5: In C3, K1, *Sl2 wyib, K2; repeat from *, end Sl1, K1.
ROW 6: In C3, K1, Sl1 wyif, *P2, Sl2 wyif; repeat from *, end K1.

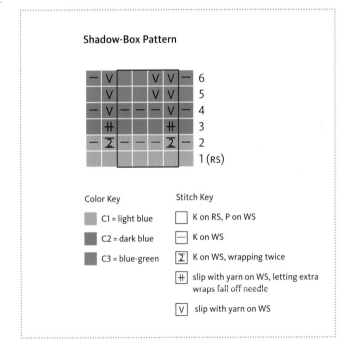

Shadow-Box Pattern

Color Key
C1 = light blue
C2 = dark blue
C3 = blue-green

Stitch Key
K on RS, P on WS
K on WS
K on WS, wrapping twice
slip with yarn on WS, letting extra wraps fall off needle
slip with yarn on WS

{Twisting and Swapping}

Working the stitches on the left needle out of order, or rearranging them before they are knit, has the same effect as rearranging stitches using a cable needle. In combination with colored stripes and extra wraps, they incorporate contrasting cables or surface decoration into the knitted fabric. Twists are tiny two-stitch cables, made without cable needles and without removing the stitches from the needle until both stitches have been worked.

Right Twist

1] Knit into the front of the second stitch.

2] Draw the yarn through, but leave the stitch on the left needle.

3] Knit into the first stitch as usual, then slide both off the needle.

Left Twist

1] Knit into the back of the second stitch. Draw the yarn through, but leave the stitch on the left needle.

2] Knit into the first stitch as usual, then slide both off the needle.

▲ *Mission accomplished!* The completed columns of right and left twists mirror each other when done correctly.

Twisted Ladder

Since these small cables have a garter stitch stripe background, the fabric doesn't curl. Slipping the cable stitches when working with the contrasting background yarn makes them a solid color. This pattern stitch is successful when worked either firmly or loosely. The cables, however, are more easily worked in a loose fabric.

Stitches: Multiple of 5, plus 4
Colors: 2

IN C1, CAST ON.

ROW 1 (RS): In C1, K1, *right twist, K3; repeat from *, end right twist, K1.

ROW 2: In C1, K1, P2, *K3, P2; repeat from *, end K1.

ROW 3: In C2, K1, *Sl2 wyib, K3; repeat from *, end Sl2 wyib, K1.

ROW 4: In C2, K1, Sl2 wyif, *K3, Sl2 wyif; repeat from *, end K1.

VARIATIONS

» Substitute left twist for right twist.

» Alternate left twist and right twist on Row 1, making the columns twist toward and away from each other.

» Use Tweed Stitch instead of twists: Knit into the second stitch, inserting your needle all the way through to the back, then wrapping the yarn and drawing it out to the front, but don't slide the stitch off the needle. Knit the first and second stitches together and finally slide both off the needle. The result looks similar to a right twist but is more easily executed.

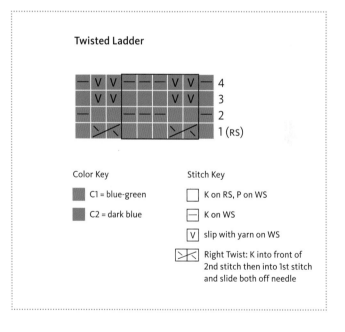

Twisted Ladder

Color Key

C1 = blue-green

C2 = dark blue

Stitch Key

K on RS, P on WS

K on WS

V slip with yarn on WS

Right Twist: K into front of 2nd stitch then into 1st stitch and slide both off needle

Executing a Swap

Drop a stitch off the needle, slip stitches to get them out of the way, then replace the dropped stitch on the needle in a different position. Don't worry about the stitches unraveling while you do this — as long as you don't stretch the knitting horizontally before placing the stitches back on the needle. To create different effects, the specific steps may vary, so follow each pattern's instructions exactly.

Gull Check

C2 forms the background and C1 the contrasting wings that cross the fabric. The best effect will be achieved by using a dark color for C2 and a lighter color for C1. Two colors of fine yarn with less contrast will create a blended effect. See chart for right and left swap directions.

Stitches: Multiple of 7, plus 1
Colors: 2

IN C1, CAST ON.
ROW 1 (WS): In C1, K3, *P2, K5; repeat from *, end last repeat K3 instead of K5.
ROW 2: In C2, K3, Sl2 wyib, *K5, Sl2 wyib; repeat from *, end K3.
ROW 3: In C2, P3, Sl2 wyif, *P5, Sl2 wyif; repeat from *, end P3.
ROWS 4 AND 5: Repeat Rows 2 and 3.
ROW 6: In C1, *K1, Right Swap, Left Swap; repeat from *, end K1.

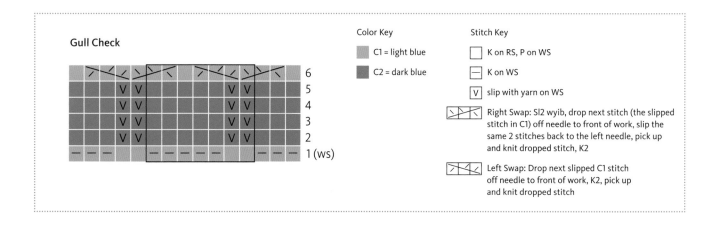

Gull Check

Color Key
C1 = light blue
C2 = dark blue

Stitch Key
K on RS, P on WS
K on WS
V slip with yarn on WS
Right Swap: Sl2 wyib, drop next stitch (the slipped stitch in C1) off needle to front of work, slip the same 2 stitches back to the left needle, pick up and knit dropped stitch, K2
Left Swap: Drop next slipped C1 stitch off needle to front of work, K2, pick up and knit dropped stitch

Winged Wave

In Winged Wave, using a variation of the technique in Gull Check, the fabric is covered with wings of both colors. This pattern combines slipped stitches, swapped stitches, and extra wraps. Drop the wraps on subsequent rows to make loose stitches, and pull the stitches taller by slipping them for several rows. Finally, rearrange the stitches to make wings. As with most pattern stitches, this one will be more dramatic with greater contrast between the colors. See chart for right and left swap directions.

Stitches: Multiple of 8, plus 2

Colors: 2

IN C1, CAST ON.

SETUP ROW 1 (WS): In C1, K4, *P2, wrapping yarn twice for each stitch, K6; repeat from *, end last repeat K4 instead of K6.

SETUP ROW 2: In C2, K4, *Sl2 wyib, dropping the extra wraps, K6; repeat from *, end last repeat K4 instead of K6.

ROW 1 (WS): In C2, K4, *Sl2 wyif, K6; repeat from *, end last repeat K4 instead of K6.

ROW 2: In C2, K4, *Sl2 wyib, K6; repeat from *, end last repeat K4 instead of K6.

ROW 3: In C2, K3, *P1, wrapping yarn twice, Sl2 wyif, P1 wrapping yarn twice, K4; repeat from *, end last repeat K3 instead of K4.

ROW 4: In C1, K1, *Right Swap, Left Swap; repeat from *, end K1.

ROWS 5–8: Repeat pattern Rows 1–4, reversing colors.

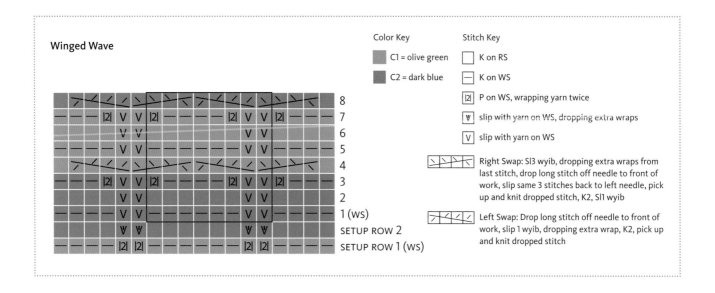

{Working into Rows Below}

You may work into rows below the current row for several reasons: to add depth and texture to the knitting, to draw colors from previous rows up higher, and to pull strands of the current color across the face of the fabric. There are several different techniques for working into these lower rows: knit below, purl below; dropping and unraveling, and dip stitches.

Knit Below

Usually you insert your right needle into the first stitch on the left needle and form a new stitch by pulling the working yarn through that single stitch. When you "knit below," you knit into the stitch one row lower instead.

After the new stitch is completed, there are two strands of yarn around its base: one strand from the lower stitch and one from the higher stitch. The strand from the higher row unravels and slumps down to form an inverted V. When these Vs are repeated using contrasting colors, they add visual interest because of the diagonal lines they create. They also add more depth to the fabric, making it both thicker and softer. Some of the patterns created this way are called *brioche stitches*.

1] Insert your right needle into the stitch directly below the first stitch all the way through to the back of the fabric.

2] Wrap or pick the yarn as usual and pull the new stitch out to the front, knitting the lower stitch together with the one on the needle, then slide the stitch off the left needle. In the same fashion, you can purl into the stitch below by bringing the yarn forward, then inserting the needle from the back of the fabric one row lower than usual.

Checked Rose Fabric

This pattern will spread in width, so be careful to cast on and bind off loosely. Both sides of the fabric are very pleasant, but the honeycomb effect is only seen on the right side. For a fabric where the checked pattern is obvious, choose two colors with very different values. Colors with little contrast will blend together. Like other stitches in the brioche family, Checked Rose Fabric is thick and fluffy. Here, C1 is the background color, while C2 forms the lattice.

Notice that C2 is worked two rows at a time, but C1 is only worked one row at a time. You must use two double-pointed needles or a circular needle and work across twice on the same side (once with C2 and again with C1), so you never need to cut the yarn. You may find it helpful to mark the right side of the fabric with a safety pin or split marker. If you find it difficult to knit into the stitch below on the first and last stitch of the row, knit the stitch instead.

Stitches: Odd number

Colors: 2

IN C1, CAST ON.

SETUP ROW (RS): In C1, knit.

ROW 1 (WS): In C2, *K1, knit below; repeat from *, end K1.

ROW 2 (RS): In C2, knit below, *K1, knit below; repeat from *.

ROW 3 (WS): In C1, *K1, knit below; repeat from *, end K1.

ROW 4 (WS): Do not turn your work; instead, slide all stitches to the other end of the needle. In C2, *knit below, K1; repeat from * and knit below.

ROW 5 (RS): In C2, K1, *knit below, K1; repeat from *.

ROW 6 (RS): Do not turn your work; instead, slide all stitches to the other end of the needle. In C1, knit below, *K1, knit below; repeat from *.

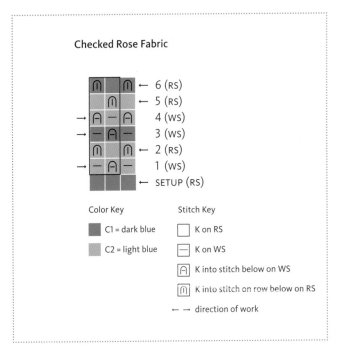

Checked Rose Fabric

← 6 (RS)
← 5 (RS)
→ 4 (WS)
→ 3 (WS)
← 2 (RS)
→ 1 (WS)
← SETUP (RS)

Color Key

◼ C1 = dark blue

◼ C2 = light blue

Stitch Key

☐ K on RS

⊟ K on WS

Ⓐ K into stitch below on WS

⋔ K into stitch on row below on RS

← → direction of work

Corrugated Brioche Rib

By knitting and purling into the row below, it's possible to produce a completely reversible Brioche or Shaker Rib, with knit ribs in one color on one side and in the other color on the reverse. This is the perfect stitch for a soft stretchy scarf, if it's cast on and bound off very loosely. The edges of the fabric tend to be loose, so be sure to tighten the yarn a bit before you begin each row. Because of these tension issues, it's important to swatch this stitch not only for gauge but so you can work it consistently once you begin your project.

Here are a few tips to make this pattern go more smoothly:

Use double-pointed or circular needles. Because you'll knit only one row at a time with each color, use two double-pointed needles or a circular needle. These allow you to work across once in each color in one direction, then turn and do the same in the other direction.

Determine direction and proper yarn. If you find it difficult to determine which direction to work or which yarn to use on any given row, look at the stitches already on the needle, which will all be in one color. Use the other color, starting from the end of the needle it's attached to.

Determine whether to knit or purl. If you can't tell whether you should knit or purl the row as you begin the row, look at the side of the fabric facing you. If the knit ribs are in the color you're working with, then you are doing a row with knits and knit belows; but if they're in the other color, you're working a row with purls and purl belows.

Corrugated Brioche Rib

→ | — | — | A | — | — | 4 (WS)
→ | | ∩ | | ∩ | | 3 (WS)
   | — | — | A | — | — | ← 2 (RS)
   | | ∩ | | ∩ | | ← 1 (RS)
→ | — | — | — | — | — | SETUP (WS)

Color Key

▪ C1 = blue-green

▪ C2 = light blue

Stitch Key

☐ K on RS, P on WS

⊟ P on RS, K on WS

Ⓐ P into stitch on row below on RS, K into stitch below on WS

ⓜ K into stitch on row below on RS, P into stitch below on WS

← → direction of work

Stitches: Odd number

Colors: 2

IN C1, CAST ON.

SETUP ROW (WS): In C1, knit.

ROW 1 (RS): In C2, K1, *knit below, K1; repeat from *. Do not turn your work; instead, slide all stitches to the other end of the needle.

ROW 2 (RS): In C1, P1, *P1, purl below; repeat from *, end P2. Turn before working next row.

ROW 3 (WS): In C2, *P1, purl below; repeat from *, end P1. Do not turn your work; instead, slide all stitches to the other end of the needle.

ROW 4 (WS): In C1, K2, *knit below, K1; repeat from *, end knit below, K2. Turn before working next row.

To end, bind off while working either Row 1 or Row 4, purling rather than knitting the plain stitches and knitting below as usual. Remember to bind off very loosely.

Drop and Unravel

A variation on knitting into the row below is to knit more than just the top two rows together. You actually unravel the stitches before knitting them together. This gathers all the loose strands together, making a pleasant change in texture from the ubiquitous stockinette stitch.

1] Drop the stitch off the left needle. Intentionally unravel the number of rows specified.

2] Insert the right needle into the highest stitch that is not unraveled, being careful to go under all the loose strands.

3] Knit the stitch and the loose strands together.

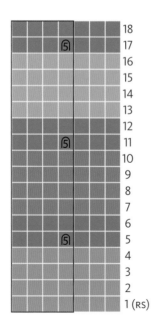

Four-Color Windowpanes

Four-Color Windowpanes

This pattern creates a stable grid, with the main color forming the lattice and the other three colors changing behind it, and has an extremely pleasing scalloped bottom edge. Its small scale is appropriate for placemats and pillows, as well as garments. Since it stretches horizontally, but not vertically, Four-Color Windowpanes is particularly good for bags. Amazingly, it doesn't curl at all, so you might even try it for a scarf. When knit firmly, the contrasting colors bubble out between the window frames. When knit loosely, it can be blocked flat. (For project using this stitch pattern, see page 90.)

Stitches: Multiple of 4, plus 3

Colors: 4

IN C1, CAST ON.

ROW 1 (RS): In C2, knit.

ROW 2: In C2, purl.

ROWS 3–4: Repeat Rows 1–2.

ROW 5: In C1, K3, *drop the next stitch, unravel 4 rows, insert needle from the front into stitch on fifth row below then knit it, catching all strands, K3; repeat from *.

ROW 6: In C1, purl.

ROWS 7–12: Repeat Rows 1–6, substituting C3 for C2.

ROWS 13–18: Repeat Rows 1–6, substituting C4 for C2.

VARIATIONS

» Use as many or as few contrast colors as you like, but maintain the same color for C1 throughout.

» Use variegated yarns for all three contrast colors, with a solid for the main color.

» Use a ribbon yarn or other novelty yarn for the main color.

Color Key

■ C1 = dark blue

■ C2 = olive green

■ C3 = blue-green

■ C4 = light blue

Stitch Key

□ K on RS, P on WS

ⓢ drop, unravel 5 rows, insert needle from RS into stitch 5 rows below and K

Dip Stitch

Dip Stitches are worked through stitches lower in the fabric, but no stitches are dropped or unraveled. Take care to work them loosely enough to avoid puckering the fabric. Dip Stitches tend to look uneven, and small holes may appear on either side of them. For this reason, they work best in a firmly knit base fabric.

1] Insert the right needle into the desired stitch from the front.

2] Wrap the working yarn around the needle and pull a new stitch out through the fabric, elongate it, and, following the instructions, either leave it on the right needle or place it on the left needle. Work this new stitch together with the next stitch to preserve the original number of stitches.

Dip-Stitch Stripes

This simple broken striped pattern has the same gauge as stockinette stitch because the dip stitch forms a new stitch on the fabric's surface, rather than distorting it. See chart for Dip Stitch instructions.

Stitches: Multiple of 6, plus 1
Colors: 2

IN C1, CAST ON.
SETUP ROW 1 (RS): In C1, knit.
SETUP ROW 2: In C1, purl.
SETUP ROW 3: In C2, knit.
ROW 1 (WS): In C2, purl.
ROW 2: In C2, knit.
ROW 3: In C2, purl.
ROW 4: In C1, K3, *work Dip Stitch, K5; repeat from *, end last repeat
K3 instead of K5.
ROW 5: In C1, purl.
ROW 6: In C1, knit.
ROW 7: In C1, purl.
ROW 8: In C2, K6, * work Dip Stitch, K5; repeat from *, end last repeat K6 instead of K5.

VARIATIONS

» Add more colors, starting new ones on Rows 4 and 8.
» Make the stripes wider or narrower, but be sure to work the dip stitch in the stitch two rows below the color change.

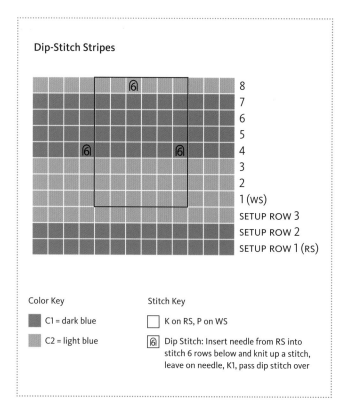

Dip-Stitch Stripes

8
7
6
5
4
3
2
1 (WS)
SETUP ROW 3
SETUP ROW 2
SETUP ROW 1 (RS)

Color Key

■ C1 = dark blue
■ C2 = light blue

Stitch Key

☐ K on RS, P on WS

ⓖ Dip Stitch: Insert needle from RS into stitch 6 rows below and knit up a stitch, leave on needle, K1, pass dip stitch over

{Manipulating Strands}

Slipping groups of stitches with the yarn on the right side of the fabric creates long horizontal strands that are caught up in stitches on later rows, leaving diagonal embellishments across the background. All of the patterns in this section are worked by slipping a series of stitches, on just one row or on several consecutive rows, while holding the working yarn on the right side of the fabric.

2] Knit them all together.

Alternately, insert the left needle under all the strands, then, using the right needle, knit the stitch and the strands together.

1] To knit the strands together with a stitch, insert the right needle under all the strands, then into the next stitch.

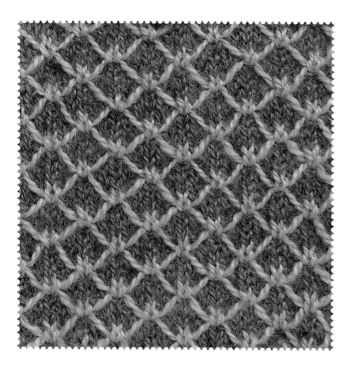

Royal Quilting

A fine web of the contrast color crosses a stockinette background. Of the many quilted patterns, this one produces the neatest results. The quality of the fabric varies a great deal depending on how tightly it's knit. Knit firmly, the fabric will be stiff and inelastic, useful for tailored garments or bags that need to keep their shape. Knit loosely, it's excellent for stretchy nonstructured garments.

Stitches: Multiple of 6, plus 3
Colors: 2

IN C1, CAST ON.
ROW 1 (WS): In C1, K1, P1, *Sl5 wyib, P1; repeat from *, end K1.
ROW 2: In C2, knit.
ROW 3: In C2, K1, purl until 1 stitch remains, end K1.
ROW 4: In C1, K1, Sl3 wyib, *insert needle under loose strand of C1 from Row 1, knit the next stitch so that this strand is caught behind it, Sl5 wyib; repeat from *, end last repeat Sl3 wyib, K1.
ROW 5: In C1, K1, Sl3 wyib, *P1, Sl5 wyib; repeat from *, end P1, Sl3 wyib, K1.
ROWS 6–7: Repeat Rows 2–3.
ROW 8: In C1, K1, *pick up loose strand from Row 5, K1 catching strand behind stitch, Sl5 wyib; repeat from *, pick up loose strand and K1, catching strand behind stitch, K1.

Royal Quilting

Color Key
C1 = light blue
C2 = blue-green

Stitch Key
K on RS
P on RS, K on WS
slip with yarn on RS
slip with yarn on WS
insert needle under loose strand and K next stitch, catching strand behind it

Butterfly Stripes

Strands from slipped stitches are gathered together into the tiny butterflies that give this pattern its name, but the overall effect is of textured diamonds.

Stitches: Multiple of 10, plus 9

Colors: 2

IN C1, CAST ON.

ROWS 1, 3, AND 5 (WS): In C1, P2, *Sl5 wyib, P5; repeat from *, end Sl5, P2.

ROWS 2 AND 4: In C1, knit.

ROW 6: In C2, K4, *insert the right needle under the three loose strands and knit the next stitch, bringing the new stitch out under the strands, K9; repeat from *, end last repeat K4 instead of K9.

ROWS 7, 9, AND 11: In C2, P7, *Sl5 wyib, P5; repeat from *, end P2.

ROWS 8 AND 10: In C2, knit.

ROW 12: In C1, K9, *lift and knit all strands together with the next stitch as on Row 6, K9; repeat from *.

VARIATION

» To add more colors, change to new color on Rows 6 and 12.

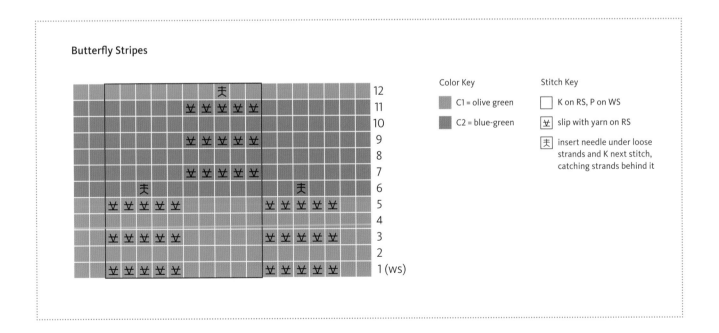

Butterfly Stripes

Color Key	Stitch Key
☐ C1 = olive green	☐ K on RS, P on WS
☐ C2 = blue-green	⊻ slip with yarn on RS
	丰 insert needle under loose strands and K next stitch, catching strands behind it

{Chevrons and Ripples}

The angular zigzags of chevrons are formed by positioning a series of decreases in columns, with increases lined up in columns between them. The curves of rippled patterns are made by placing groups of decreases on one row between groups of increases from a previous row or rows.

Welted Stripes Fantastic

All the shaping for this chevron pattern is worked in the stockinette sections, and the garter-stitch stripes bend to match on their own. The fabric doesn't curl, which makes it perfect for times when you don't want to add borders. C1 is used for the garter stitch, C2 for the stockinette.

Stitches: Multiple of 11

Colors: 2

IN C1, CAST ON.

ROW 1 (WS): In C1, knit.

ROWS 2–5: In C1, knit.

ROWS 6, 8, AND 10: In C2, *K2tog, K2, knit into front and back of the next 2 stitches, K3, ssk; repeat from *.

ROWS 7, 9, AND 11: In C2, purl.

ROW 12: In C1, repeat Row 6.

VARIATION

» Use more than two colors, which is particularly effective if one color is used for the stockinette stripes while the garter-stitch stripes change, or vice versa. If a textured yarn is used in the garter-stitch sections, its qualities will be highlighted.

Welted Stripes Fantastic

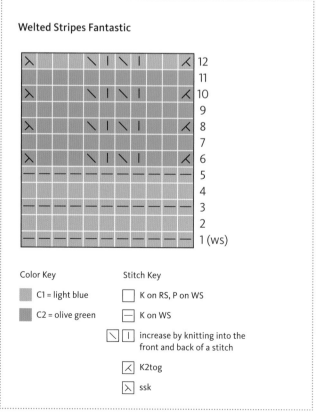

Color Key

- C1 = light blue
- C2 = olive green

Stitch Key

- K on RS, P on WS
- K on WS
- increase by knitting into the front and back of a stitch
- K2tog
- ssk

Afghan Stitch

This is the knitted version of the traditional crocheted ripple afghan stitch. Use just three or four horizontal repeats of the pattern for a scarf, or as many as you like for a blanket. Every row is knitted, so there is no curling and decorative points form at both ends of the fabric. Note that the number of stitches decreases on Rows 1 and 3, but returns to the original count on Rows 2 and 4. To ensure that the points at the bind off are crisp, bind off on a wrong-side row, in pattern. That is, when you reach the K1-yo-K1 increase, bind it off as you go: K1, pass the previous stitch over, yarn over, pass the K1 over, K1, pass the yarn over over, and so on across the row.

Stitches: Multiple of 12, plus 3
Colors: At least 2

IN C1, CAST ON.
SETUP ROW (WS): In C1, knit.
ROW 1 (RS): In C2, K1, ssk, *K9, Sl2, K1, P2sso; repeat from *, end K9, K2tog, K1.
ROW 2: In C2, K1, *P1, K4, K1-yo-K1 in next stitch, K4; repeat from *, end P1, K1.
ROWS 3–4: In C1, repeat Rows 1–2.

VARIATIONS

- To incorporate more colors, start each new color on Row 1 of the pattern.
- Vary the width of the stripes by working them for any even number of rows.
- Adjust the width of the chevrons by reducing or increasing the number of stitches between the columns of increases and decreases. Always add or subtract an even number of stitches in each pattern repeat.

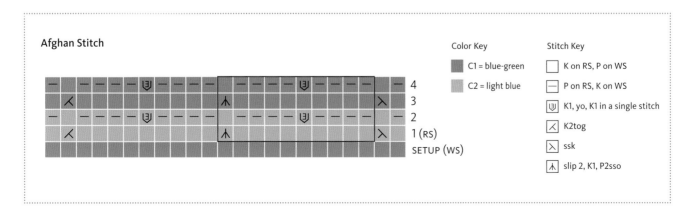

Afghan Stitch

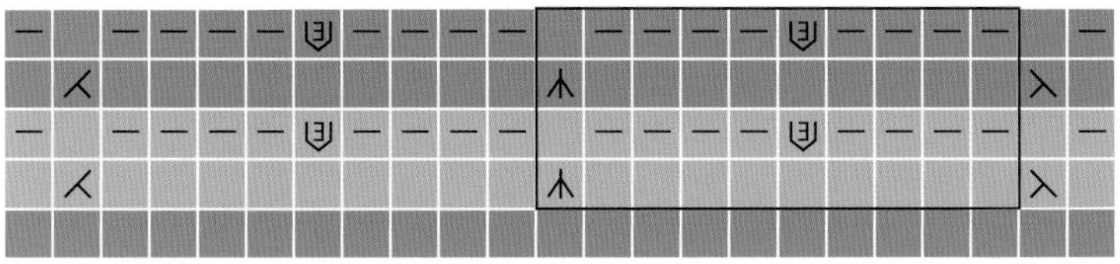

Color Key
C1 = blue-green
C2 = light blue

Stitch Key
K on RS, P on WS
P on RS, K on WS
K1, yo, K1 in a single stitch
K2tog
ssk
slip 2, K1, P2sso

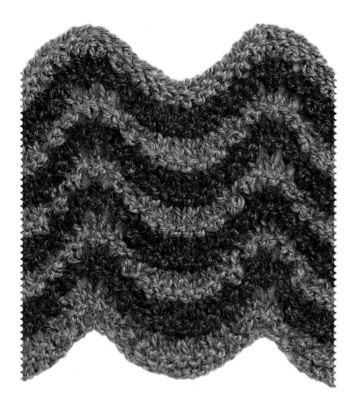

Old Shale

Old Shale is a traditional Shetland pattern, very simple to work, but with maximum impact for the small amount of effort involved. A scalloped edge forms at the cast on, making this the perfect bottom border for vests or sweaters, as well as lacy shawls and scarves.

Stitches: Multiple of 18, plus 1
Colors: At least 2

IN C1, CAST ON.

ROW 1 (RS): In C1, *K1, K2tog 3 times, [yo, K1] 5 times, yo, K2tog 3 times; repeat from *, end K1.

ROW 2: In C1, knit.

ROW 3: In C1, knit.

ROW 4: In C1, purl.

ROWS 5–8: In C2, repeat Rows 1–4.

VARIATIONS

» Make narrower stripes by changing colors on Rows 3 and 7 as well as on Rows 1 and 5.

» Make the pattern all garter stitch by knitting on Rows 4 and 8.

» Make Old Shale's more symmetrical stockinette stitch cousin, Shell Pattern, by substituting K2tog tbl or ssk for the last three decreases in each repeat and purl Rows 3 and 7.

» Eliminate the eyelets by knitting into the back of each yarn over on the following row.

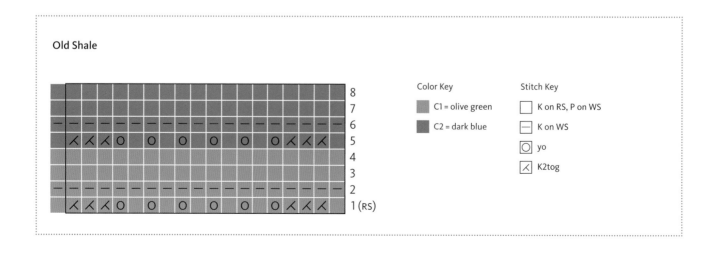

Old Shale

Color Key
C1 = olive green
C2 = dark blue

Stitch Key
K on RS, P on WS
K on WS
yo
K2tog

{Picots and Bobbles}

Contrasting bobbles and picots added to the surface of the fabric render both texture and color more interesting. *Picots* are made by increasing rapidly, then decreasing slowly. During both the increase and decrease, care is taken to make the picot neat and symmetrical. *Bobbles* are little bumps that protrude from the surface of your knitting, and you can make them in numerous ways. Like picots, the bobble is made by increasing rapidly but then decreasing just as rapidly back to the original number of stitches.

Picots

Picots are little points that pop up from a ridge of garter stitch. Making the picots and shaping the rest of the fabric around them takes place over several complete rows of knitting. Rows 1 and 2 are worked with the picot color, the other rows in the background color. The eyelet at the center of the picot can be used as a small button-hole, if you like.

ROW 1 (RS): Using the contrast color, knit until you come to the stitch where the picot will be located. [K1, yo, K1, yo, K1, yo, K1] into this stitch to make 7 stitches in it, knit to the position for the next picot, or to the end of the row.

ROW 2: In the same color, knit the entire row, including the picot stitches.

ROW 3: Change to the background and knit until 1 stitch remains before the picot stitches, K2tog, K5, ssk, knit to end of row, repeating for each picot.

ROW 4: Purl until you reach the ssk from the previous row, ssp, P1, Sl1 wyif, P1, P2tog, purl to end of row, repeating for each picot.

ROW 5: Knit until you reach the P2tog from the previous row, K2tog, Sl1 wyib, ssk, knit to end of row, repeating for each picot.

ROW 6: Still using the background color, purl.

Small Bobble

Because this small bobble takes just one row to complete, it's a very convenient addition to a pattern in a single or final row of a color. It makes a neat little bobble, one that stands up nicely on the surface of the fabric. (See bottom row of both swatches on opposite page.)

1] Use the knitted cast on to add 5 new stitches to the left needle.

2] Knit 6 (the new stitches plus one more).

3] Pass the second stitch off over the first, then pass the third, fourth, fifth, and sixth stitches over in succession, until only the original stitch is left.

Medium Bobble

This bobble is one of my favorites because it holds its shape. It differs from many because the instructions include the stitch following the bobble, which helps to get rid of the small hole that forms at the base and prevents the bobble from twisting and flattening. Note that you start working this bobble a stitch earlier than you might expect. (See middle row of both swatches on oposite page.) On the right side, work until you come to the stitch before the one where you want to position the bobble.

ROW 1: Knit into front, back, front, back, front of the next stitch (making 5 stitches in 1), K1, turn.

ROW 2: P5, turn.

ROW 3: K5, turn.

ROW 4: P5, then pass the second, third, fourth, and fifth stitches over the first stitch, turn.

ROW 5: Knit into back of the stitch.

Large Bobble

This is a very big bobble, worked over two stitches to give it more stability, and is useful when you want to make a very bold statement. Work across on the right side until you come to the two stitches where you want to place the bobble. (See top row of both swatches on opposite page.)

ROW 1: (K1, yo, K1, yo, K1) to make 5 stitches in the first stitch, repeat for the second stitch, turn.

ROW 2: Purl the bobble stitches, turn (3 bobbles stitches).

ROW 3: Ssk twice, K2, K2tog twice, turn (6 bobble stitches).

ROW 4: Purl the bobble stitches; turn.

ROW 5: Ssk twice, K2tog; turn.

ROW 6: Purl the bobble stitches; turn.

ROW 7: K1, K2tog; 2 bobble stitches remain.

VARIATIONS

» On the following row or round, you may want to work into back of bobble stitches to twist them and anchor the bobble more firmly.

» Make bobbles larger or smaller by increasing more or fewer stitches initially.

Bobble Notes and Inspirations

Single-row bobbles, while smaller than the others, can be worked much more quickly. Learning to knit backward will save you the time and effort of turning repeatedly on large, multiple-row bobbles. If you'd like more texture, make multirow bobbles and knit across the wrong-side rows, so the purls make the fabric bumpier. You can place bobbles very close together to provide allover texture, or spread them far apart.

Now that you know how to make bobbles, how do you control the color as you place them on the fabric?

TO ACCENTUATE PATTERNS. You can work a bobble any-where on the face of the fabric when you happen to already be using that yarn. For example, you could place bobbles at the center point of a chevron, to high-light the wavy ridge that punctuates Old Shale, or as finials on the intersections of a lattice.

USE A GARTER-STITCH RIDGE. You can make a garter-stitch ridge across the fabric where you want the bobbles by knitting all the stitches in the bobble color and working the bobbles as you go. Then knit across the wrong side with the same color before switching back to the background color.

FREE FLOATING. If you want your bobble to float free in a sea of the background color, change to the bobble color and knit the first stitch of the row to anchor the yarn. Slip the stitches before, after, and between the bobbles, keeping the yarn behind the fabric and tak-ing care to leave the strand loose so the fabric doesn't pucker. It's best not to slip more than 4 or 5 stitches at a time, so if your bobbles will be farther apart, consider knitting 1 stitch in the bobble color halfway between each bobble. To get the yarn back to the other edge of the fabric, work the row after the bobbles with the same color, knitting into the bobble stitches and slip-ping the intervening stitches.

Going
Beyond!

Pattern Stitch Design and Inspiration

You may find a pattern stitch that is exactly what you want — just the right number of colors, just the right width and height, and just the right scale for your project. But what if you can't? Find something close to what you want, then change it.

Remember to suit your fabric to your project, using thicker, less stretchy fabrics for things you want to hold their shape, like bags; medium fabrics for basic garments like hats and sweaters; and light, very stretchy fabrics for things that need a lot of stretch and drape, like shawls. For more information on designing, both fabric and garments, see chapter 9.

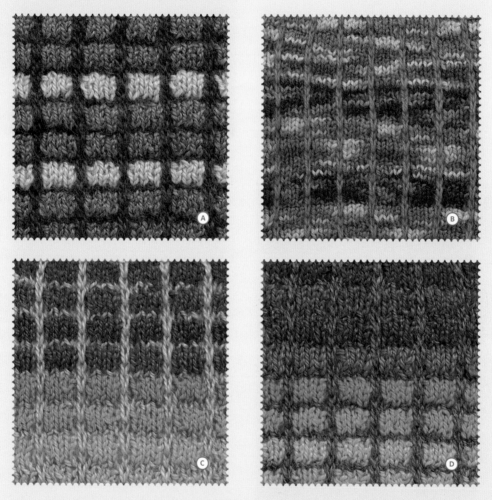

VARIATIONS ON FOUR-COLOR WINDOWPANES (page 74). The simplest change you can make is to adjust the number or occurrence of the colors. The Four-Color Windowpanes pattern could be completed in just two colors or in as many as you like. Above, I've explored several options. The original pattern is shown in shades of green (A), using a single self-striping yarn in place of all the contrasting colors (B), then changing colors gradually from yellow to purple, with a light aqua (C) and an olive background (D). For a project using this stitch pattern, see page 90.

VARIATIONS ON RIDGE CHECK (page 56). In horizontal patterns, you can almost always vary the width of the stripes. The original Ridge Check Pattern is shown in olive and dark gray-green (A). Variations include working wider and narrower stripes of each color (B) and (C), and swapping stitches to make the ridges run diagonally (D).

Going
Beyond!

Pattern Stitch Design and Inspiration *(continued)*

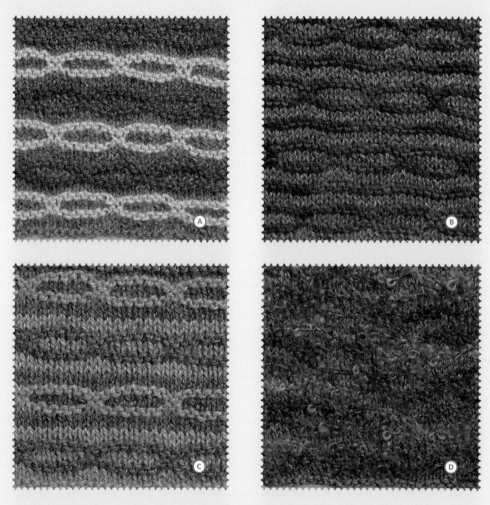

VARIATIONS ON CHAIN STRIPES (page 60). Chain Stripes (A) calls for two contrast colors alternating on a solid background, with the chains shifted each time the color changes. Variations shown are: a single variegated yarn for the contrast colors plus a garter ridge in this color between each chain (B), a two-color version reversing background and foreground colors in each repeat and lining up all the chains (C), and a single variegated bouclé in place of the contrast colors (D).

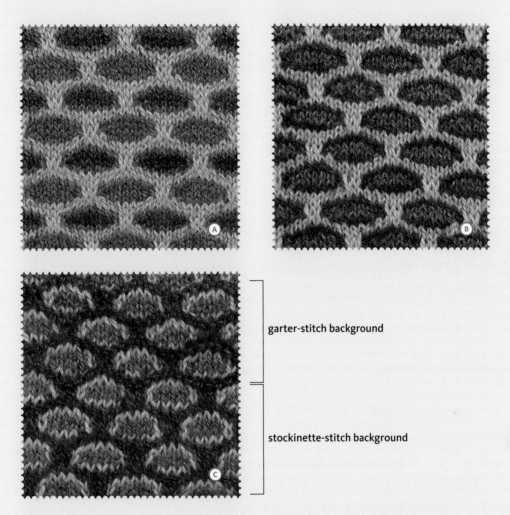

garter-stitch background

stockinette-stitch background

VARIATIONS ON OUTLINED CHECK (page 62). Light aqua forms the background in A and B, but in A the centers of the ovals alternate between medium green and dark gray-blue. In B, the darkest color, gray-blue, outlines the two medium colors for a more organized effect. In C, the width of the pattern has been altered to make the center ovals only 4 stitches wide, rather than 6, changing the proportion of the pattern. The top half of this swatch explores a further variation, knitting the second row of the background color between each set of ovals to outline them with a garter-stitch ridge. This makes the pattern more angular and gives it greater depth.

WINDOWPANE BAG

The windowpane-stitch pattern creates a fabric with little stretch, making it perfect for a bag. The comfortable handles are worked in a slip-stitch pattern, creating a firm fabric with even less stretch. The handles are designed so that the long one slips through the short one to provide easy, secure closure.

Measurements   10" (25 cm) wide × 9½" (24 cm) tall; one strap is 24" (61 cm) long and the other is 10" (25 cm) long.

Yarn   Kid Hollow semi-worsted, 50% wool/50% mohair, 4 oz (113 g)/180 yd (164.5 m), one skein of each of the following: C1: Moss Green Heather; C2: Indian Yellow; C3: Wild Strawberry; C4: Scarlet Blend; C5: UVA Orange; C6: Dark Red; C7: Plums; C8: Violet Heather; C9: UVA Blue

Needles   One US #4 (3.5 mm) circular needle, 16" (41 cm) long, *or size needed to achieve correct gauge*

Gauge   20 stitches = 4" (10 cm) in pattern stitch (For Four-Color Windowpanes Pattern Stitch, see page 74.)

Knitting the Bag

Using C1, cast on 80 stitches. Join the beginning and end of round being careful not to twist the cast on.

ROUNDS 1–2:   Using C1, knit around.

ROUNDS 3–6:   Using C2, knit around.

ROUND 7:   Using C1, K3 *drop the next stitch, unravel 4 rows, insert needle from the front into the stitch on the fifth row below (which will be in C1), then knit it, catching all the unravelled strands as you do so; K3; repeat from * around.

ROUND 8:   Continuing in C1, knit around.

ROUNDS 9–14:   Repeat Rounds 3–8.

ROUNDS 15–26:   Repeat Rounds 3–14, using C3 in place of C2.

ROUNDS 27–38:   Repeat Rounds 3–14, using C4 in place of C2.

ROUNDS 39–50:   Repeat Rounds 3–14, using C5 in place of C2.

ROUNDS 51–62:   Repeat Rounds 3–14, using C6 in place of C2.

ROUNDS 63–74:   Repeat Rounds 3–14, using C7 in place of C2.

ROUNDS 75–86:   Repeat Rounds 3–14, using C8 in place of C2.

ROUNDS 87–98:   Repeat Rounds 3–14, using C9 in place of C2.

ROUNDS 99–100:   Using C1, knit around.

I-Cord Bind Off

For more information and photos of Binding Off with I-Cord, see page 249.

Turn the bag so that the wrong side faces you.

Using C1, cast on 3 stitches at the beginning of the left needle point.

*Knit 2, slip 1 knitwise, knit the first stitch to be bound off, pass the slipped stitch over (this works the last stitch of the cord together with the first stitch to be bound off). Slip all 3 stitches back to the left needle purlwise. Do not turn.

Repeat from * until the top of the bag has been bound off and only the I-cord stitches remain. Work a second round of I-cord. Cut yarn, pull end through all stitches, and stitch firmly to beginning of I-cord.

Knitting the Straps

For tips on working this stitch, see Tricolor Fabric Stitch, page 51. Note that you never cut any of the colors; just carry them up the edge of the strap whenever you need them. The straps shown use colors C1, C4, and C9, but you could use any combination of three colors from the body of the bag that you prefer. Swatch to see what works best!

Using C1, cast on 11 stitches.

SETUP ROW (WS):   Purl to end of row.

ROW 1 (RS):   In C4, K1, *Sl1 wyif, K1; repeat from *.

ROW 2:   In C9, K1, P1, *Sl1 wyib, P1; repeat from *, end K1.

ROW 3:   In C1, repeat Row 1.

ROW 4:   In C4, repeat Row 2.

ROW 5:   In C9, repeat Row 1.

ROW 6:   In C1, repeat Row 2.

Repeat these 6 rows until the strap measures 24" (61 cm).

Make another strap identical to the first, measuring 10" (25 cm).

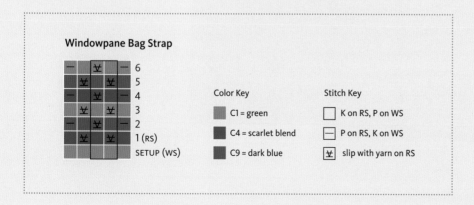

Windowpane Bag Strap

Color Key

C1 = green
C4 = scarlet blend
C9 = dark blue

Stitch Key

K on RS, P on WS
P on RS, K on WS
slip with yarn on RS

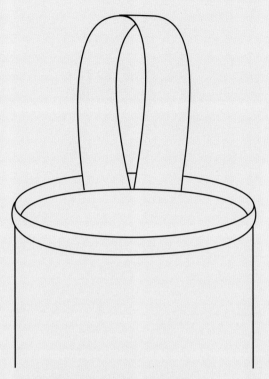

Attached straps with corners abutting.

Finishing the Bag

Fold the straps in half, and sew the ends securely to the inside of the I-cord bind off, one at each side of the top, as shown in the drawing.

With wrong sides facing, use C1 and backstitch to sew the bottom of the bag closed.

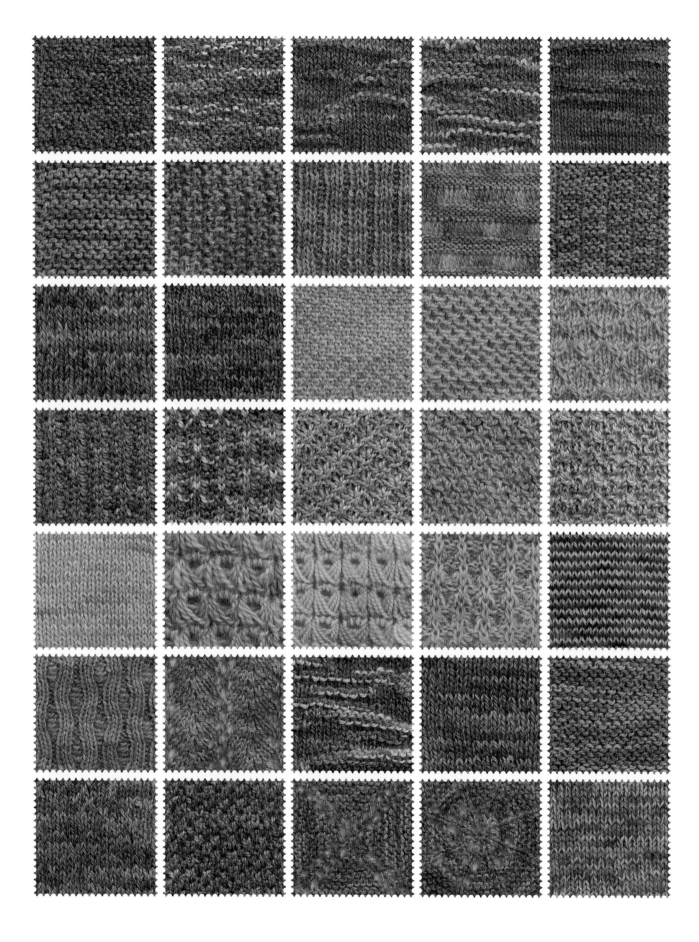

4 MULTICOLOR YARNS

Multicolor yarns are often the eye candy of the yarn store, and they come in so many different forms that it's impossible to generalize about them. Some are variegated, with solid colors changing abruptly or gradually. The color segments may be as short as half an inch or as long as several yards. Some have a striking variety of hues and a great deal of contrast between colors, while others are monochromatic or have so little variation in value that the colors all blend together in the knitted fabric. Some are marled, with different colored plies twisted together, and others, like bouclé, have complex structures that add texture and change the appearance of the colors. If the colors were combined before the fiber was spun into yarn, the yarns may be heathery (if well blended), the color changes may be very gradual along the length of each ply, or you may even see small beads (called *garnets*) of color distributed throughout the yarn. Handspun yarn from dyed fiber may be marled in sections, variegated, garneted, or a combination of all three. This chapter explores how the characteristics of multicolor yarn affect the appearance of the finished fabric, and it also provides tools for manipulating those characteristics to change the appearance.

{Variegated Yarns}

In commercially dyed and handpainted yarns, the colors usually repeat regularly throughout the skein or ball. The colors in handspun yarns don't generally have a regular, identifiable repeat, even though they may be distributed evenly throughout the skein. What these yarns have in common, however, is that they almost always look wonderful in the ball or skein — enticing us to buy them — but knit up, they frequently don't live up to their full potential. I hear the same complaints about variegated yarns time and again: the skein was beautiful but the knitted fabric has ugly stripes or the colors pool unattractively. Your variegated yarn may never look as good in plain old stockinette as it did when you were lured by the siren call of the skein or ball. The good news is that you can use numerous techniques to showcase the yarn in your finished project.

The Importance of Swatching

The key to optimizing your yarn's appearance is experimentation. A yarn may be lovely worked with a particular pattern stitch on a particular size needle, but not on needles two sizes bigger or smaller. The colors may align themselves strikingly in a narrow piece of knitting, but pool or stripe terribly in a wider piece, or quite the opposite may happen. Pattern stitches can bring out breathtaking aspects of the yarn's character, but the combination of color and pattern may just look muddy or confused. Trying different combinations of yarn, needle, and stitch pattern is the only way to discover the effects. While you experiment, you'll also be auditioning techniques to see which ones you enjoy and which ones produce the best results while bringing you the most knitting pleasure. There's no point in spending hours doing something that drives you crazy, so it's important to find techniques you can live with.

Working with Different Color Repeat Lengths

Experimentation with swatches probably won't tell you everything you need to know about the color repeat. For very short repeats, a swatch may look much like the finished product, but longer repeats won't show their true colors until you work the full width of your fabric. The length of the color repeat, combined with the needle size and number of stitches, controls how often and where the colors appear in your knitted fabric. For example, if you use larger needles, each stitch takes more yarn. If you use smaller needles, each stitch uses less yarn. The effect, even with the same number of stitches, is that you'll get to the end of the color repeat sooner on larger needles.

Experience, however, does give us an idea of what to expect from variegated yarns: spirals of color in circular knitting and colors alternating from side to side in flat knitting. The appearance of your knitting will vary according to a combination of the following:

Width or circumference. The outcome changes significantly depending upon the width of the piece you're working on.

Variations in the yarn. Even within a straight piece, you may see variations caused by the yarn itself. Some sections of hand-painted skeins may have a shorter circumference, so the color repeats are shorter.

Variations in your knitting. Were you tense or relaxed when you knitted?

Differences in your environment. Even humidity can affect the results. Was there one day when those wooden needles felt sticky?

In sleeves and other tapered tubes, the color spirals in one direction at the bottom, pools when the circumference of the sleeve matches the length of the color repeat, and then spirals in the opposite direction as the circumference grows larger near the top. You can expect the same kind of pooling to occur on the opposite sleeve, but since it will be attached to the other side of the sweater, it will fall in the opposite position (back or front) from the first sleeve.

Working with Different Color Segment Lengths

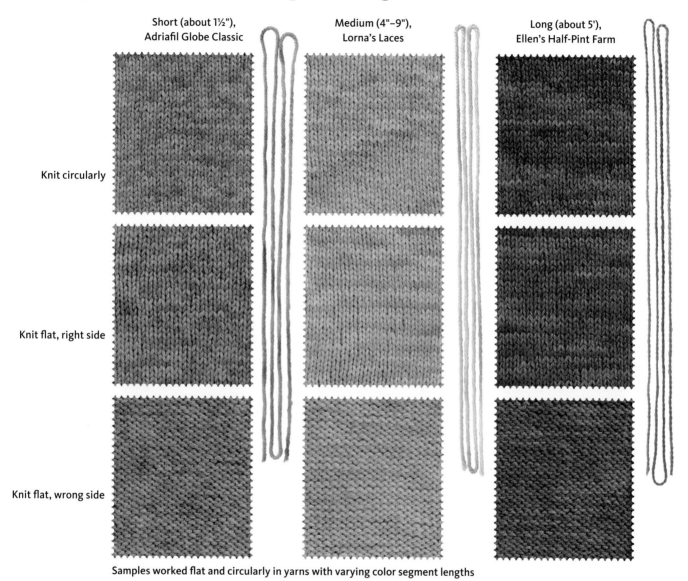

Samples worked flat and circularly in yarns with varying color segment lengths

▲ *Effect of color segment length.* The length of each color segment affects how many consecutive stitches appear in each color. If the segments are very short, a color will show up in only one or two stitches before it changes. The longer the color segment, the longer the row of stitches will be. For a flecked effect, select a yarn with shorter color segments; for longer stripes, choose longer segments. Self-striping yarns carry this concept out the farthest, with the length of each color segment designed to make a solid stripe around or across the garment.

Examine the knitted samples above. Stockinette stitch creates a smooth surface, so the most noticeable element is the changing color of the yarn. Any striping or pooling is quite visible. See the difference in the way the colors fall in the flat swatches versus the circular swatches. Look at the wrong side of the stockinette swatches: reverse stockinette is highly textured and breaks up the colors, but long-segment yarns still produce noticeable stripes. If you don't like the results of your first swatch, try a different needle size; the change in stitch size may improve the look of the fabric.

{Pattern Stitch Interplay}

You can explore a broad range of possibilities for using purling, slipped stitches, and other pattern stitches to get the best effect from your multicolored yarn. The effect of each pattern stitch varies depending on the length of the color segments of your yarn, the frequency of the color repeats, the width of your knitting, and your gauge, as well as on the amount of contrast between the colors. Small-scale swatches usually don't show the same color effect as the final garment. Sometimes you need to knit the full width of the garment to see how the finished product will look. Remember: Experimentation is the key to success.

Creating Effects with Random Purls

In addition to fragmenting the color of a stockinette background, purled stitches add surface texture. This affects the appearance of the colors by creating highlights and casting shadows, making a single hue appear to be a range of tints and shades.

If the project you're planning doesn't lend itself to an organized pattern stitch, then an easy option is to add random purl stitches to the stockinette fabric. Knitting is such a rhythmic, repetitive process that it's difficult to do anything truly random without going to a lot of trouble. This approach doesn't actually produce random purl stitches, but it looks unpredictable. Make up a pattern repeat, in knits and purls, that doesn't match the number of stitches in your knitting. For example, if you have 80 stitches, use something with a multiple of 7, such as K5, P2, and repeat this all the away across or around your knitting. When you get to the end of the row or round, keep on going in the same pattern. It won't line up with what you did on the previous row, which creates the random look.

If you lose your place, don't even try to figure out where you were in the pattern, just start again with K5, P2, and it will add to the inconsistency. Work on the piece when there are distractions (talk to people, watch TV or sporting events, and so on), to introduce even more "mistakes." Check often to see if the purl stitches are beginning to form a pattern — diagonals, for example. If

they are, change to a different pattern that also doesn't go evenly into your number of stitches (for example: K1, P2) and begin working that, allowing interruptions to disrupt the pattern. Continue this process throughout your knitting.

If you want a less bumpy texture with fewer purl stitches, try knitting the right-side rows and work your "pattern" on the wrong side only. Keep in mind, though, that one of the benefits of working the purl stitches on every row is that the fabric will be reversible — an advantage for shawls and scarves. In circular knitting, you could knit every other round. But don't be too careful — if you accidentally mess up the alternation, it just contributes to the unpredictability. The arbitrary stitch changes create a random-looking bouclé.

▲ *Working random purls for textural interest.* Notice the difference between swatch A, which has shorter color segments and less contrast, and swatch B, which has long segments and a great deal more contrast between the colors. In swatch A, the colors blend and there's an overall textured effect. In swatch B, individual stitches are far more obvious where light and dark colors interact.

Letting the yarn tell you when to purl is another technique for achieving randomness. Pick a specific color in the yarn, and whenever a stitch of that color is on the left needle waiting to be worked, purl it. If purling so many consecutive stitches in one color looks ugly, purl every second or third stitch instead. You may work this "pattern" on every row, alternating rows, or even every third or fourth row. Your purled stitches may line up with each other on repeated rows. To avoid something that looks like ribbing, make it a rule not to purl directly over a recently purled stitch; instead, knit it and purl the next stitch in that color. Depending on the color you choose, this technique could either emphasize or de-emphasize the color, so experiment to see what it does. To add more variation, change the purling color every few rows.

▲ *Purl according to the color of the working yarn.* For a different effect, decide when to purl based on the color of the yarn you are about to knit with as is shown in swatches E and F. Rather than watching the color of the next stitch on the needle, pay attention to the color of your working yarn where it is attached to the needle and purl whenever you come to this color. You can use all the same variations when purling based on the color of the yarn as I suggested for purling based on the color of the stitch. The differences between these two are very subtle. Note that the ridges in the chosen color face down rather than up when you choose this method.

▲ *Purl according to the color that's on the needle.* The amount of texture varies considerably depending on the proportion of the color you choose to purl in the yarn. In swatch C, the shorter color segments result in a more blended effect than in swatch D.

Using Knit and Purl Patterns for Textural Effects

Maintaining a random pattern can require a good deal of attention, so you may find it easier to produce a similar effect by working a simple, repetitive knit/purl pattern stitch instead.

▲ *For simplicity, garter stitch.* Sometimes the simplest solution is best. It's amazing how good garter stitch can look in a variegated yarn. It breaks up the stripes, camouflages pooling colors, and adds texture — which casts shadows, making it look like there are more color variations in the yarn. Worked firmly, it creates a dense fabric with a lot of texture. Worked loosely, it stretches and leaves distinct horizontal ridges across the fabric. It's worth trying garter stitch to see how it works with your yarn. You can compensate for the fact that garter stitch is wider than stockinette by using a smaller needle, but the fabric will be thicker. Even in garter stitch, striping and pooling are more noticeable in swatch A, which has longer color segments than those in swatch B.

▲ *Seed Stitch effects.* If garter stitch is too striped for your taste, or the very horizontal nature of the stitch doesn't appeal, try Seed Stitch to break up the stripes and pools of color. Cast on an odd number of stitches and work K1, P1 repeatedly across. Repeat this on every row. In circular knitting, you can make a seamless fabric in Seed Stitch by working it on an odd number of stitches. Alternate K1, P1, and the knits and purls will miraculously align themselves to form the pattern. The result is a tiny checkerboard of knitted and purled stitches. Many knitters find Seed Stitch tedious, so you may not want to make a commitment to working it over large areas. Luckily, it can be quite effective in small sections of a garment. Be aware that, like garter stitch, it is often wider than stockinette worked on the same number of stitches on the same needles.

▲ *Ribbing rules.* For a stretchy noncurling fabric, you really can't beat ribbing. Amazing transformations can take place in wider ribs. Depending on the length of the color segment and color repeat in your yarn, relaxed ribbing can make it look like you're changing colors when it's really just the yarn at work. It's worth experimenting to see the different effects of various ribbed combinations, changing the stitch count for the knit or purl ribs (or both) to make them wider or narrower. Ribbing will look different depending on whether it is relaxed, as in swatch A, or stretched, as in swatch B.

▲ *Broken garter, a combo.* This stitch is a variation on both garter stitch and ribbing. The fabric is ridged like garter stitch, but with the apparent color changes of ribbing. To work this, choose a number of stitches (columns 3–5 stitches wide work very well) and alternate this number of stitches in knit and purl across or around (for example: K3, P3). On the next row or round, purl the knit stitches and knit the purl stitches. The outcome is narrow columns of garter stitch that shift up and down in relation to each other. This pattern lends itself to many variations in width. Experiment with different widths for the columns of stitches. For example, alternate columns of 3 stitches and 5 stitches. Be sure to work broken garter firmly, or the pattern won't be noticeable. Most effective in yarns with medium to long color segments, broken garter looks like you're changing colors across each row.

An advantage of this stitch pattern is that it stretches easily in length without changing in width, so socks or sweater sleeves knit with it adapt to fit the wearer. When working broken garter circularly, use an odd multiple of the stitches in each rib so that the pattern repeats seamlessly on every round. For a pattern using broken garter, see page 138.

{Slipped Stitches}

Slipped stitches help break up the striping characteristic of medium to long color segments by pulling a stitch up across two rows, carrying the working yarn horizontally across the surface of the fabric, or both. Slipping adds a smaller amount of surface texture than purling. It stretches the stitches and tightens the fabric as a result. You can add a small number of slipped stitches without a noticeable change in the hand or drape of the fabric, but a large number will result in a tighter, thicker, less stretchy fabric. If you are slipping a high proportion of stitches, you can produce a more elastic fabric with a nice drape by using larger needles. The swatches displayed here demonstrate several different methods of slipping and their effects. You'll want to try them all to see which ones give you the best results with the yarn you're working with.

Slipping by the Rules

You can employ all the same techniques discussed in Creating Effects with Random Purls (pages 98–99) when slipping stitches. It works best, however, if you slip stitches only on every other row or round to prevent the fabric from becoming too tight and to avoid a situation where you're slipping the same stitch over numerous rows, distorting the fabric. Also keep in mind that you cannot slip every stitch. Slip every second or third stitch in your chosen color as you work across. Slip purlwise, or your stitches will be twisted and the fabric will become very tight. (For more information on slipping stitches, see pages 44–45).

▲ *Randomized slips.* Create a random pattern of slipped stitches with the working yarn always kept on the wrong side of the fabric. The surface will be slightly more textured than plain stockinette, and horizontal stripes of color are fragmented by the taller slipped stitches, which are most noticeable when they fall against a contrasting background. All the colors in this swatch were slipped equally, so no particular color is emphasized.

▲ *Slipping based on stitch color.* Choose a color and slip whenever it appears in the next stitch on the left needle. Since stitches in this color are pulled taller, the color is emphasized. As with randomized slips, the working yarn is always hidden on the wrong side of the fabric while slipping. Purple was the slipped color here, so the taller purple stitches are noticeable throughout the swatch.

▲ *Slipping based on working yarn color.* Slip the next stitch whenever your working yarn (rather than the next stitch) is the chosen color. This tends to hide and fragment the color because the working yarn is hidden on the wrong side of the fabric. In this example, the working yarn was purple. The slipped stitches are most noticeable where the color pulled up from the row below is lighter, serving as a background to alternating purple stitches. There is less purple on the surface of the fabric, but the alternating stitches are eye-catching.

▲ *Varying yarn position.* When the working yarn is held on the right side of the fabric rather than the wrong side while slipping, the effect is quite different. A horizontal strand of the working yarn cuts across the taller slipped stitch, adding texture to the surface. Slipped stitches were randomized in this swatch, so no one color is emphasized.

Linen Stitch

Linen Stitch is identical to Tricolor Fabric Stitch, but worked with just one strand of yarn. Both sides of this pattern are very attractive. To keep track of the right versus the wrong side when starting, fasten a safety pin or split marker to the right side. Cast on and bind off firmly, or the top and bottom will flare.

Stitches: Odd number

ROW 1 (RS): K1, *Sl1 wyif, K1; repeat from *.
ROW 2: K1, P1, *Sl1 wyib, P1; repeat from *, end K1.

Linen Stitch

Stitch Key

K on RS, P on WS

K on WS

slip with yarn on RS

Slipped Honeycomb

This is one of my favorite pattern stitches. Based on garter stitch, it does not curl and requires no borders. Carrying the yarn across the back of the slipped stitch makes a longer section visible, highlighting the yarn's surface texture and structure. It's very versatile, because smaller needles can produce a dense fabric, ideal for placemats, pot holders, bags, and collars, while larger ones create a drapier fabric that is perfect for sweaters, scarves, and cozy afghans.

Stitches: Odd number

ROW 1 (RS): Knit.
ROW 2: K1, *Sl1 wyib, K1; repeat from *.
ROW 3: Knit.
ROW 4: K1, *K1, Sl1 wyib; repeat from *, end K2.

VARIATION

» Work Rows 1–2 only to make a close stitch. All the longer strands will line up in columns, and the back of the fabric will look like a purled ribbing.

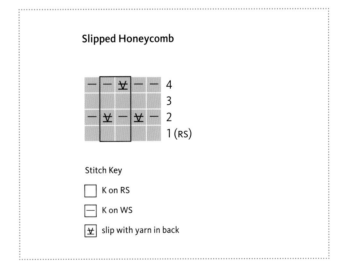

Slipped Honeycomb

Stitch Key

K on RS

K on WS

slip with yarn in back

Mock Honeycomb

One of the delights of this pattern stitch is the two long strands of yarn that are lifted and knit with a later row. They stretch diagonally across the front of the fabric, creating the same diagonal overlays that attract us to balls of variegated yarn in the first place. Mock Honeycomb is an excellent choice if you're looking for a pattern stitch with more depth than stockinette.

When slipping the stitches, carry the yarn across the front of the fabric. Carrying it loosely will produce a flatter fabric. Carrying it tightly will pucker the fabric, making the honeycomb deeper. (For more information on knitting the loose strands with a stitch, see Manipulating Strands, page 77.)

Stitches: Multiple of 4, plus 5

ROW 1 (AND ALL WS ROWS): Purl.
ROW 2: K1, *Sl3 wyif, K1; repeat from *.
ROW 4: Repeat Row 2.
ROW 6: K2, *insert needle under the two loose strands from Rows 2 and 4 and knit the next stitch catching the strands behind it, K3; repeat from *, end last repeat K2 instead of K3.
ROW 8: Knit 3, *Sl3 wyif, K1; repeat from *, end K2.
ROW 10: Repeat Row 8.
ROW 12: K4, *insert needle under the two loose strands of Rows 8 and 10 and knit the next stitch, catching the strands behind it, K3; repeat from *, end K1.

Mock Honeycomb

Stitch Key

☐ K on RS, P on WS

⊻ slip wyif

🛨 insert needle under loose strands and K next stitch, catching strands behind it

{Brioche Stitches}

One of the appeals of variegated yarn in the ball or skein is the overlapping diagonals. We see longer strands of yarn than in the knitted fabric and lots of relief, with each strand casting a shadow on the strands it crosses and a honeycomb of multicolored strands beneath. Brioche stitches produce the same effect because strands from one row below are pulled up diagonally on either side of a stitch. These stitches tend to create very soft, loose, stretchy fabrics — for a firmer fabric, use smaller needles. (For more information on this technique, see Knit Below, page 70.)

Rose Fabric stitch adds diagonals and greater texture to the fabric of this shell, while garter stitch creates horizontals on a field of stockinette. (Yarn: Cherry Tree Hill)

Rose Fabric

Rose Fabric can look either neatly tailored or nubbly, depending on the twist of the yarn and the gauge of the knitting. In a multicolor yarn, however, you notice the interplay of the colors rather than the pattern stitch. See how different the effect is in the two swatches. At the top, knit in a yarn with shorter color segments and much less contrast, the colors blend together. At the bottom, with longer color segments and more contrast, the colors appear to alternate, producing an effect almost like switching between two colors of yarn across the row.

It can be difficult to tell what row you are on in this pattern. Each time you begin a right-side row, look two rows below for the larger inverted V formed by knitting into the stitch below on the previous pattern row. Make sure that you don't work the next knit-below directly above this.

Stitches: Odd number

ROW 1 (WS): Knit.
ROW 2: K1, *knit below, K1; repeat from *.
ROW 3: Knit.
ROW 4: K1, *K1, knit below; repeat from *, end K2.

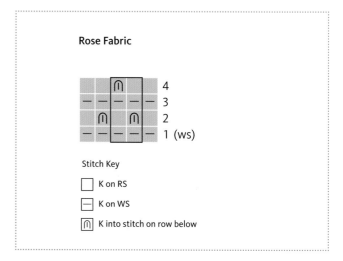

Rose Fabric

Stitch Key

☐ K on RS

─ K on WS

𝝥 K into stitch on row below

Garter Ladders

Garter Ladders is yet another pattern based on garter stitch, so it doesn't curl. It's a good choice when you want a flat fabric with a noticeable vertical rib. The ribs are separated by larger Vs of color, broken by garter stitch at their center. The Vs are far more apparent in the bottom swatch, with more contrast and longer color segments. Since this fabric lacks the elasticity of a true ribbing, it should not be substituted for ribbing in the borders of a garment. This faux rib spreads horizontally more than you may expect, so cast on and bind off loosely to avoid puckering.

Stitches: Multiple of 3

ROW 1 (WS): Knit.
ROW 2: K1, *knit below, K2; repeat from *, end knit below, K1.

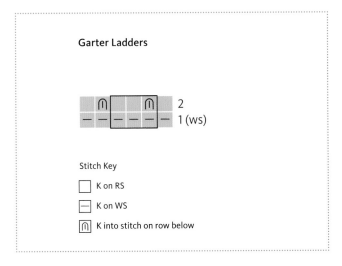

Garter Ladders

Stitch Key

☐ K on RS

⊟ K on WS

⋒ K into stitch on row below

{Lace Patterns}

Pattern stitches that incorporate increases and decreases, including lace, help disguise the striping that is so often a problem with variegated yarns. For every increase in the pattern, there is a corresponding decrease, in order to maintain the proper number of stitches over the course of the pattern repeat. Every decrease overlaps two or more stitches, elongates some strands, and pulls them diagonally. Every increase pushes two stitches farther apart and creates either a twisted stitch (making still more diagonals), or an eyelet (breaking up the stripes).

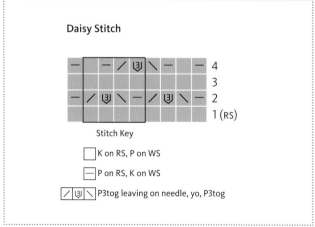

Daisy Stitch

Stitch Key

☐ K on RS, P on WS

⊟ P on RS, K on WS

⧄⊔⧅ P3tog leaving on needle, yo, P3tog

Daisy Stitch

Working P3tog-yo-P3tog into one stitch on Rows 2 and 4 creates the daisylike fan shape. To work this special combination stitch, purl 3 together but leave the stitches on the left needle, wrap the yarn all the way around the needle to make the yarn over and bring it back to the front again, then purl 3 together again into the same three stitches and slide them off the needle. Work loosely, or you may find you can't purl the three stitches together. Needles with long tapered points will make manipulating these stitches much easier.

Stitches: Multiple of 4, plus 5

ROW 1 (RS): Knit.
ROW 2: K1, *P3tog-yo-P3tog into the next 3 stitches, K1; repeat from *.
ROW 3: Knit.
ROW 4: K1, P1, K1, *P3tog-YO-P3tog into the next 3 stitches, K1; repeat from *, end P1, K1.

Lace Background Stitch

This simple lace knits up surprisingly quickly, and the short pattern repeat is easily memorized. When knit on the usual-size needles for the yarn, it produces a fairly solid fabric, and the increases, decreases, and crossed stitches blend the colors. When knit more loosely and blocked open, the colors are broken into smaller dots rather than blended.

Knitting needles with long tapered points make it easier to manipulate the stitches. Note that the stitch count increases when you work Rows 1 and 3, then returns to the original count after Rows 2 and 4.

Stitches: Odd number

ROW 1 (RS): K1, *yo, Sl1 knitwise wyib, K1, yo, pass the slipped stitch over both the knit stitch and the yarn over; repeat from *.

ROW 2: *P2, drop the yo of the preceding row off the needle; repeat from *, end P1.

ROW 3: K2, *yo, Sl1 knitwise wyib, K1, yo, psso both the knit stitch and the yo; repeat from *, end K1.

ROW 4: P3, *drop the yo of the preceding row, P2; repeat from *.

Note: This pattern stitch does not lend itself to charting because of the changing number of stitches.

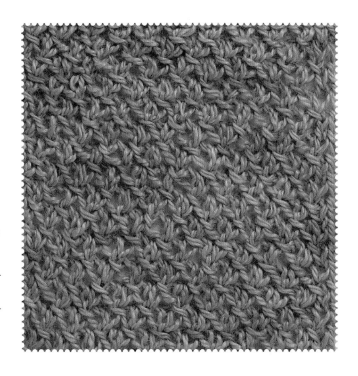

Right side

Wrong side

Lace Rib

Lace Rib doesn't look knitted at first glance, but it's easy to see that it's based on K1, P3 ribbing when you look at the back of the fabric. It can be left unblocked, to take advantage of the natural relief of the ribbing, or blocked, to open out the lace and flatten the fabric. Working Lace Rib on the needle size recommended for the yarn results in a tighter fabric and more blending of the colors. Larger needles create a lacier fabric, with large holes breaking up any stripes. The double decrease at the center of each knit rib pulls the yarn into longer diagonals to good effect.

When working Row 3 of this stitch pattern, it's easy to forget to pass the slipped stitch over. If you discover this on the following row, simply lift the extra stitch over before working the center stitch of the 3 purl stitches.

Stitches: Multiple of 4, plus 1

ROW 1 (RS): P1, *K3, P1; repeat from *.
ROW 2: *K1, P3; repeat from *, end K1.
ROW 3: P1, *yo, Sl1, K2tog, psso, yo, P1; repeat from *.
ROW 4: *K1, P3; repeat from *, end K1.

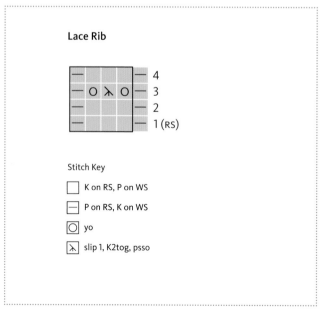

Lace Rib

Stitch Key

☐ K on RS, P on WS

☐ P on RS, K on WS

☐ yo

☐ slip 1, K2tog, psso

It's Got a Bend in It!

Ripple and chevron patterns bend the straight stripes of longer color segments into Vs and curves and, at the same time, add surface texture. The ripple and chevron patterns in chapter 3 lend themselves nicely to multicolor yarns without the necessity of changing colors. Yarns with longer color segments show the structure of the pattern best, while yarns with shorter stretches of each color simply appear more interesting because the stitches tilt to one side or the other, are partially obscured by decreases, and appear as small dots of color in increases.

Vine Lace

Simply shifting the pattern from Row 2 one stitch to the right on Row 4 staggers the increases and decreases, creating the undulating chevron pattern in Vine Lace (shown below).

Stitches: Multiple of 9, plus 4

CAST ON LOOSELY.

ROW 1 (WS): Purl.

ROW 2: K2, * K1, yo, K2, ssk, K2tog, K2, yo; repeat from *, end K2.

ROW 3: Purl.

ROW 4: K2, *yo, K2, ssk, K2tog, K2, yo, K1; repeat from *, end K2.

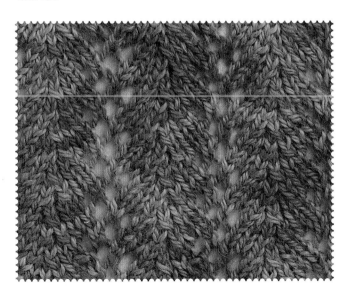

Variation

Stitches: Multiple of 9, plus 4

» To make Feather Lace, loosely cast on and then work just Rows 3–4 (ending with a K1 instead of a K2). This produces a very tailored vertical lace pattern with a pronounced grain to the "feathers."

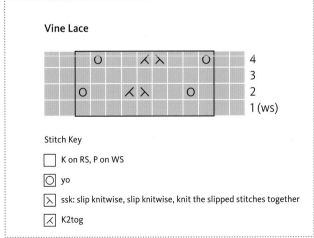

Vine Lace

Stitch Key

☐ K on RS, P on WS

Ⓞ yo

⋋ ssk: slip knitwise, slip knitwise, knit the slipped stitches together

⋌ K2tog

{Dropped-Stitch Patterns}

Extra wraps of yarn are used to create tall stitches that can be manipulated by twisting or crossing — mitigating striping and showing off the surface of the yarn. (For more information on extra wraps, dropped stitches, and slipped stitches, see chapter 3.)

Openwork Stripes

Long vertical strands alternate with horizontal ridges of garter stitch. Since it's based on garter stitch, there's no curling and no borders are needed. Since it's reversible, it's a doubly perfect stitch for a scarf, especially in a textured yarn.

Don't try this stitch on double-pointed needles: the extra wraps on Row 7 quickly fill the needles and fall off the ends!

Stitches: Any number

ROWS 1–6: Knit.
ROW 7: K1, knit, wrapping three times for each stitch until one stitch remains, K1.
ROW 8: Knit, dropping all the extra wraps.

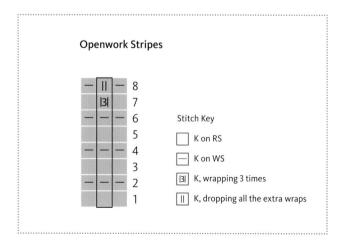

Openwork Stripes

Stitch Key

☐ K on RS

— K on WS

|3| K, wrapping 3 times

|| K, dropping all the extra wraps

Drop-Stitch Ribs

The back of this openwork rib is similar to the front but with just one knitted stitch in each rib, making it a perfect choice for scarves, shawls, or blankets where both sides will be seen.

This stitch is best worked firmly. If you're a loose knitter, drop down a needle size or two from your usual one for the yarn.

Stitches: Multiple of 8, plus 2

SETUP ROW (RS): K2, *P2, K2; repeat from *.

ROW 1 (WS): P2, *K1, yo, K1, P2, K2, P2; repeat from *.

ROW 2: *K2, P2, K2, P3; repeat from *, end K2.

ROW 3: P2, *K3, P2, K2, P2; repeat from *.

ROWS 4 AND 5: Repeat Rows 2 and 3.

ROW 6: *K2, P2, K2, P1, drop next stitch off needle and unravel 5 rows down to yo, P1; repeat from *, end K2.

ROW 7: P2, *K2, P2, K1, yo, K1, P2; repeat from *.

ROW 8: *K2, P3, K2, P2; repeat from *, end K2.

ROW 9: P2, *K2, P2, K3, P2; repeat from *.

ROWS 10 AND 11: Repeat Rows 8 and 9.

ROW 12: *K2, P1, drop next stitch off needle and unravel 5 rows down to yo, P1, K2, P2; repeat from *, end K2.

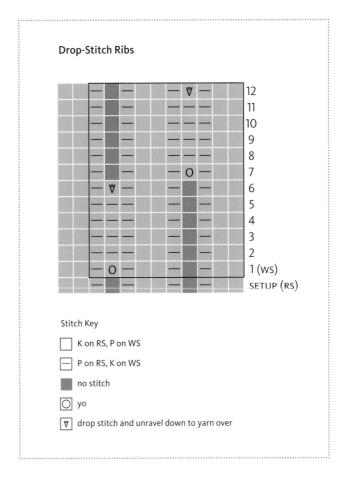

Drop-Stitch Ribs

Stitch Key

☐ K on RS, P on WS

⊟ P on RS, K on WS

▨ no stitch

⊙ yo

Ⅴ drop stitch and unravel down to yarn over

Estonian Shell Stitch

This wonderful swirled stitch is a variation of an Estonian long-eye stitch. It shows off variegated yarns in ways unlike any other pattern stitch I've run across, and lends itself to many variations in spacing and size. It's most effective with thinner, elastic yarns (as in the bottom swatch; yarn from Claudia Handpaints). For best results, knit firmly, and remember to always slip purlwise. It's easy to slip all three of the stitches together, saving time.

Thicker, loosely plied yarn

Thin, tightly plied yarn

Stitches: Multiple of 4, plus 1

ROW 1 (RS): P1, *K3 wrapping the yarn 4 times in each stitch, P1; repeat from *.
ROW 2: *K1, Sl3 wyif, dropping all the extra wraps; repeat from *, end K1.
ROW 3: P1, *Sl3 wyib, P1; repeat from *.
ROW 4: *K1, Sl3 wyif; repeat from *, end K1.
ROW 5: P1, *K3tog tbl, leaving the stitches on the needle, yo, K3tog tbl again in the same stitches and slide off needle, P1; repeat from *.
ROW 6: Purl.

VARIATIONS

» If the swirled strands seem too long and look messy, especially in thicker yarns, shorten them by wrapping only three times in each knit stitch on Row 1.

» Depending on the twist of your yarn, this pattern stitch may look better if the K3tog-yo-K3tog into the three slipped stitches on Row 5 is worked normally rather than into the back of the loops, which will cause the shell to twist in the opposite direction from the instructions as written.

» Stagger the shells so that they are centered between those in the previous pattern repeat.

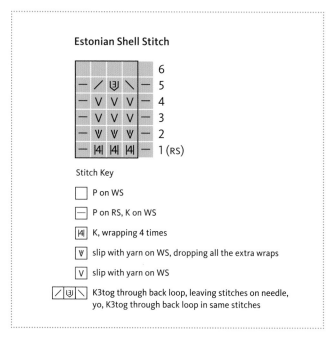

Estonian Shell Stitch

Stitch Key

☐ P on WS

— P on RS, K on WS

|4| K, wrapping 4 times

Ⓥ slip with yarn on WS, dropping all the extra wraps

V slip with yarn on WS

╱ ⓤ ╲ K3tog through back loop, leaving stitches on needle, yo, K3tog through back loop in same stitches

Raveled Ribs

This makes an incredibly fluffy fabric with lots of relief, and the back is just as interesting as the front. (For more information on dropping and unraveling stitches, see page 73.)

Stitches: Multiple of 3, plus 2

ROW 1 (WS): K2, *P1, K2; repeat from *.
ROW 2: Purl.
ROW 3: Knit.
ROWS 4–5: Repeat Rows 2–3.
ROW 6: *P2, drop next stitch off needle and unravel the 4 rows in reverse stockinette, knit into the knit stitch on the fifth row under all 4 loose strands and catch them in the stitch; repeat from *, end P2.

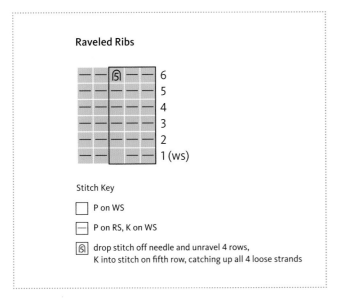

Raveled Ribs

Stitch Key

☐ P on WS

— P on RS, K on WS

⑤ drop stitch off needle and unravel 4 rows,
K into stitch on fifth row, catching up all 4 loose strands

Right side

Wrong side

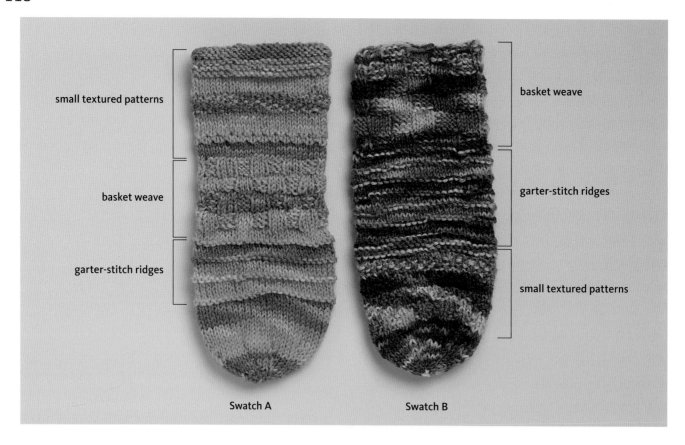

small textured patterns

basket weave

garter-stitch ridges

basket weave

garter-stitch ridges

small textured patterns

Swatch A

Swatch B

{Self-Striping Yarns}

While self-striping yarns remove the difficulty of changing colors to make stripes, they can be a bit boring to work with when there's nothing to do but plain knitting. These yarns also present special challenges when the shaping of the garment changes the width of the stripes in unappealing ways.

Making the Most of Self-Striping Sock Yarn

Introduce simple pattern stitches into the stripes to make it look like you've worked something complex. The sock swatches above show the effects of changing the pattern stitch whenever a new color appears in the yarn. When putting this technique to work, don't worry about where the beginning and end of round falls — instead, change your pattern stitch immediately as soon as the color changes.

Garter stitch. To highlight the color change itself, work a ridge of garter stitch by purling one round. If you do this as soon as the color changes, the interlocking stitches in the ridge show bumps of both the old and the new color (see swatch B). Swatch A demonstrates the slightly different effect when you knit one round in the new color, followed by a purl round.

Basket weave. When each stripe is about the same width, basket weave works very well. First, establish a ribbed pattern. Whenever the color changes, knit one complete round, then reverse the knits and purls in your ribs. K3, P3 basket weave appears in the middle of swatch A; K4, P4 basket weave is shown at the top of swatch B.

Random pattern stitches. Small pattern stitches used at random or with a different one assigned to each color are fun to work and add textural interest. Alternate between small pattern stitches or rotate through all of them. As with basket weave, these stitches look best when you knit one complete round whenever the color changes, then begin the new pattern stitch on the next round. Small textured patterns such as this appear at the top of swatch A and near the toe of swatch B.

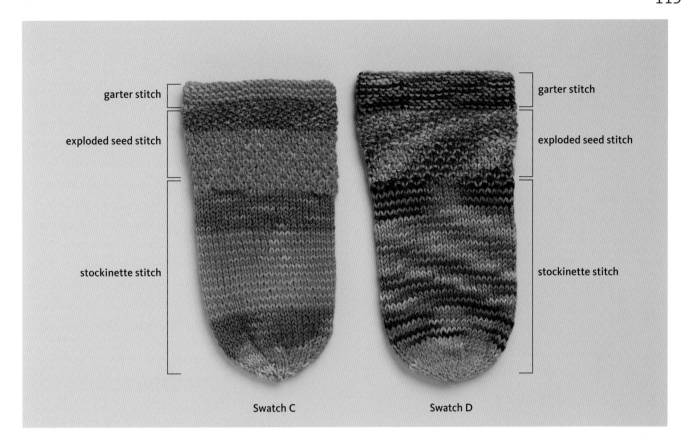

garter stitch

exploded seed stitch

stockinette stitch

Swatch C

garter stitch

exploded seed stitch

stockinette stitch

Swatch D

Other Patterning Possibilities for Self-Striping Sock Yarns

Helix-knit socks. Self-striping yarns also lend themselves to helix knitting, where they are worked on alternate rows with another yarn. The sock swatches above use the same self-striping yarns as used for the swatches on the facing page. In swatch C, the orange/pink/blue yarn is alternated with a solid pumpkin-colored yarn. In swatch D, it's knit with the blue/green self-striping yarn. Both examples show the effect in plain stockinette, in an exploded Seed Stitch (where there is a plain knit round between each knit/purl round), and in garter stitch. Notice how the seeding causes the warm colors to blend in swatch A, while the contrasting colors show off the pattern stitch in swatch B. (For more information on this technique, see Helix Knitting, page 198.)

Self-Striping Sweater Yarns

Fair-Isle patterns. Self-striping yarns are also fun to use with a second solid yarn for Fair-Isle patterning: it looks like you're changing colors as the sections of striping follow one another. You'll find more about Fair Isle and stranded knitting in chapter 5. Entrelac, modular knitting, or any other technique that incorporates strips or blocks where the grain of the knitting travels in different directions can all be used to good effect. (See also chapter 7, and Putting Geometry to Work, page 125.)

Listening to your yarn. Allowing the color of the yarn to dictate the pattern stitch works with self-striping sweater yarns just as well as with sock yarns. When the transition from one color to the next is gradual, however, it can be difficult to know when to start the new pattern stitch. Avoid a tight slipped-stitch pattern adjacent to wider garter stitch, unless you want the garment to vary in width.

In pattern stitches. Use a self-striping yarn in color pattern stitches such as those in chapter 3. For example, substitute one yarn for all the contrast colors in the bag on page 91.

PATTERN STITCH INS AND OUTS

The scarf above takes advantage of the characteristics of different pattern stitches to create an undulating profile. Slipped Honeycomb (page 105) makes the fabric narrower and supports both ends of the scarf. Brioche Rib (below) is light, fluffy, and much wider, creating the medallion effect. The two pattern stitches alternately emphasize the horizontal and the vertical. (Yarn by Lorna's Laces.)

No-Purl Brioche Pattern Stitch

Even number of stitches

SETUP ROW: Knit.

ROW 1: *Knit into stitch below, K1; repeat from *.

ROW 2: Repeat Row 1.

Stitch Key

☐	K on RS
⊟	K on WS
Ⓐ	K into stitch below on WS
⋒	K into stitch below on RS

```
⋒  2
Ⓐ ⊟ 1 (ws)
   SETUP
```

{Texture and Fiber}

When multicolor yarns are also highly textured, there is an additional level of complexity. You'll need to experiment to show off both the color and the texture of the yarn. As a general rule, textured and fuzzy yarns are most attractive in patterns that include purled stitches. But the more interesting the yarn, the less any pattern will show, so the simplest choices are frequently the best. Some pattern stitches are nearly impossible to see in a highly textured yarn, which is fine if it makes the yarn look good, but extremely annoying if you can't see the pattern well enough to knit it! You'll need to balance the difficulty of the knitting against the effect you want to produce when deciding the best approach to each particular yarn.

Comparing Stitch Effects on Different Yarns

All of the swatches shown on the following pages were knit with the same simple pattern stitches in the same order: (from bottom to top):

1. Garter stitch
2. Stockinette stitch
3. Slipped Honeycomb (page 105)
4. Reverse Stockinette
5. Rose Fabric (page 108)
6. Seed Stitch

The yarns used, although very different in fiber content and construction, were all dyed in the same colors by Mountain Colors.

Swatch A. Mountain Colors, Mountain Goat: 55% mohair/
45% wool 2-ply

▶ *Swatches A and B.* You can see the patterns clearly in
swatches A and B, which are worked in smooth yarns. The
stitch definition is best in swatch B for two reasons: (1) it's
a 3-ply yarn, which is rounder and shows off the stitches
better than the 2-ply yarn in swatch A; (2) it's 100% wool,
while the yarn used in swatch A is a wool-mohair blend.
Wool has greater elasticity than other fibers, and its
springiness results in greater relief in pattern stitches.
On the other hand, the shine of the mohair in swatch A
shows off the stitches more than yarn made from a less
reflective fiber. In these two yarns, the main effect of the
pattern stitches is to change the way the colors appear.
Some break up the colors into small points, some create a
bumpy fabric, some emphasize the horizontal, and some
show off the vertical. Any of the pattern stitches could
be used successfully in either of these yarns, so you can
choose based on the visual effect you want, the feel and
thickness of the fabric, and whether curling is acceptable.

Swatch B. Mountain Colors, New 3-Ply Wool: 100% wool 3-ply

Note: For explanation of numbered stitch patterns, see page 120.

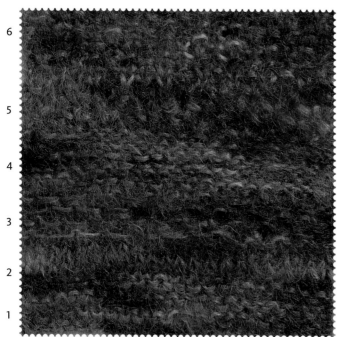

6
5
4
3
2
1

Swatch C. Mountain Colors, Mohair: 78% mohair/13% wool/
9% nylon, brushed

6
5
4
3
2
1

Swatch D. Mountain Colors, Wooly Feathers: 65% kid mohair/
35% nylon eyelash

▲ *Swatch C is a brushed mohair blend.* The stitches are not quite as clear as in swatches A and E because the colors are softened by a halo of mohair. Least effective visually is Rose Fabric stitch (5), which can barely be seen through the haze. The plain stockinette section is the least fuzzy, since the mohair tends to pop out on the purl side of any stitch. If you want to maximize the halo of the yarn, select one of the patterns with plenty of purl stitches. Garter stitch (1) and reverse stockinette (4) both emphasize the horizontal, with the ridges spaced farther apart in garter stitch. Choose between them based on the spacing, but go for garter if you don't want the fabric to curl. To avoid noticeable horizontal lines, choose Seed Stitch (6).

▲ *Swatch D.* The long strands of "eyelash" completely obscure the pattern stitches and make it impossible to see what you're doing as you work. Your best choice with this yarn is garter stitch. (See also the hints for working with loopy mohair on the facing page.)

Note: For explanation of numbered stitch patterns, see page 120.

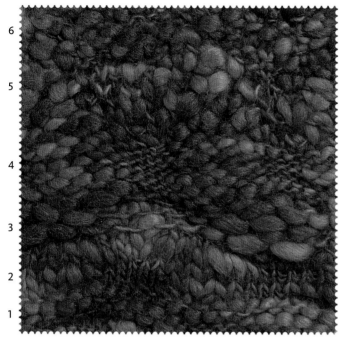

6
5
4
3
2
1

Swatch E. Mountain Colors, Homespun: 85% wool/15% silk single-ply thick-and-thin

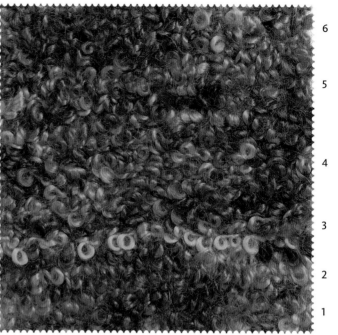

6
5
4
3
2
1

Swatch F. Mountain Colors, Mohair Loop: 93% mohair/4% wool/3% nylon bouclé

▲ *Swatch E.* Here, the thick and thin yarn entirely overshadows all pattern stitches. Whatever you knit using a yarn like this is going to be about the yarn, not the pattern. The swatch does show interesting properties of the yarn, though, in the garter (1), stockinette (2), and reverse stockinette (4) sections. The garter-stitch section at the bottom of the swatch undulates, forced into curves by the thick and thin yarn. This could be exploited in a design by alternating

garter stitch and stockinette stitch stripes. Where thick areas converge on several rows in stockinette, the fabric fans out and accentuates the colors in the larger stitches. In reverse stockinette, where thick spots fall at the same point on four or five consecutive rows, the yarn actually pops out like a bobble, responding to the natural curl of the fabric. If the fabric were knit more loosely or blocked firmly, these lumps would disappear.

▲ *Swatch F.* The loopy mohair yarn is just as unresponsive to variations in pattern stitch as the eyelash yarn. It appears less loopy in stockinette (2), but otherwise it looks almost identical regardless of the pattern stitch used. It's nearly impossible to see the pattern stitches while you are knitting this yarn, and it's not easy to knit because the tips of the needles catch in the loops. For all those reasons, I would work anything made from this

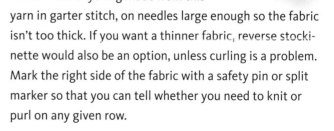

yarn in garter stitch, on needles large enough so the fabric isn't too thick. If you want a thinner fabric, reverse stockinette would also be an option, unless curling is a problem. Mark the right side of the fabric with a safety pin or split marker so that you can tell whether you need to knit or purl on any given row.

A. Coughlin's Homespun

B. Plymouth

C. Plymouth

D. Schoeller Stahl

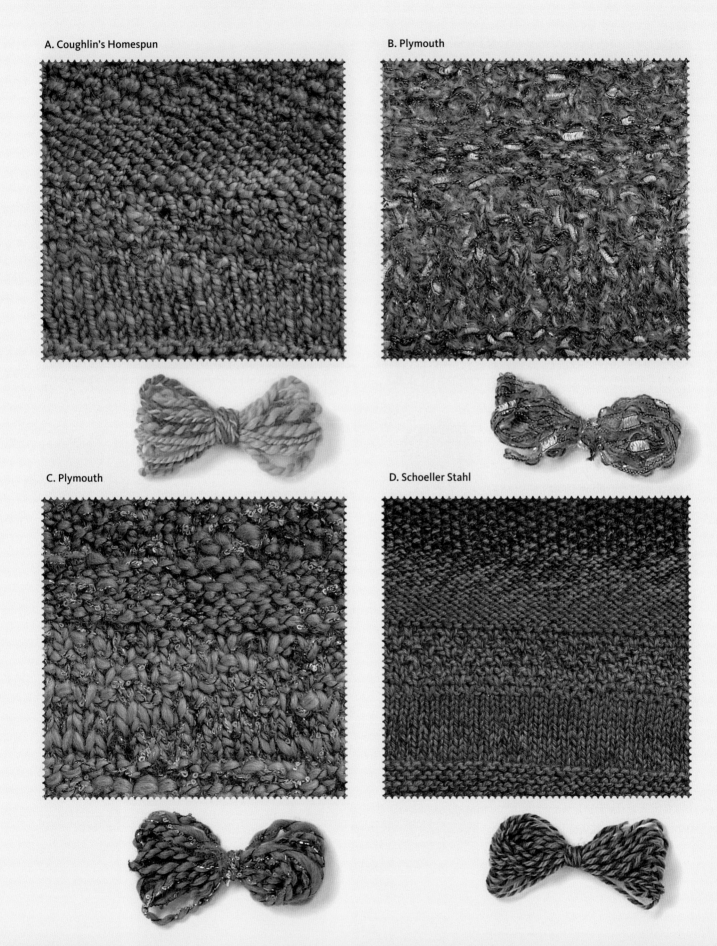

Complex Yarns

The yarns I've showcased so far in this chapter are all handpainted or space dyed. Although their colors and the lengths of their color segments and repeats may vary, they all have one thing in common: at any given point, the yarn color is solid. Where the color in a yarn isn't solid, it has been incorporated at the structural level, during fiber preparation, spinning, or plying, rather than painted or printed onto the yarn later. Color incorporated at the structural level looks different in the finished knitting.

The swatches shown on the facing page only sample the many types of yarns with color as an integral part of the spinning process that are now available. Some combine changing colors over their length with multiple plies in different colors throughout; others have slubs or bumps of contrasting colors. You can be certain that each new season will bring the release of yarns with still different structures into yarn shops around the world. Some of these yarns have beautiful textures or twists that are shown off best with a pattern stitch, while others are so textured that they overpower any pattern. Have fun experimenting with needle size and pattern stitch to find the best way to show off complex yarns like these.

{Putting Geometry to Work}

By knitting your garment in sections, you can exploit the characteristics of variegated yarns that are not shown to advantage in traditional garments, constructed with one-piece front, back, and sleeves. These sections can include strips, a patchwork of squares and rectangles, or smaller modules composed of triangles, mitered squares, or other geometric shapes. When you break a garment (or other knitting project) into modules, you can change the direction of the grain of the fabric in each module, also changing the orientation of any stripes caused by the yarn. This effect can be seen in entrelac and modular knitting (see chapter 7), as well as in larger intarsia color-blocks (see chapter 6). Knitting the modules independently in triangles, mitered squares, or circles has added advantages: it requires shaping that causes each row to have a different number of stitches, which in turn affects the placement of the colors in the fabric and prevents repetitive striping or blotching. Pieces that are knit circularly, like mitered squares, bend the stripes, emphasizing the structure of the module.

Geometric Shapes: Triangles, Squares, and Beyond

The swatches shown on the following pages were all knit in garter stitch because it simplifies the shaping. The triangular swatches were knit flat, but the others were knit circularly from the center out, using yarn overs for shaping so the increases are easy to see. You can, of course, use a different increase technique that doesn't create eyelets. Because the center portion of the swatch is worked on very few stitches, you'll need to use a set of double-pointed needles or two circular needles. When the shapes grow to 5 or 6" (13–15 cm) across, they will fit on a 16" (40 cm) long circular needle. As the knitting grows still larger, however, you will find it more comfortable to change to an even longer circular needle.

Right Triangle

Work two of these to create a square. Use any increase you like, but it's best if you increase after the first stitch of the row, so the edge doesn't become too tight. A single triangle can grow large enough to be a shawl.

CAST ON 2 STITCHES.

ROW 1: Knit 1, increase 1, knit to the end of the row.

Repeat this row over and over to make your triangle grow larger, 1 stitch every row.

When the piece is as large as you want it, bind off.

VARIATIONS

» Repeatedly change yarns to make stripes.

» To work a square, increase to the desired dimension, then begin decreasing at the beginning of every row until you have just 1 stitch left. Make it as big as a blanket — or as small as a coaster.

» If you work a square, switch yarns at the widest point, when you begin decreasing, to divide the resulting square exactly in half.

A FEW NOTES ON INCREASES FOR SQUARES, CIRCLES, AND OCTAGONS

Knitting into the front and back of the stitch doesn't work well in the modules, because it steals yarn from the existing stitches. On the first increase round, where you are doubling the number of stitches, this increase causes the knitting to become too tight and makes it difficult to work. This can also be a problem if you use the lifted Make 1 (M1) increase. Instead, increase with an M1 using the working yarn (not lifted from the row below) or a yarn over (yo). Where M1 increases occur in pairs, in a square or octagon for example, it's best to alternate left and right twists for symmetry.

Mitered Square

CAST ON 8 STITCHES, using either double-pointed or two circular needles, and join the beginning and end of the cast on, being careful not to twist. Place a split marker or safety pin in the first, third, fifth, and seventh stitches.

ROUND 1: Purl.

ROUND 2: Increase before and after every marked stitch. On this first increase round, you'll need to increase at the beginning of the round and between every stitch (16 stitches).

REPEAT ROUNDS 1–2. Move the four markers up closer to the needles as the piece grows. Continue alternating these rounds until the square is the size you want, ending after working Round 2.

Bind off loosely in purl, or turn the square over and bind off in knitting, working back around in the opposite direction. Cut your yarn after binding off and use the tail to close the gap between the beginning and end of the bind off. Use the tail left at the cast on to close up the hole at the center of the square.

VARIATION

» Knit the marked stitch on every round, creating a column of knit stitches highlighting each corner. This technique was used for the octagon on page 129.

WORKING FROM THE OUTSIDE IN

By casting on enough stitches for the perimeter, you can also knit squares, circles, and octagons from the outside to the center, instead of from the center out. To work from the outside, you must first work a gauge swatch and calculate the number of stitches needed to go all the way around. Round this to the nearest multiple of 8. Decrease as described for increasing in the directions for each shape, until you get down to 8 stitches at the center. Cut the yarn and pull it through all the remaining stitches, pulling them together to avoid a hole at the center.

Circle

If you work yarn overs for the increases, you'll see the swirl of eyelets, as shown in the swatch here. If you work closed increases, there won't be any eyelets, but the swirled structure will still be noticeable. If you prefer to camouflage your increases and do away with the swirl, shift your increases to a different position each time you work them. On the first two increase rounds, you won't have a choice of where to put them, but on the third increase round, move them so that they fall between the last two sets of increases. Continue making this adjustment on each increase round. As long as they don't line up, they will not be noticeable.

CAST ON 8 STITCHES, using either double-pointed or two circular needles, and join the beginning and end of the cast on, being careful not to twist.

ROUND 1 AND ALL ODD-NUMBERED ROUNDS: Purl.
ROUND 2: *K1, inc 1; repeat from * (16 stitches).
ROUND 4: *K2, inc 1; repeat from * (24 stitches).
ROUND 6: *K3, inc 1; repeat from * (32 stitches).
Continue in this manner, knitting one additional stitch between increases on each subsequent increase round. Remember to purl the plain rounds between increase rounds.

When the circle is the size you want, stop after working an increase round.

Bind off loosely in purl or turn the circle over and bind off in knitting, working back around in the opposite direction. Cut your yarn after binding off and use the tail to close the gap between the beginning and end of the bind off. Use the tail left at the cast on to close up the hole at the center of the circle, if desired.

Octagon

CAST ON 8 STITCHES, using either double-pointed or two circular needles, and join the beginning and end of the cast on, being careful not to twist. Place a split marker or safety pin in each of the 8 stitches.

SETUP ROW: Knit around, increasing before every stitch (16 stitches).

ROUND 1: Purl the unmarked stitches and knit the marked stitches (Note: Work P1, K1 all the way around the first time).

ROUND 2: Knit.

ROUND 3: Purl the unmarked stitches and knit the marked stitches.

ROUND 4: Knit around, increasing before and after every marked stitch (32 stitches). (Note: The first time you will increase at the beginning of the round and between every stitch.)

REPEAT ROUNDS 1–4. Remember to knit the marked stitches and purl all the other stitches on Rounds 1 and 3. Whenever you work Round 4, you will increase 16 stitches, one on each side of the eight marked stitches. Move the eight markers up closer to the needles as the piece grows. Continue until the octagon is the size you want, and stop after working Round 4.

Bind off loosely in purl or turn the octagon over and bind off in knitting, working back around in the opposite direction. Cut your yarn after binding off and use the tail to close the gap between the beginning and end of the bind off. Use the tail left at the cast on to close up the hole at the center of the octagon.

VARIATION

» Purl all the stitches on Rounds 1 and 3, which will make the corners of the octagon less noticeable. You can see this effect in the corners of the mitered square (page 127).

Garter Rules!

The rule of thumb in garter stitch for squares, circles, and octagons is to increase at a rate of 8 stitches every other round. These shapes must be knit loosely enough that they lie flat. If knit too tightly, they may be distorted, with a protruding center or curling outer edge.

» *For triangles.* Increase 1 stitch at both edges every other row.

» *For squares.* Since these are made from four triangles, you need to make the increases for all four triangles. Two stitches for each triangle equates to 8 stitches every other round. These are worked in pairs at each corner.

» *For octagons.* Pair increases so there are 16 on every increase round. To make the increasing continue at the correct rate, these are spaced four rounds apart instead of two. This works because in garter stitch, one stitch measures the same as two rows.

Working Geometric Shapes in Patterns Other Than Garter Stitch

If you want to knit the same shapes in any other pattern, including stockinette stitch, you need to figure out the ratio of stitches to rows. Knit a swatch in your pattern stitch and then measure it over several inches or centimeters for accuracy. For example, measure the number of stitches in 2" (5 cm) and the number of rows in 2" (5 cm). In stockinette stitch, using worsted weight yarn, this is likely to be 10 stitches and 14 rows, in which case your ratio would be 10:14. Simplify the ratio by dividing by any common factors. That is, divide both numbers by the same number so you can work with the smallest numbers possible. In this case, both numbers are even, so divide by 2 to get a ratio of 5 stitches to 7 rows.

For triangles in stockinette stitch. Assuming you get the same ratio (5:7), you must increase one stitch at each edge on 5 out of every 7 rows as evenly as possible to make a right triangle. You can do this by casting on 2 or 3 stitches and increasing at both edges on Rows 1–3 and Rows 5–6. Work Rows 4 and 7 without increasing. Repeat this same sequence of 7 rows until your triangle is the size you want. If you've measured accurately, your triangle will have a perfect right angle.

For circles in stockinette stitch. Increase at 8 points, just as in the garter stitch circle example (page 128), but do it only on 5 out of every 7 rounds.

For squares in stockinette stitch. Cast on 8 stitches, mark the 4 corner stitches, and then increase on both sides of them on 5 out of every 7 rounds, just like for the triangle.

For octagons in stockinette stitch. This is a bit trickier: You must increase 16 stitches at a time, but half as often, so you increase on 5 out of every 14 rounds. Plan to increase every third round 4 times, and then on the second round once. This places the increases on Rounds 3, 6, 9, 11, and 14.

Remember, your numbers may not be the same as mine. In fact, the numbers will vary depending on the pattern stitch you choose. Once you've figured out your ratio of stitches to rows, the easiest way to work out an increase plan is to make a table like the one below. Spread out the increase rows as evenly as you can and it will work just fine.

Sample Plan for Increases

Row Number	Increase
1	yes
2	yes
3	yes
4	no
5	yes
6	yes
7	no
7 rows	5 increases

{Using Geometric Shapes}

You can make any of these shapes whatever size you like. A single square can grow large enough to be a pillow, a blanket, or the front or back of a sweater. If it needs to be shaped in some way, you can bind off some of the stitches and continue with others.

Some Sample Designs

For set-in sleeve:

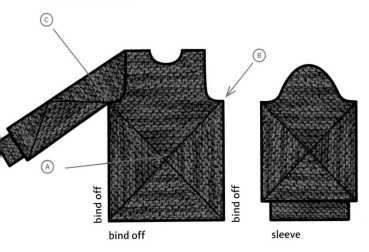

bind off

bind off

bind off

sleeve

For drop shoulder:

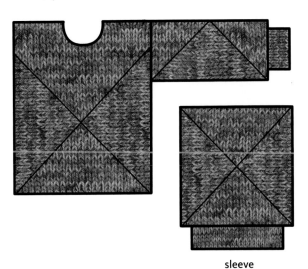

sleeve

For example, make a square starting from the center (A) and work until it is the right width for a sweater back from side to side. Work across one side without any more increasing. Begin binding off an inch or two before the corner on this first side (B). Continue binding off all the way around the other three sides of the square, and then bind off another inch or two at the beginning of the first side (C).

You've now got the back of a sweater worked up to the bind off at the underarm. Continue working up the back of the sweater, shaping the armholes and the neckline using whatever method you prefer. Make a second piece like the first, but shape the neckline for the front of the sweater. Sleeves can be made in the same fashion, starting with a mitered square and adding sleeve-cap shaping at the top instead of an armhole or neckline. If you want a tapered sleeve, it's easiest to make the mitered square, then continue with the stitches along the sides to add shallow triangles for shaping from cuff to underarm. Making a drop shoulder sweater is even simpler, since there is no armhole or sleeve-cap shaping (above right).

Circles and octagons can be used as the basis for sweaters as well. When you've knit them wide enough for the sweater front or back, add triangles to fill out the corners. Wherever you want to add a triangle, continue working, decreasing at both edges until it comes to a point rather than binding off. Now you have a square, and the same shaping notes apply as for a garment based on mitered squares.

If you prefer casting on at the outer edge and then decreasing to the center, you can still construct garment-sized pieces. Make the main piece, then go back and pick up stitches along the outer edge anywhere that you want to add another section. Another construction technique that makes it unnecessary either to cast on or to pick up a lot of stitches is to begin at all four corners, making four separate triangles by increasing from 2 or 3 cast on stitches. Join all four triangles on a circular needle and decrease to the center, in a circle or octagon, to complete your square.

Strips and Blocks

If you find the more complicated geometric modules daunting, working with rectangular strips is an easier approach to sweater construction. While you can plan strip or block construction in advance, working a gauge swatch and calculating the number of stitches for each section, you can also indulge in "organic" design, which means that you make it up as you go. The basic concept is to knit a strip as long as you want it. Bind off, then pick up stitches along one or both edges and work sections at right angles to the original strip.

For example, if you want to make a sweater, knit the center panel first (A). Start by casting on some stitches. For a narrow center panel, cast on fewer stitches; for a wider one, cast on more. Work this center panel in any pattern stitch you like: garter stitch, stockinette, one or more cables, a textured pattern, or lace. When it is the length of your sweater from the bottom edge up to where you envision the neckline, bind it off. If you plan to add borders to the neck or bottom later, stop short to allow for these. Now go back and pick up stitches all along the side of the center panel. (For more information on picking up stitches, see chapter 8.) If you plan to work the sides in the same pattern stitch, measure the gauge on that first panel and figure out how many stitches to pick up. If you want to use a different pattern stitch, work a swatch in that pattern and measure the number of stitches per inch to ensure that you pick up the correct number along your center panel. (For information on sideways sweater construction, see pages 283.)

Another approach is to work horizontally: Knit a strip until it reaches the desired length across or around the garment (B), and then pick up stitches and knit up or down from there. This works for sweaters and hats, where the strip can serve as either a central element or the bottom border, as well as for socks and mittens, where the strip can serve as the cuff.

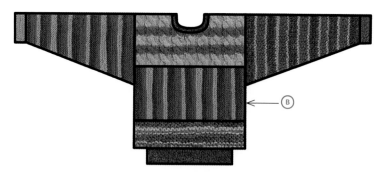

Assemble an entire garment out of strips. This is particularly effective in self-striping yarns, which produce variable blocks of color within each strip. Work a center strip, then strips of varying widths, until all of them placed side by side are wide enough to make the garment piece. Strips at the sides can stop at the underarm or end in triangles to provide armhole shaping. Sleeves can be shaped this way as well. Joining these strips can be daunting, so refer to pages 236–240 for ideas on how to accomplish this.

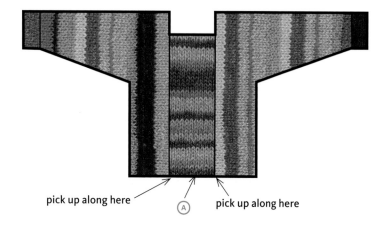

pick up along here   Ⓐ   pick up along here

{Using Multiple Yarns}

Combining multicolor yarns with other yarns, both solid and variegated, offers many opportunities for creativity, especially when you capitalize on the various color knitting techniques available. As you see here, you can select yarns that coordinate or contrast, choose one or several solid colors that match the colors in your variegated yarn, or put color harmonies to work for you.

▶ *Stranded knitting.* Consider working a Fair Isle or stranded pattern using a solid background color and a variegated pattern color or using two variegated yarns. Make sure that the yarns you select don't share any of the same hues and that they are also very different in value. This is necessary to provide enough contrast so that the pattern will be visible. (For stranded knitting, see chapter 5.) The subtly graded color changes are an ideal choice to evoke the feeling of sand and ocean in this seashore-themed stranded sweater. (Yarns by Lorna's Laces)

▲ *Mosaic knitting.* Multicolor yarns can be used in mosaic knitting, pattern stitches, and entrelac. In fact, they can be used anywhere you'd use a solid-colored yarn. You're only limited by your creativity. (For mosaic and entrelac, see chapter 7; for pattern stitches, see chapter 3.) Multicolored yarns give these whimsical bags a delightful sparkle. (Yarns by Unger and Oak Grove [left] and by Oak Grove [right])

▲ *Intarsia knitting.* Multicolor yarns can, of course, also be used in intarsia knitting. They add frequent variations in color that are difficult to achieve by changing between solid yarns. As with stranded knitting, choose multicolor yarns whose values and hues differ from neighboring colors to ensure good contrast. This boldly radiating vest design is softened by the use of monochromatic variegated yarns. (Yarns by Kathleen Hughes)

Three Simple Techniques with Multicolors

In addition to the formal techniques we've just been examining, you have the option of using more than one strand of yarn in much simpler ways. Holding two strands of yarn together while knitting, alternating rows of each color, or designing striped patterns using multicolor yarns can all be extremely effective, although the results differ depending on the hue and contrast of the colors.

▲ *A muting effect.* Solid purple yarn was knitted with the handpainted yarn. Since the purple matches one of the colors in the yarn, the two blend together in much of the swatch. Only the green, orange, and gold of the hand-painted yarn are visible, and then only when they're on top of the purple yarn. The overall effect is to tone down the handpainted yarn.

A BAGFUL OF COLOR. Holding two different variegated yarns together while knitting results in dynamic color interplay in this shoulder bag. (For pattern, see page 143; yarns from Cherry Tree Hill.)

Holding two strands together. Knitting with two strands of yarn — whether it's two ends of the same center-pull ball, two balls of the same yarn, or two completely different yarns — can have surprisingly effective results. Before you start, estimate the correct needle size, because using two strands of the same-weight yarn will be thicker than you might expect. You may want to knit it on larger needles to make the fabric looser and thinner, or substitute a fine yarn for one of the strands. (For estimating needle size and working with multiple strands, see pages 22–23.

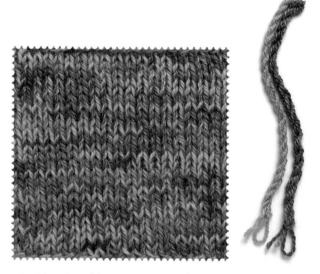

▲ *Livening things up.* A second variegated yarn in warm oranges with a little green is knit with the same variegated yarn as in the swatch above. The colors mix together, creating a fabric that is warm and variegated throughout.

Alternating rows. You can also use two strands of yarn alternately to make stripes. Alternating rows of the same yarn is very helpful for blending together different dye lots or for camouflaging variations in skeins of handpainted yarns. This technique is also useful for stretching out small amounts of yarn to finish a project and for combining colors in interesting ways. (For more ideas and techniques, see chapter 2.)

▲ *A solid with a handpaint.* A handpainted yarn was knit in alternating one-row stripes with a solid yarn that matched one of its colors. The result is that the other colors are spread out, creating a very subtle stripe. The striping itself isn't very bold because the values of the two yarns are close enough to create little contrast.

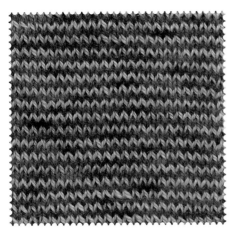

▲ *Two variegateds.* The same variegated yarn used on the facing page was knit with a second variegated yarn, in dark burgundies and greens. There is a great difference in value between the two yarns, and the combined colors form a triad from the hue families of the secondary colors — orange, purple, and green — to vibrant effect.

▲ *Creating stripes with texture and pattern.* You can make stripes any width you like and use different-textured pattern stitches in each stripe. The swatch above is the preliminary fabric design for a sweater, showing the ridged striped pattern for the sleeve and body and the mosaic pattern used in the borders. Random stripes would, of course, work just as well as formal ones. Bouclé stripes knit in reverse stockinette show off this heavily textured yarn to best advantage. The colors for the solid stripes and the gold yarn in the cuff were matched to colors in the variegated bouclé. (Yarns by Oak Grove)

{Solving Problems}

Some phenomena that crop up when working with variegated yarns can be perplexing. Here are a few ideas for dealing with problems like maintaining (or preventing) color repeats, interventions for pooling and striping, and making matched pairs.

Matching Color Repeats

When you change to a new ball, you could start at the beginning and relinquish control of the colors. This may look fine, but it may be unpleasantly disruptive if a color repeat is already noticeable. Assuming that the two balls are dyed consistently, you have the option of maintaining the existing color repeat. When you get about 3 yards from the end of the original ball, stretch the yarn out so you can see all that's remaining. Pull out the beginning of the new ball and lay it alongside the end of the old one until you find a section where the colors match. Use an overhand knot to tie the beginning of the new yarn to the old one, leaving a tail. If the colors don't match up now that you've tied the knot, slide the knot until they do. Knit the old yarn up to the knot, then switch to the new yarn. Trim off any excess yarn, leaving tails to be woven in later. If the skeins are not dyed consistently, line up the colors as well as you can.

Variations in Color Repeats

Variations in the length of the color repeat can occur within a skein or in different skeins. This problem is more common with hand-dyed yarns than commercially printed yarns. When the yarn is wound into a skein, the inner layers of the skein are a tiny bit shorter than the outer layers. Variations between skeins can occur if one is simply wound under a little more tension than another. These small disparities can be quite noticeable if they occur in a straight section of a garment. Variations in the knitter's tension can also disturb the color repeats. Where there is shaping, the color placement changes as the stitch count changes, and variations in the length of the color repeat will be less noticeable.

If any of these discrepancies become a problem, you can disguise it by alternating rows of the same variegated yarn, either knitting from both ends of a center-pull ball or knitting from two different balls. This usually disrupts the color repeats enough so that further variations, due either to the yarn or to the knitter, won't be noticeable.

Shoulder Area Looks Different

When a garment is shaped in the armhole and neck area, the rows are shorter and less yarn is used in each row, so any repeating color pattern is disturbed. If this interruption is unpleasant, pull out a few inches of yarn at the beginning of the row every so often and leave it to be secured later. In self-striping yarns, where stripes may suddenly become three or four times as wide as they were below the armholes, cut the yarn and skip to the next color in the ball when each stripe seems wide enough to you.

Pooling and Striping

If pooling and striping plague you in the course of a project — in spite of any pattern stitches you're using to prevent them — pull a couple of inches of yarn out at the beginning of every row or every few rows, and the color placement will shift (unfortunately this may merely shift the problem to another place on the fabric). You will, of course, need to weave in the additional ends later.

Making Two of Anything Match

Some knitters embrace the differences in pairs of socks, mittens, left and right sleeves, and left and right sweater fronts; they don't worry if the pairs are identical twins or not. Others find that the differences grate on their nerves. To make two of anything the same, begin each garment or piece at the same point in the color repeat of the yarn and shape them identically. With some yarns it may matter which end of the ball or skein you begin with, so be sure the colors repeat in the same sequence (not the reverse!) on the second of the pair. If they don't, unravel and begin again with the other end of the yarn.

Sleeves present a special challenge. Because they are attached to the sweater facing in opposite directions, you see the right half of one and the left half of the other regardless of whether you're looking at the front or back of the sweater. When sleeves are knit circularly, there will frequently be a noticeable pool of color in the upper arm area, which will face front on one sleeve and back on the other. There are several ways to avoid or mitigate this problem. The first is to knit the sleeves flat. The second is to watch for any noticeable pooling of color and bring it to a halt by pulling out a few inches of yarn at the beginning of several rows (or rounds) as soon as it appears. A third, more challenging, solution is to knit the second sleeve in the opposite direction from the first. In circular knitting, this can be accomplished (in stockinette) by purling the entire sleeve and turning it right-side out when it's complete. In flat knitting, unless you are adept at knitting and purling backwards, this is not a workable solution.

{Inspiration for Design}

I have found that it's best to take inspiration from the yarn itself when working with multicolor yarns. The ideas in this chapter for working with these challenging yarns are the ones I have found most effective, and any of them will serve as a good starting point. As I said at the beginning of the chapter, the key to success is experimentation; you never know how a yarn will look until you try it out.

Modifying Existing Patterns

Once you discover the best way to show off your yarn, you can either design a project from scratch or make modifications to a pattern you already have. You'll find discussions of both approaches in chapter 9, but here are some ideas to get you started.

Assuming that your multicolor yarn knits up at the same gauge and is made of the same material as the yarn called for in the instructions, you can substitute that yarn for the entire garment. If the fiber content is different, you may still be able to substitute, but you run the risk of the garment either being too elastic (if it was designed for cotton, and you knit it in wool), or stretching out of shape (if it was designed for wool, and you knit it in cotton).

If you'd like to substitute a pattern stitch for whatever is called for in the original pattern, that should also be possible if the new stitch knits up at the same gauge as the old one, and if the fabric created is similar in thickness, drape, and elasticity. You can also add bands of pattern stitches, adjusting the stitch count or needle size in that section if necessary, to ensure that the width of the fabric doesn't change. Regardless of the type of yarn, you can always add embellishments: ruffles, cords, fringes, bindings, and so on. For more ideas, take a look at chapter 8.

HIKER SOCKS

The Broken Garter Stitch Pattern makes a thick and comfy sock. The fabric also stretches beautifully to fit growing feet, so they make the perfect sock for kids. This is an excellent pattern stitch for showing off variegated yarns to great effect.

Measurements

Small   5.75"–7.5" (14.5–19 cm) foot length, 6.5"–8" (16.5–20.5) foot circumference

Medium   7.75"–9.5" (19.5–24 cm) foot length, 7"–9" (18–23 cm) foot circumference

Large   9.5"–11.25" (19.5–28.5 cm) foot length, 8.5"–10.5" (21.5–26.5 cm) foot circumference

Yarn   Tess Designer Yarns Superwash Merino, 100% wool, 8 oz (228 g)/560 yds (512 m), Spring Garden, 1 skein

Needles   One set of US 4 (3.5 mm) double-pointed needles, *or size needed to achieve correct gauge*

Gauge   22 stitches = 4" (10 cm) in Broken Garter Stitch Pattern

---

Broken Garter Stitch Pattern
ROUND 1   K3, *P3, K3; repeat from *.
ROUND 2   P3, *K3, P3; repeat from *.
Repeat Rounds 1 and 2 for pattern.

Knitting the Leg

	Small	Medium	Large
SETUP ROW Cast on	33 sts	39 sts	45 sts
Arrange stitches on 3 double-pointed needles as follows:			
NEEDLE 1	15 sts	18 sts	21 sts
NEEDLE 2	9 sts	12 sts	12 sts
NEEDLE 3	9 sts	9 sts	12 sts

Join into a round, being careful not to twist stitches.

	Small	Medium	Large
Work in Broken Garter Stitch Pattern until measurement from cast on is	5" (12.5 cm)	6" (15 cm)	7" (17.5 cm)

End with Round 2 of pattern.

Knitting the Heel Flap

Slip all stitches from Needle 3 onto Needle 2. You now have stitches on 2 needles as follows:

	Small	Medium	Large
NEEDLE 1	15 sts	18 sts	21 sts

Knitting the Heel Flap (cont'd)

	Small	Medium	Large
NEEDLE 2	18 sts	21 sts	24 sts
Turn and work back and forth on Needle 2 stitches only.			
ROW 1 (WS)	*P3, K3; repeat from *	P3, *K3, P3; repeat from *	*P3, K3; repeat from *
ROW 2 (RS)	*K3, P3; repeat from *	P3, *K3, P3; repeat from *	*K3, P3; repeat from *
Repeat Rows 1 and 2 until you have completed	19 rows	23 rows	27 rows

Shaping the Heel

Note: The heel is knit in plain garter stitch.

	Small	Medium	Large
ROW 1 (RS) Knit _____, K2tog, K1, turn.	11 sts	13 sts	14 sts
ROW 2 (WS) Slip 1, knit _____, K2tog, K1, turn.	5 sts	6 sts	5 sts
ROW 3 Slip 1, knit to 1 stitch before the gap formed by last turn, K2tog, K1, turn.			
Repeat Row 3 on both right- and wrong-side rows until all heel stitches have been worked.			
Note: On the last 2 rows you may not have enough stitches to work the last K1. If this happens, simply ignore the K1, turn and work the next row. For heel stitches, *you now have*	12 sts	13 sts	14 sts
This is the Bottom Needle. The stitches you have not been working are on the Top Needle. Break yarn. Using an empty needle, attach yarn and work across Top Needle in Broken Garter Stitch Pattern as established.			
Using an empty needle, now called the First Side Needle, pick up and knit along the edge of the heel flap:	11 sts	13 sts	15 sts
With same needle, knit about half the stitches from Bottom Needle.			
Using an empty needle, now called Second Side Needle, knit the remaining stitches from Bottom Needle and with the same needle pick up and knit along the other edge of the heel flap:	11 sts	13 sts	15 sts

	Small	Medium	Large
Mark this point as the beginning of the round. You now have the stitches on 3 needles as follows:			
TOP NEEDLE	15 sts	18 sts	21 sts
DIVIDED BETWEEN TWO SIDE NEEDLES	34 sts	39 sts	44 sts
TOTAL	49 sts	57 sts	65 sts

Knitting the Gussets

ROUND 1

TOP NEEDLE   Work Broken Garter Stitch Pattern as established.

FIRST SIDE NEEDLE   Purl.

SECOND SIDE NEEDLE   Purl.

ROUND 2

TOP NEEDLE   Work Broken Garter Stitch Pattern as established.

FIRST SIDE NEEDLE   K2tog, knit to end.

SECOND SIDE NEEDLE   Knit to last 2 stitches, K2tog.

	Small	Medium	Large
Repeat Rounds 1 and 2 until you have a total of	33 sts	39 sts	45 sts
Leave stitches on Top Needle as they are and redistribute stitches between side needles so you have stitches on 3 needles as follows:			
TOP NEEDLE	15 sts	18 sts	21 sts
FIRST SIDE NEEDLE	9 sts	12 sts	12 sts
SECOND SIDE NEEDLE	9 sts	9 sts	12 sts

Knitting the Foot

	Small	Medium	Large
Continue in Broken Garter Stitch Pattern on all stitches until foot measures ____ less than desired finished length.	1" (2.5 cm)	1.5" (3.75 cm)	1.75" (4.5 cm)

End your last round after completing stitches on First Side Needle. Beginning of round is now between the two side needles, at the center bottom of the foot.

	Small	Medium	Large

Shaping the Toe

NEEDLE 1   Knit to last 3 stitches, K2tog, K1.

NEEDLE 2   Knit.

NEEDLE 3   K1, ssk, K___, K2tog. You may need to knit a few stitches from Needle 1 to Needle 3; or you may have a few stitches left on Needle 3. If so, slip them to Needle 1.

	Small	Medium	Large
	4 sts	6 sts	7 sts
You now have a total of	30 sts	36 sts	42 sts

These are arranged with half on Needle 2 and the other half divided evenly between Needle 1 and Needle 3.

ROUND 1

NEEDLE 1   Knit to last 3 stitches, K2tog, K1.

NEEDLE 2   K1, ssk, knit to last 3 stitches, K2tog, K1.

NEEDLE 3   K1, ssk, knit to end of needle.

ROUND 2: Knit.

	Small	Medium	Large
Repeat these 2 rounds for a total of	3 times	4 times	5 times
You now have	18 sts	20 sts	22 sts
Work Round 1 twice. *You now have*	10 sts	12 sts	14 sts

Knit the stitches from Needle 1 onto Needle 3. Your stitches are now evenly divided between 2 needles.

Finishing

Cut the yarn, leaving a 12" (30 cm) tail and graft toe stitches together with Kitchener stitch (see page 298). Weave in ends.

DOUBLE-TROUBLE BAG

This slouchy bag puts to work a number of techniques described in this chapter. Two strands of handpainted yarn are knit together so their colors blend. This also produces a thicker fabric, which helps the bag keep its shape. Construction of the bag combines the concepts of starting from a strip (which forms the sides, bottom, and strap) and using geometry to make the variegated yarns more interesting. Each side of the bag is three-quarters of a mitered square, missing the top triangle, which means that it can be worked flat.

Measurements   7" (18 cm) wide × 6½" (16 cm) tall × 2" (5 cm) deep; strap is 28" (71 cm) long

Yarn   Cherry Tree Hill Super Sock DK, 100% wool, 4 oz (113 g)/340 yd (311 m), one skein each of Winterberry and Cabin Fever

Needles   One US 6 (4 mm) circular needle 24" (60 cm) long, *or size needed to achieve correct gauge,* and a pair of double-pointed needles the same size

Gauge   20 stitches = 4" (10 cm) in stockinette using a double strand of yarn

Other Supplies   Safety pins or split markers, two buttons about 1" (2.5 cm) in diameter, yarn needle

Note   Hold two strands of yarn (one of each color) together throughout this project.

Knitting the Strap

Holding two strands of yarn (one of each color) together, cast on 10 stitches.

Work in garter stitch for 228 ridges (456 rows). Strip will be about 50" (1.3 m) long.

Bind off.

Sew the two ends of the strip together, being careful not to twist it. The seam will be at the center bottom of the bag.

Setting Up to Work the Bag Front

Count 53 ridges away from the center bottom seam in both directions, and place safety pins or split markers in both ends of both of these ridges. These points are the top corners of the bag.

With the right side of the strap facing you, pick up and knit 106 stitches between the two safety pins along one edge of the strip: pick up one stitch for every ridge.

ROW 1 (WS)   Knit.

ROW 2   K1, ssk, K31, Sl2 tog, K1, p2sso, place split marker (or safety pin) in the last stitch worked, K32, Sl2 tog, K1, p2sso, place split marker (or safety pin) in the last stitch worked, K31, K2tog, K1. *You now have* 100 stitches.

Knitting the Bag Front

ROW 1 (WS)   Purl.

ROW 2   K1, ssk, (knit until 1 stitch remains before marked stitch, Sl2 tog, K1, p2sso) twice, knit until 3 stitches remain, K2tog, K1.

ROW 3   Purl.

ROW 4   Repeat Row 2

ROW 5   Purl.

ROW 6   Repeat Row 2.

ROW 7   Knit.

ROW 8   Repeat Row 2.

Repeat these 8 rows until 10 stitches remain, ending with a wrong-side row.

NEXT ROW   Ssk, (slip 2 tog, K1, p2sso) twice, K2tog. *You now have* 4 stitches.

NEXT ROW   Purl.

Cut yarn, leaving a 4" (10 cm) tail, pull tail through remaining 4 stitches, then weave it in on the wrong side.

Knitting the Bag Back

With the right side of the strap facing you, pick up and knit 106 stitches between the two safety pins or markers on the other edge of the strap: Pick up one stitch for every ridge. Work the Bag Back as for Bag Front.

Working the Top Band

With right side of bag facing you, pick up and knit 36 stitches along the top edge of one side of bag.

ROW 1 (WS)   K16, K2tog twice, knit to end of row. *You now have* 34 stitches.

ROW 2   Purl.

ROW 3   Knit.

ROW 4   Purl.

On wrong side, bind off firmly in knitting.

Cut the yarn, leaving an 18" (46 cm) tail. Turn the band to the inside and using a yarn needle, sew the end of the band to the strap, sew the band to the inside across the top of the bag, and sew the other end to the strap. Weave in end on inside of bag.

Repeat for other side of bag.

Working the Closure

Still using both strands of yarn, cast on 3 stitches, and make an I-cord 6½" (16.5 cm) long. Cut the yarn leaving a 12" (30 cm) tail. Using this tail and a yarn needle, pull the tail through the 3 stitches to secure them, then sew to the beginning of the I-cord to form a loop.

Flatten the loop so that the seam is centered along the opposite side and join together with a few stitches to make a double loop or figure 8. Wrap the yarn firmly around this join several times to hide the seam. Knot it unobtrusively and pull both tails of yarn to the inside of the I-cord. Trim any excess yarn.

Sew a button on each side of the bag, centered just below the top border. Insert both buttons through the double I-cord loop to close the bag.

5 STRANDED KNITTING

Stranded knitting is most familiar to us from color-patterned Fair Isle and Scandinavian sweaters. It's named for the loose yarn carried across the back of the fabric between stitches. Stranded knitting usually features small patterns and uses the same colors repeatedly for the length of each row. The strands, also called *floats*, create a thick warm fabric, making it ideal for the yoke, bottom edge, and cuffs of sweaters to protect the wearer from cold. The strands also make it less elastic than single-color knitting. Although stranded knitting is frequently referred to as Fair Isle knitting, the two are not synonymous; Fair Isle knitting is just one example of stranded knitting. In traditional Fair Isle, traditional patterns are used, colors are limited, and there are never more than two colors per row. Contemporary Fair Isle knitting has branched out into a broad range of colors and patterns but is still restricted to two colors per row.

{Basic Techniques}

Stranded knitting is one of those wonderful techniques that appears much more complicated than it actually is. If you can knit, you can strand. Once mastered, stranded knitting opens up exciting opportunities for complex play with color: changing background or foreground colors (or both) on every row, shading subtly from light to dark, and adding bright complementary highlights.

INS AND OUTS OF STRANDING. **The inside of this hat shows the way the yarns are carried along in back of the knitting until used again. For hat pattern, see page 170.**

Knitting with Two Colors

Stranded color patterns are usually represented by charts, which may be printed in full color, with symbols representing each color, or in black and white leaving the knitter free to choose the colors for each row. (See page 304.)

Circular knitting lends itself to stranding because you are always working on the knit side of the fabric, which makes it easier to manage your yarns and follow charts. Sections of garments (between the armholes, for example) may need to be worked flat, which requires purling the wrong-side rows. In many stranded garments, to avoid working on the wrong side, *steeks* are used. Steeks are extra stitches cast on to bridge openings like armholes so that you can continue knitting in the round. After the piece is completed, these extra stitches are cut up the center, trimmed of loose ends, and stitched down on the inside of the garment.

The finished product of all the techniques described here is nearly identical, so feel free to choose the method that suits you best. Each has its own advantages and you may find that one works better than another for a particular project. For example, when you work with one yarn in each hand, it doesn't matter whether they are used in equal amounts because the two yarns flow independently. When you work with the yarns in just one hand and aren't using them in equal amounts, it can be difficult to maintain even tension on both yarns, and constant adjustments become necessary.

Efficiently handling your yarns isn't dependent on which hand(s) you hold them in or how you tension them, but on holding them all the time rather than dropping the unused yarn between stitches. If you can keep them tensioned properly in your hand, you don't have to hunt for, pick up, and tension the yarn each time it's used. Maintaining consistent tension also makes for more even knitting.

Holding One Color in Each Hand

Knitting with both hands is quick and rhythmic and also prevents the yarns from twisting around each other, so you don't need to stop and untangle them. The concept is really quite simple, but before you begin, you need to know how to knit using both the English method (with the yarn in the right hand) and the Continental method (with the yarn in the left hand). You already use one of these techniques, but may need some practice to become adept at the other. (For instructions, see Knit Stitch and Purl Stitch, pages 299 and 301.) To practice, cast on using yarn and needles that are easy to work with: good-quality, stretchy, 100 percent wool and wooden needles with fairly sharp points. Follow the directions for the method you don't yet know and knit with a single color.

Experiment with various ways of holding and tensioning the yarn until you find one that works for you. Expect your stitches to be very loose, very tight, or completely inconsistent at first, but stick to your knitting until it begins to feel comfortable and your tension is consistent. You may need to practice a few days until you begin to feel comfortable. To keep in practice as time goes by, use the inexperienced hand whenever you need to knit plain garter stitch or to work stockinette in the round. Take a critical look at your work. Do you knit more tightly or more loosely with this hand than the other? If you do, consciously loosen or tighten up just a bit until they match.

Next, try knitting with both hands at the same time. If one color is used more frequently than the other in your pattern, hold it in your more experienced hand. See Positioning the Yarns (page 152) for some important precautions.

1] Hold one yarn in each hand. Keep both index fingers free for knitting and hold the needles with the other fingers and thumbs.

2] When you need a stitch in the right-hand color, insert the needle and wrap the yarn with the right hand.

3] When you need a stitch in the left-hand color, insert the needle and either pick or wrap the yarn in the left hand.

Holding Both Yarns in Your Left Hand

If you normally knit with the yarn in your left hand, try holding both yarns in this hand. Any one of the following techniques may work for you:

▲ *Yarns over left index finger.* Keep the yarns in the same position all the time so that they don't twist around each other. When you knit, make sure that you put only the correct color around the needle to form the new stitch.

▲ *Alternatively, use a yarn guide or knitting thimble.* These may help you keep the yarns in place; adjust the angle of the guide so that the yarns are in a convenient position.

▲ *Yarns tensioned against palm.* You could also hold both yarns tensioned against your palm, slipping your index finger under the desired yarn whenever you need it.

▲ *Yarns over two fingers.* Hold one yarn over your index finger and one over your middle finger.

Holding Both Yarns in Your Right Hand

If you normally knit with the yarn in your right hand, all of the suggestions for the left hand will also work for you. You might also hold both yarns tensioned against your palm, one over the index finger and the other pinched between thumb and index when you want to use it.

▲ *Both yarns over right index finger.* As with the left hand, be sure to knit with the correct color and not to twist the yarns as you work.

▲ *Yarns tensioned against palm.* Slip your index finger under the desired yarn when you need it.

▲ *Yarns over two fingers.* One yarn is over your index finger and the other over your middle finger.

Practice, Practice, Practice

To try stranded knitting, begin with just two colors of yarn. They should be the same thickness and knit up at the same gauge. Use a 16" (40 cm) long circular needle, in a size appropriate for your yarn. Choosing comfortable needles and good-quality yarn (such as a nice, stretchy 100% wool) will make your first effort at stranded knitting much more pleasant.

Using your main color, cast on a multiple of 8 stitches plus 7. There should be enough stitches to go comfortably from end to end of the needle without severe stretching. Make sure the cast on isn't twisted and join the beginning and end of the round. Work some ribbing or just knit a few rounds in the main color so that you have a comfortable base to begin with.

Begin working with both colors: Pick up your contrast color yarn, leaving a 6" (15 cm) tail hanging down, and knit one stitch with the contrasting yarn. Then, knit a stitch with your main color. Keep alternating, knitting 1 stitch of each color. While you practice keep these things in mind:

» Don't twist the yarns.
» Each time you change colors, smooth the stitches just completed out to the right.
» Don't pull hard on the new yarn — just let it lie softly across the back of stitches in the other color.

Keep alternating colors until you are comfortable working with two yarns, your tension is even, and your knitting isn't loose and loopy or tight and puckered. The stranded part of your knitting will pull in and the plain section below may ruffle a bit as a result. This is perfectly normal. Because you're working with an odd number of stitches, your knitting automatically makes a tiny checkerboard called "salt and pepper."

When you are comfortable knitting 1 stitch in each color, increase 1 stitch at the beginning of the next round (so you have a multiple of 8 stitches) and begin knitting 2 stitches in each color. Continue working until once again you and your tension are both comfortable. Every two rounds, switch colors to form a checkerboard.

Next, try knitting 4 stitches in each color. You need to be very aware of spreading out the stitches on the right needle and keeping the yarn loose as you work the first stitch in each color. Switch colors every 4 rounds to make a checkerboard. Again, keep doing this until it feels comfortable and you've resolved any tension issues.

Finally, try knitting from a chart (see Using Charts, page 304) or making up a simple pattern of zigzags or diamonds. In this lively design, the colors move one stitch away from the center up to the middle of the bag, then reverse, creating an eye-catching zigzag pattern.

Positioning the Yarns

It's important to be consistent in how you position the yarns because this affects the size of the stitches in each color. First, there may well be a difference in tension between the two strands, because one hand knits just a bit more loosely than the other. Also, as you work, one color is carried below the other across the back of the fabric. If you're working with one color in each hand, the color in the left hand is the lower color. If you are holding just one yarn at a time, to avoid twisting you will pick up one color to the left and the other to the right: the left color is the lower color. If you're holding both colors in one hand, then just look at the back of your knitting to see which strand travels below the other. Note the position of this color in or on your hand.

WORKING WITH MORE THAN TWO COLORS

Although traditional Fair-Isle knitting is restricted to two colors per row, other knitting traditions — or personal preference — allow you to use more colors. If you can knit with both hands, you may want to hold two colors in one hand and one in the other. Many knitters find it easiest to keep the background color in one hand and to hold all the other colors in the other hand. If one color is used less often than the others, you can drop it and then pick it up when needed, or if the color is used very infrequently, add it using duplicate stitch after the knitting is completed.

The stitches made with the lower strand are just a bit taller than the stitches made with the higher strand. When the foreground pattern is worked with the lower yarn, these stitches are more prominent and stitches neighboring each other diagonally actually touch so the pattern looks continuous. If the foreground color is worked with the higher yarn, then it is less prominent and diagonal stitches appear to be slightly separated. Be careful not to change the yarn position in the course of your project, because the change can be very noticeable.

▲ *Examining the effect of how yarns are held.* At the bottom of this swatch, the light color was held lower than the dark color, with the dark color tensioned more tightly; in the middle, the dark color was held lower than the light color; at the top, the light color was held lower, with both colors tensioned equally.

{Yarn Management}

You may expect dealing with multiple balls of yarn to be daunting, but with a little care you'll be able to keep them under control.

Joining Yarn for New Colors

When starting a new color, simply leave the end dangling at the beginning of the row or round. In traditional Fair Isle sweaters, to conserve yarn, ends were knotted together leaving a short tail and left to felt. For a cleaner finish, weave in the ends (see page 182) or braid them (see page 241). Ends at a steek (see below) will be cut off when the steek is cut, so no finishing is needed. If you need to start a new ball or deal with a knot in the middle of a row or round, either leave the ends dangling to be woven in later or splice the new ball to the end of the old and keep right on knitting.

Avoiding Twists and Tangles

When knitting flat with only two balls of yarn attached to your work, you can avoid twisting by being careful to turn the work one way at the end of one row and the other way at the end of the next row. When working circularly, the yarns should rarely twist around each other. If they do, you are changing their positions, from right to left hand, or from top to bottom as you work. Place one ball of yarn to your left and one to your right, especially if you knit with one yarn in each hand. This will make it much more noticeable when the yarns begin to twist, so you can prevent it immediately.

When you are working with several yarns at the same time, wind them into center-pull balls. Sit in front of a table, or place them in a box where they'll fit snugly, with the left (or lower) yarn on the left, the right (higher) yarn on the right, and any other yarns between them. You can also put each ball of yarn in a small jar inside the box, which is handy when they are small and tend to lift into the air. Boxes with dividers (such as sock drawer organizers) work well, too. This is similar to the method shown for organizing your yarns while working intarsia (see Keeping Things in Order, page 177). Whenever you change yarns, make sure that the strands aren't twisting around each other. If they do, correct the problem as soon as it occurs.

Cutting Your Yarn

If you are using a yarn on every row or round, never cut it. It's possible, if the background color remains the same throughout, that you'll use a continuous strand of yarn from beginning to end, assuming your ball of yarn is big enough. If you're working with a yarn every other row or round, you may also carry it up without cutting, but the stitches at the beginning and end will be a bit distorted. Where these stitches don't show (at an underarm "seam" or at the center of a steek), the distortion isn't a problem. When there are more than one or two rows in other colors, however, it's best to cut, knot the end of the old color together with the new one, and deal with the ends later.

{Solving Problems}

You may run into problems with the way your knitting looks and feels, as well as discover outright mistakes. In the next few pages solutions to the most frequent problems are suggested.

Disguising Jogs

When you knit circularly in stranded knitting, as when you work plain stripes, there will be a jog or stair step wherever a new color begins or ends. There are several ways to make this less noticeable.

Place beginning of the round in a less obvious place. For example, place the color change at the side seam or within a steek on a pullover or cardigan, and either at the center back or along the inside of the leg and down the center of the bottom of the foot on socks. On hats, all sides are equally visible, so place the beginning of a round at the center back so that you, at least, can't see it, even though anyone behind you can. When the background color changes, disguise and minimize the jog using the methods described on pages 31–32.

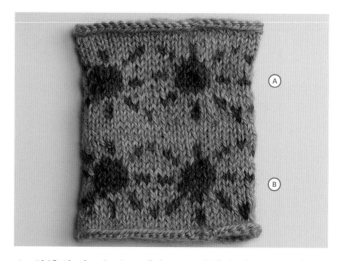

▲ *Shift the beginning of the round.* If the foreground color appears in separate motifs, shift the beginning of the round to fall between the motifs or to a position within the motif where it will be less noticeable. For example, if half of a motif falls before the end of the round and half after, ignore the motif completely when you first encounter it at the beginning of the round. Instead, continue working in the background color. You may end up with a long strand of the foreground color at this point. (For ways to deal with this, see Weaving the Strands, page 182.) Begin working with the foreground color when you come to the first full occurrence of the motif. When you eventually return to the troublesome motif at the end of the round, knit the whole thing. You've shifted the beginning of the round so that it follows this motif. Compare the motif at the top of the swatch (A) to the one at the bottom (B). The transition between the suns is smoother at the bottom, but the sun on the right in B is a bit misshapen because the beginning of the round cuts it in half.

In A, the rays don't line up between suns, because the beginning of the round falls between them, but both suns are nice and round.

Correcting Mistakes in Patterning

If you notice a mistake on the last row or round you completed, pick out just this one stitch when you come to it and reknit it with the correct color. Frequently, it has been reversed with an adjacent stitch, so pull out and reknit that one as well and the yarn used will even out. If there's just one stitch to be corrected, there's usually enough slack in the stranding to accommodate it. If there are more than a few stitches in one color that must be corrected, it's usually best to unravel the entire row and work it over.

Corrections to rows further back in the knitting are so problematic when dealing with multiple colors that it's easiest to fix them by ripping back to the mistake and reworking the whole piece from that point. For smaller problems involving just a few stitches, duplicate stitch can most easily be used to camouflage a mistake in the color pattern.

Because of the difficulties inherent in fixing mistakes made too far back in your knitting, stop periodically to take a good look at it. It's amazing how many details show up from across the room that aren't visible at an arm's length.

Dealing with Unevenness

Changes in tension while working the different strands of yarn can cause some unevenness. If stitches in one color are consistently tighter than the other, evaluate your knitting style to see if you're holding that color more tightly or failing to spread the stitches out across the right needle before working the first stitch in that color every time you use it. Occasional looser or tighter stitches will make the surface of the knitting look uneven, but these are normal and will be smoothed out by blocking under slight tension.

Too tight. If your knitting in one color puckers up between stitches in the other, your strands are too tight. Whenever you switch colors, spread the knitting out smoothly on your right needle before you knit the first stitch of the new color. Tight stranding is more of a problem when working a wide piece of knitting on a short needle, so use the longest needle that suits your project. You can also loosen your tension when working a tube on a short circular needle or on double-pointed needles by turning it inside out, pushing the knitting through the center and out the other side. Continue knitting on the right side of the fabric, just as you were before.

INSIDE-OUT KNITTING. With the tube turned inside out, all strands of yarn must travel around the outside, following a slightly longer and looser path.

Too loose. If the stranding on the back of your fabric shows through on the front, your knitting is too loose. You need either to use smaller needles to match your yarn or to find thicker yarn to match your needles, if you need to match a particular gauge. Even if the stranding doesn't show, individual stitches in the foreground color may be puffy and enlarged. A bit of looseness in the foreground stitches is normal. If stretching the fabric gently is enough to get them under control, blocking will even out your stitches. If the problem is more severe, you're making the strands between stitches too loose. When you start the first stitch of a color, make sure that the fabric is smoothed out flat on the right needle, but not stretched, and that the strand is just long enough to lie smoothly across the back of the fabric.

Managing Long Floats

When a color lies unused for too many stitches, the floats can become so long that the wearer's fingers get caught in them, which is a particular problem in infants' clothing. The stitches at both ends of the long float may also appear loose and puffy. You should catch these long strands on the back of the fabric to secure them. There's no absolute rule for when this is necessary, but here are some guidelines:

» *With a bulky yarn* that felts easily, like Icelandic Lopi, you can leave very long strands because they will adhere to the back of the fabric at the first wearing.

» *With a fine yarn,* because the stitches are so small, you may leave strands across more stitches than with a thicker yarn.

When a color goes unused for 5 or more stitches, you need to at least consider catching it at the center of the strand. Whether you do or not is really a matter of personal preference, taking into account whether the loose strand will cause problems, how much extra time and effort it will take to catch or weave in the strands, and what effect the weaving will have on the finished fabric. You'll need to decide on a case-by-case basis how to handle the floats on each project.

There are two ways to deal with the long strands: weave them in on the back of the fabric as you go, or catch them on the following row or round. Either way, there's no need to twist the yarn, so weaving or catching still doesn't mean your yarns will get tangled.

▲ *Weaving in as you go, knit side, right handed.* When the working yarn is in your right hand or carried above, lift the yarn not in use up just a bit and insert your right needle under it while knitting the next stitch. (If you hold both yarns in one hand, insert the needle into the stitch, lay the unused yarn over the top of the needle, then knit the stitch with the working yarn.)

▲ *Weaving in as you go, purl side, right handed.* Follow exactly the same procedure as you use for working on the knit side when you are on the purl side of the fabric.

▲ *Weaving in as you go, knit side, left handed.* When the working yarn is in your left hand or carried below, insert the right needle into the next stitch and wrap the higher yarn in the right hand around the point of the needle counterclockwise (A). Wrap the working yarn around as usual (counterclockwise). Unwrap the nonworking yarn (B). Knit the new stitch out through the old one.

Catching the yarn just once at the center of a long strand is enough to secure it. You may catch the unused strand as often as every other stitch, which has the effect of weaving the strand in and out, but this changes the hand and appearance of the fabric, making it less flexible than it would be otherwise. Avoid securing the strand on the stitch immediately before or after the color is knitted, because it will distort the pattern stitch in that color. Whether you choose to weave constantly or occasionally, be consistent throughout the garment. Too much consistency, however, is a bad thing. If you catch the stranded yarn at the same column of stitches on every row or round, it will be quite noticeable, so shift it at least a stitch earlier or later to prevent all the catches from lining up.

CATCHING FLOATS ON SUBSEQUENT ROWS/ROUNDS

Here's a simpler solution for managing both yarns at once, or when working on the purl side: wait until the next row or round and then insert the tip of the needle under the strand when working a stitch at or near its center. This technique is also handy if you simply forgot to catch that strand on the previous row. It's best not to catch a strand this way more than once, because it will stretch the strand and distort the fabric.

{Details, Details}

Now that you've learned the basics of stranded knitting, turn your attention to the little details that contribute to the quality of really excellent knitting, like perfect shaping, cast on, textured highlights, and borders.

Shaping

Use any increases and decreases you like in stranded knitting, but be aware that some increases can noticeably disrupt the color pattern, while others help to maintain it. The knit-into-the-front-and-back increase, for example, should not be worked on the row where a color change takes place, because this increase pulls a bead of the old color up into the new color.

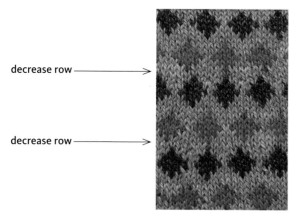

decrease row ———→

decrease row ———→

▲ *Decrease or increase in plain-colored areas.* It's best to position increases and decreases in an area that's all one color: either the background or a solid area of the foreground color. If the color patterns are knit in horizontal bands, you can work decreases or increases in the plain areas between the bands. If decreases are worked all the way across or around the garment, pattern motifs may no longer line up vertically, unless the motifs themselves change size so that the number of repeats is maintained. In the example here, the motifs no longer line up after the decrease rounds, but the motifs themselves are unchanged.

The Make 1 (M1) increase using the working yarn is the easiest to fit into a color pattern without distorting the colors from the previous row. When you reach the increase point, simply use the working yarn in the required color for the increase. The only drawback to the M1 is that it fits tightly around the needle and can, therefore, be difficult to work on the following row. An alternative is to work a yarn over instead of the normal twisted loop, then knit into the back of it on the next row to twist it, preventing a hole.

▲ *Adding two stitches at the same point in the row requires a double increase.* These are most frequently used on the crowns of hats worked from the center out. Many double increases make holes or bumps and should be avoided. The easiest way to deal with this is to work two M1 increases on either side of a center stitch, being careful to twist the two in opposite directions so they are symmetrical (A). Work into the back of one stitch of the pair on the following row to prevent it from twisting more than the other. Another option is to use the increase decoratively. The bobblelike increase on the swatch above was made by working knit-purl-knit into a single stitch (B).

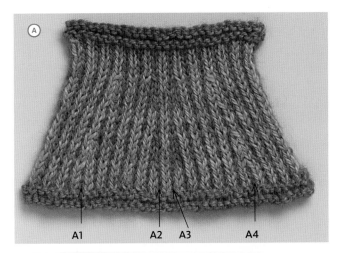

you don't want a raised effect and you want to avoid a noticeable slant, work a pair of K2tog and ssk decreases, as shown at the center of swatch A.

CROWNING GLORY. Form and function work together here as raised double decreases ornament and shape the crown of this hat. (For project, see page 170.)

▲ *Decreasing in patterns.* Working neat decreases in color patterns is simpler than increasing; however, you need to be aware of which color will end up on top and which direction the decrease will slant. When you knit 2 together (K2tog), the second stitch shows and the decrease slants to the right. With slip, slip, knit (ssk) or slip 1, knit 1, pass slipped stitch over (skp), the first stitch shows and it slants to the left (A). In swatch A, K2tog is used at A1 to keep the turquoise stitch on top and at A3 to keep the blue stitch on top. Ssk is used at A2 and A4. Notice the way that placing K2tog and ssk on either side of the center stitch highlight it.

A raised or centered double decrease (Sl2, K1, p2sso) shows the center color prominently (B1). To work this, slip 2 stitches together knitwise (as if working a K2tog), knit 1, pass the two slipped stitches over. The simpler-to-work Sl1, K2tog, psso will show the first stitch on top and slants to the left (B2). Be sure to slip the first stitch knitwise. If

Casting On

If you will be working corrugated ribbing (see page 160), a firm cast on is required. Otherwise, you can use any cast on, plain or decorative, that you like. Alternating colors while you cast on or using different colors for the two strands of the long-tail cast on are both nice embellishments at the edge of the knitting. You may also work the long-tail cast on with multiple strands of different colors in place of the single bottom strand. All of these cast on variations are discussed in chapter 8.

Adding Texture

Stranded knitting is normally worked in smooth stockinette stitch. If you want to add texture, however, it's just a purl stitch away! There are two things to keep in mind. First, moving the yarn to the front and back to purl when you change colors can slow you down substantially. Second, whenever you purl a new color over an old one, you get a color "bump." You can avoid this by only purling a stitch when it's the same color as the one below it, as shown in the photo below.

Accenting a stranded pattern.

Designing Dynamic Borders

Plain ribbed borders can be quite pleasing and are the easiest choice for button bands, but a border that incorporates all the colors in your garment can be the highlight of the project. Striped ribbing (see chapter 2), Seed Stitch, Moss Stitch, and garter stitch also make excellent borders. A multicolor version of Seed Stitch can be made working one color at a time using mosaic knitting techniques. (For ideas, see page 208.)

▲ *Hems as borders.* Hems and bindings make neat finishes, cover up loose ends, and do not need to be ribbed to prevent curling (See pages 242–43.)

▲ *Corrugated ribbing as a border.* The pinnacle of borders for stranded knitting is *corrugated ribbing,* which is worked with one color for the knit ribs and another for the purl ribs. Corrugated ribbing can be quite time-consuming to work, so many stranded garments are made with plain ribbing. The stranding across the back of corrugated ribbing makes it tighter and less elastic than the customary one-color ribbing, so you can usually work it on the same number of stitches as the garment and on the same-size needles. Test out the ribbing on your swatch to prevent painful surprises in the actual garment.

Work corrugated ribbing just like stranded knitting in stockinette, but bring the yarn forward to purl and return it to the back before knitting with the other color. If you forget, you can fix it on the next row or round. Just slip the intervening knit stitches off the needle, pop the strand over them to the back, and slip them back on the needle. If you've worked farther, however, you'll have to unravel to move the strand to the back. For a photo of K2, P2 corrugated ribbing, see the bag on page 152.

Preventing curled edges. Corrugated ribbing sometimes curls up at the outer edge, but there are ways to prevent this problem:

» *Use a firm cast-on.* If your normal cast on tends to be tight, then it should be perfect for corrugated ribbing. If not, use a needle one or two sizes smaller, or try the cable or crocheted cast on.

» *Use a ribbed cast-on,* either the ribbed cable cast on for K1, P1 ribbing or the long-tail cast on for K1, P1 or K2, P2 ribbing.

» *Begin ribbing immediately* on the row above the cast on or work one row of garter stitch. If you use the cable cast on, the knit side will be facing you as you work the first row, so purl across to create garter stitch. If you use the long-tail cast on, the purl side will be facing you, so knit the first row.

» *Work ribbing in cast-on color.* If you don't like the way the first row of purled stitches looks in a contrasting color, work a row of ribbing in the cast-on color, then introduce the second color on the next row, or cast on in the color of the purl ribs.

» *Use K2, P2 ribbing* because it curls less than K1, P1 and is quicker to work.

» *Use a provisional cast on,* and begin your project above the ribbing. When it's complete, remove the cast on and add the ribbed borders. Finish them with a firm bind off.

WORKING BUTTONHOLES INTO CORRUGATED RIBBING

The challenges of buttonholes in corrugated ribbing are fitting the holes neatly into the ribs and dealing with the stranded yarn so that it doesn't fall across the hole.

» *Small buttons.* A simple yarn-over buttonhole will do for small buttons. Before you begin, place a safety pin or split marker wherever you want a buttonhole and stop to work one as you come to each marker. It looks best if you've marked a knitted stitch, rather than a purled stitch. Work until one stitch remains before the marker, yarn over using both strands, and K2tog using the color of the marked stitch. On the next row, treat the double strand of the yarn over as a single stitch and knit it.

» *Large buttons.* Make a horizontal buttonhole as wide as you like. On a right-side row, work the first stitch of the buttonhole in the appropriate color. Slip the next stitch purlwise and bind off by passing the knitted stitch over it. Continue to slip one stitch at a time and pass the previous stitch over it until you've bound off enough stitches for your button to fit. Slip the last stitch back to the left needle purlwise and turn to the wrong side. Use the cable cast on, alternating the colors in pattern and twisting the strands between each stitch until you've cast on as many stitches as you bound off. Turn to the right side, twist the yarns once more, and continue across the row.

{Finishing Techniques}

Most finishing for stranded knitting is identical to that for all other types of knitting. There are few places, however, where specific finishing techniques are either required or desirable.

Binding off. When you're finishing off a border of corrugated ribbing, a firm bind off is required to prevent it from curling. You can bind off using a single color or in your color pattern. To match the color below the bind off as closely as possible, shift the color pattern one stitch to the right. That is, knit the color one stitch early. Then, when it is passed over the following stitch, it falls directly above the stitch of the same color (see page 248).

Dealing with ends. How you finish off the ends inside your garment depends on the situation. They can be knotted, with short ends left to felt, if they're in a location that won't show and you've used natural animal fibers. If a lot of ends fall along an edge near an opening, like the front of a cardigan, you may want to make a double border or a hem and enclose them inside it. At the beginning of the round, where you want the pattern to appear continuous, use the ends to help disguise the jog, using duplicate stitch on the wrong side of the fabric (see page 32).

Blocking. For stranded knitting, washing your work and letting it dry under tension is a requirement. This will smooth out unevenness and begin the process of slight felting that will prevent steeks from unraveling. Traditionally, Fair Isle sweaters are blocked on woolly boards (see page 244), which adjust to fit the size of the garment. (For more information, see Blocking Methods, page 244.)

{Demystifying Steeks}

Steeks are extra stitches knit at armholes, necks, and cardigan fronts to be cut open after the garment has been completed. Steeks allow you to make an entire garment circularly, so that you can work the color patterns from the knit side throughout. They work best in garments of natural wool, because the cut ends will felt, thus preventing unraveling. If you have some sewing experience, you'll recognize that the extra fabric, once the steeks are cut open, is used as a seam allowance.

Planning a Steek

Here's an overview of how steeks fit into garment construction, so that you'll know what to expect before you start. On the following pages, I show you exactly how to work a steek. If you're making a cardigan, the center-front steek begins when you cast on at the bottom of the sweater, and the beginning of the round is at the center of this steek. When you cast on, the steek stitches are in addition to the stitches required for the body of the garment. I like to work with an odd number of stitches and prefer to make steeks 9 stitches wide. This gives me a center stitch, which disappears when cut, thus leaving 4 stitches on either side as a seam allowance. At least one of these stitches disappears when the edge is trimmed before sewing it down, leaving a margin of just 3 stitches. Some knitters cast on more stitches; others, as few as three stitches for their steeks. More stitches in the steek mean more work to complete the garment, but using only a few stitches requires you to take extra measures to secure the steek before cutting.

If you're making a pullover, cast on the body as usual and work until you get up to either the underarms or the neck opening, whichever comes first.

For either a cardigan or a pullover, when it's time to bind off for the underarms, go ahead and do it. How many stitches you bind off at the underarm depends on the requirements of your garment shaping. Before you bind off, make sure that the pattern is centered on the front and back between the two underarms. Bind off one underarm, continue around in pattern, and bind off the other underarm exactly halfway around. If you're working a pullover with the beginning of the round at one of the side seams, you'll need to center the first underarm bind off over the beginning of the round. Note that to do this you must begin the bind off before you reach the end of the previous round. Before you proceed any further, check again that the pattern is centered on the front and back. Continue around until you reach the first underarm bind off. Cast on 9 stitches for the steek, or however many you prefer. The easiest cast on to use is the simple half hitch or loop cast on. If this is a round where you are working two colors, alternate them in the cast on.

If you need to change colors before beginning the next round, change in the middle of the steek, knotting the beginning of the new ball of yarn to the end of the one it is replacing. These 9 stitches are the bottom edge of your steek. On a pullover, the beginning of the round will be at the center of the first armhole that was bound off. On a cardigan, the beginning of the round will remain at the center front.

This small V-neck vest has steeks at the center front and armholes. The steek at the left has not yet been cut. The steek at the neck opening has been cut. The steek at the right has been finished with a ribbed border.

Working the Steek

Steek stitches are usually knitted in vertical stripes or in a tiny checkerboard to distinguish them from the body of the garment. Alternating colors across the steek makes it firmer, less likely to unravel when cut, and carries both yarns across to the next section of the body. I prefer vertical stripes because they provide a clear center cutting line. If you're working with only one color, just knit across the steek with that color. As you continue, keep the steek stitches in their pattern and maintain the garment stitches in their own pattern. Use markers on either side of each steek, if necessary, to prevent confusion.

Dealing with shaping. There will be times when you need to work shaping near the steek stitches, such as the sloped shaping of an armhole or a neck opening. These decreases are worked in the body of the garment, not the steek. Whenever you need to work a decrease, work the steek, then one stitch of the garment, then work your decrease; work across that section of the garment in pattern, stopping 3 stitches before the next steek. Work the corresponding decrease, then one edge stitch, then the next steek. Leaving a stitch between the decreases and the steek provides a smooth, visible column of stitches in the garment where you will pick up the stitches for the border or sleeve after cutting the steek open. You may make your decreases slant either toward or away from this edge stitch by using the K2tog or the ssk decrease. Whichever one you use at one edge, use the opposite at the other so that they'll be symmetrical. In fine yarns, you may prefer to place increases or decreases several stitches over, so they appear a bit farther from the edge.

Neck-opening shaping. If you're making a pullover, at some point you will need to begin the neck opening. *For a V-neck,* you may place one stitch at the center front on a safety pin or split marker: this is picked up later to become the center point of the neck border. *For a round neck,* bind off stitches as needed to shape your garment, just as you did for the underarms. When you reach the neck opening on the next round, cast on your 9 steek stitches, regardless of how many (or how few) stitches you bound off. *For a cardigan,* of course, you have already started the front steek. Bind it off when you bind off for the neck, then cast on again above the original steek. Any further shaping along a round neck must be done by decreasing rather than by binding off. As described for the underarms, work any shaping in the body of the garment, not in the steek itself.

Ending the Steek

When you reach the shoulders of the garment, on the last round, bind off all the steek stitches and knit across all the shoulder stitches. Once your steeks have been secured, use the three-needle bind off to join the shoulders of the sweater together (See page 243).

Securing the Steek

Now that your garment is off the needles, it's best to block the steeks, which discourages them from unraveling when they are cut. Mist the steeks with water from a spray bottle and leave them to dry; wash the garment, roll it in a towel to remove excess moisture, and leave it to dry; or use a steamer or steam iron on the sections that will be cut.

If you are working with natural wool (as opposed to superwash, or machine-washable wool), alpaca, mohair, or other animal fiber, all of which have a tendency to felt, you may cut the steeks without further preparation. When working with a fiber that is either slippery or won't felt (such as superwash wool, cotton, rayon, or silk) secure the stitches before cutting. Set your sewing machine to very small stitches so that it catches the strands of every row

of knitting as you sew. Sew a line of stitches along each side of the center of the steek. If you don't have a sewing machine, you may secure the knitting by hand: using sewing thread and a needle, sew through each strand of yarn along both sides of the center line.

Cutting the Steek

Cut the knitting along the center line of the steek. Use sharp sewing shears because dull ones will pull the yarn and may cause unraveling. Be very careful not to accidentally cut through the strands on the far side of the garment. To protect these strands, fold up a newspaper to the dimensions of the garment and slide it inside. Cut one steek at a time, complete the border or sleeve, and sew down the steek on the inside of the garment as soon as possible.

Picking Up Stitches

The steek, worked in stockinette stitch, naturally curls to the inside once cut. There are two techniques for picking up stitches for the edging that finishes the opening.

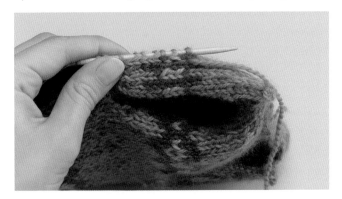

▲ *Pickup method 1.* Hold the garment with the right side facing you and the steek rolled to the inside. Pick up and knit stitches under the last stitch of the garment next to the steek. Be sure to work underneath both halves of the edge stitch. Knitting under just one strand of the stitch will pull it loose, leaving gaps between the edge of the fabric and the border or sleeve. In the photo above, the garment has been turned to the wrong side so the steek is visible.

▲ *Pickup method 2.* Uncurl the edge of the steek, carry the yarn along the back of the fabric, and insert the needle between two stitches to the back of the fabric to knit up the yarn. This method is a bit more awkward to work, but results in slightly less bulk along the fold.

Overcasting the Steek

Complete the border or sleeve, then turn the garment inside out.

▲ *Fastening the steek in place.* The remains of the steek will have unraveled a bit. Using sharp sewing shears, trim the straggly ends to neaten the edge, then using a yarn, tapestry, or darning needle and whichever color of yarn shows the least, overcast all the way around. If you are working with a thick yarn (worsted weight or thicker), flatten the steek against the inside of the garment, sew around in one direction, then return in the opposite direction, forming Xs of overcast yarn, securing the edge and preventing it from unraveling further. If you are working with a thinner fabric, turn the edge of the steek under like a hem, and sew around just once to hold it in place. You can also enclose the steek completely for a neater finish on the inside of the garment, if you've secured the edges with machine or hand sewing (see Binding the Edges, pages 242-243).

Other Kinds of Steeks

There are several other ways to work steeks. You might work a wrapped steek by wrapping the yarns in use around the needle several times rather than knitting them. When cutting this steek, snip up the center of all the loose strands. Wrapping is quicker than knitting, but you must secure all of the individual strands by knotting them together, weaving them in on the inside of the garment, or sewing along the edge.

Another method is to crochet the steek. In this case, you need a steek that's only 3 stitches wide, which means less knitting. On either side of a center stitch, twist the knitted stitches (either intentionally while knitting the garment, or by running them down and working them back up to the top using a crochet hook, twisting each stitch). Then work chains of stitches along both sides of the steek, through all the twisted stitches, using a crochet hook and another strand of yarn. Finally, cut the center column of stitches. It will immediately fray, but won't unravel past the crocheted chain.

After cutting when you use either of these methods, pick up stitches around the opening and then add a border or a sleeve.

What, No Steeks?

It is, of course, perfectly possible to make a garment without steeks. Sections with openings are worked flat, either by knitting across on the right side and purling back on the wrong side, or knitting every row on the right side, breaking the yarns, knotting them together to prevent unraveling, then sliding the knitting to the opposite end of the needle and knitting across again on the right side. In Norwegian knitting, sweaters are knit in tubes and then cut without adding any stitches for steeks or seam allowances — a method that is best practiced on natural wool to take advantage of its propensity to felt. Making a circular yoked sweater is another way to avoid the need for steeks, because the entire sweater is worked seamlessly in the round. (See page 282.)

{Inspiration for Design}

A number of key details must be considered when designing a stranded garment. These include planning the structure of the garment, selecting the type of yarn and colors, designing the pattern and fabric, keeping track of the colors, and calculating how much yarn will be needed.

Garment Architecture

As you've seen in this chapter, stranded knitting, while it can be worked flat, really lends itself to circular knitting. Unless you have a reason to choose flat garment construction, it makes sense to use a circular garment structure. Several circular sweater architectures are discussed in chapter 9. Underarm gussets, although not discussed in chapter 9, are part of the traditional gansey shape that is frequently used for stranded sweaters, without any additional armhole shaping. Many contemporary designs, however, substitute shaped armholes and have no underarm gussets.

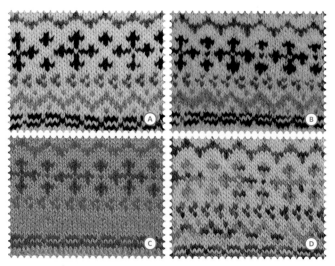

Yarn manufacturers are (A) Reynolds, (B) Yarns International, (C) Kid Hollow Farm, and (D) Lorna's Laces.

Choosing Yarn

Keep in mind that yarn type affects the appearance of the fabric. For clear, precise color patterns, choose a smooth, solid-colored yarn. For colors that blend, choose a fuzzier yarn. Highly textured yarns, like bouclé, may obscure the color patterns completely, and the effect of the pattern is very different in a fine yarn than it is in a bulky one.

Choosing Colors

Use any colors you like. You'll need at least two, one for the foreground and one for the background. Or you can go wild with multiple shades and hues. If you want the color pattern to be clear, make sure there's plenty of contrast between your foreground and background colors throughout. When using variegated yarn, remember that for good visibility none of the colors should match any of your other colors of yarn.

▲ *Different effects.* The wrister on the left is worked with a strong solid-color contrast yarn, while the one on the right is done with a multicolor yarn, making it appear that you've changed colors even more often. When you make projects like this, be sure to pick a multicolor yarn that has no colors in common with the main color, or the pattern will be lost. (Yarns by Kid Hollow Farm [left] and Cascade and Tess Designer Yarns [right].)

If you choose to use a lot of colors, spend some time deciding which will be foreground and which will be background colors, and plan whether to use them in a particular order or at random. Refer to pages 18–19 for hints on how to organize colors into groups to make this task easier. You may want to relegate all the darker colors to the background and use all the brighter colors in the foreground, or you may want to reverse dark and light as you work through the garment. Gradations of colors and contrasts as you work toward the center of a pattern can give it more depth or can obscure it completely if not handled well. And don't forget the magic that complementary colors can work in bringing other colors to life. If the colors you've selected seem to be lacking something, take a look at Color Harmonies (page 15) to see if there's a color or two you can add to perk them up.

Experimenting to find the best placement of your colors can be very time consuming, so consider wrapping cards (page 20) rather than knitting a swatch, which allows you to quickly adjust the order and proportion of colors. Decide on the color sequence (if any) and the proportion of your background colors and foreground colors and wrap one card with each of them. Hold the foreground card over the background card and evaluate how they work together. Is there enough contrast on any given row? Do you like the way the colors interact? Make adjustments and try it again. When you think it looks best, take your foreground colors and weave them into the background card to get a better sense of how they'll interact in the fabric.

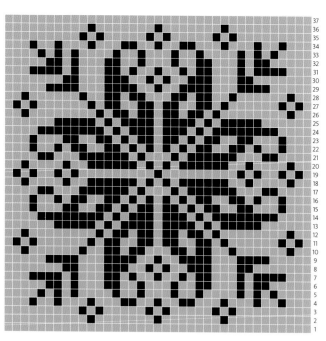

The swatches at left were all knit from this chart, varying the colors and color placement.

▲ *The final test.* Knit swatches in your pattern stitch to see which color arrangement you prefer.

Swatching

Making swatches serves several purposes. It tests the color interactions. It allows you to adjust the needle size to determine how tightly or loosely the yarn should be knit to create the kind of fabric you want. And it provides a sample so you can measure your gauge. When you're designing, gauge is only one consideration. You may need to work several swatches using your colors in different positions within the pattern before you're satisfied. A quick way to change color placement is to duplicate stitch one color over another on half of the swatch for comparison purposes.

What if all this planning and testing is just too much to deal with? What if it stifles your creativity? Decide what order you think you'd like to use the colors in or organize them into groups. Knit at least a small patterned swatch to determine your gauge and test your needle size. Then,

forge ahead, combining colors and changing patterns as you knit. This approach works better with small patterns than large ones. Let your imagination lead you as you knit, but also let your judgment tell you if you need to backtrack. If you don't like the look of something, unravel it and try a different color or a different pattern. If there's a problem with the finished project (one color pattern really needs just a touch of a complimentary color, for example), then duplicate stitch that color in to fix it.

Designing Borders

If you already have an idea for the border, but don't know what you want for the body, play with the border first and use it as inspiration for color interactions in the stranded patterns. On the other hand, if you know what you want in your main pattern stitch, use that as a guide to help you design the borders. In either case, if there is anything complicated in the border, you will need to swatch the border as well as the main pattern to test them both.

Keying Your Colors

Keeping track of just a few colors isn't difficult. When you're using several shades of individual colors, however, it can be easy to confuse them and use them out of order. Sometimes you won't discover the mistake until the garment is finished. Once you've settled on your color progression, keep your wrapped card and your final swatch handy for reference. You can also create a key, attaching samples of each color to your chart with staples or tape, or tying them through punched holes near the edge.

Centering Patterns

With small patterns (up to about a 4-stitch repeat), you won't need to worry too much about centering them on the garment, except at key points (for example, when you begin a V-neck). Larger patterns, however, need to be centered on the front, back, and sleeves. It is easiest to make the body an even multiple of the largest pattern repeat you plan to use. When you start the steek for the center front or when you divide for the underarms, make sure that the pattern is placed on the front and back in an aesthetically pleasing position. Be aware of how the patterns will interact when they meet at the shoulder. Plan your armhole placement so that the shoulder seam falls at the center of a large pattern or between two patterns. You may need to sketch this out or chart the shaped areas of your garment.

Sources for Charted Patterns

Browse bookstores, knitting stores, and libraries for stranded knitting books that include reference sections of charts, from tiny one- and two-row filler patterns to large stars and flowers that will fill the whole front of a sweater. You can, of course, chart your own patterns on paper or using software. Regular graph paper with square cells can be used for your charts, because stranded knitting is a bit narrower horizontally than stockinette knit in one color. (See Creating Your Own, page 306.)

How Much Yarn?

It can be difficult to calculate yarn requirements for stranded knitting because you must allow for the yarn consumed by stranding between stitches. It's best to estimate based on the total yarn needed for the sweater. A sweater made with stranded knitting throughout requires about 50 percent more yarn than a sweater made in single-color stockinette. Estimate how much yarn a plain sweater would require, add 50 percent to this amount, and then divide the total between colors based on the proportion of each in your pattern. It's a good idea to have more yarn on hand than you think you'll need. Leftovers can always be used for future projects, such as matching mittens and hats.

KNITTING A CIRCULAR SWATCH

Many knitters have a different tension when knitting than purling, so your gauge in circular knitting (which is all knit stitches) may be significantly tighter or looser than your gauge in flat knitting (which is half purl stitches). To accommodate this tendency, knit a circular swatch so it will accurately represent the fabric of the finished product. Try any of these approaches:

» **Knit a narrow tube** on a set of double-pointed needles or on two circular needles.

» **Make a flat swatch** working all the rows on the right side by knitting across, breaking off the yarn, and then going back to the beginning of the row and knitting across again. If you hate to waste yarn (or suspect you'll need to unravel the swatch and knit it again), instead of cutting the yarn, pull it very loosely across the back of the swatch, leaving long enough strands that the swatch can be laid flat to measure.

STRANDED HAT

The stranding technique makes particularly warm winter hats because of the extra thickness created by carrying strands of yarn across the back while knitting the color pattern.

Measurements 21" (53.3 cm) in circumference and 8" (20 cm) tall, with bottom band folded up

Yarn Kid Hollow semi-worsted, 50% wool/50% mohair, 4 oz (113 g)/180 yd (164.5 m): MC: 125 yards Turquoise; C1: 45 yards Violet Heather; C2: 13 yards Bright Milling Blue; C3: 8 yards Burnt Orange

Needles One US 7 (4.5 mm) circular needle 16" (36 cm) long, *or size needed to achieve correct gauge,* and one set of double-pointed needles the same size

Gauge 20 stitches = 4" (10 cm) in stranded pattern

Knitting the Bottom Band

Note that the band is worked flat (back and forth in rows).

SETUP: Using MC, cast on 96 stitches.

ROWS 1 AND 2: Using C2, knit.

ROWS 3 AND 4: Using MC, knit.

ROWS 5 AND 6: Using C3, knit.

ROWS 7 AND 8: Using MC, knit.

ROWS 9 AND 10: Using C1, knit.

ROWS 11 AND 12: Using MC, knit.

Knitting the Sides

Note that the sides are worked circularly.

Join beginning and end of round, being careful not to twist and making sure knitting is right-side out. The wrong side of the bottom band will show on the right side at this point, ready to be turned up when the hat is completed.

SETUP ROUNDS Continuing in MC, knit 12 rounds.

ROUNDS 1–29 Continuing in stockinette stitch and using colors as designated in chart, work Rounds 1–29 of the Stranded Hat chart. (See pages 304–305 for information on how to work from charts.)

Knitting the Crown

See Crown Decreasing Made Easy for advice on working crown shaping.

ROUNDS 30–42   Continuing in stockinette, work Rounds 30–42 of the Stranded Hat chart, working decreases in each repeat of pattern where indicated. At the end of the chart, *you will have* 12 stitches remaining.

Crown Decreasing Made Easy

» At the beginning of each decrease round, knit the first stitch in MC, then work the chart as written. When you reach the end of the round, work the final decrease using the last two stitches at the end of round, plus the first stitch of the next round.

» On the double decreases, be sure to slip 2 stitches together knitwise, K1, then pass both slipped stitches over. This makes a double decrease with the center stitch on top.

» When the crown becomes too small to work comfortably on the circular needle, switch to double-pointed needles.

Finishing

Cut yarn. Use a yarn needle to pull the end through the remaining stitches and pull to inside of hat. Sew ends of bottom band together (see Mattress Stitch, page 300). Weave in ends on inside.

Stranded Hat

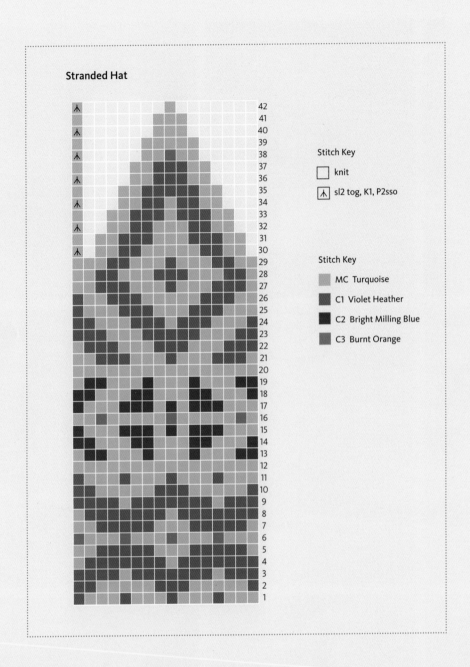

Stitch Key

☐ knit

⅄ sl2 tog, K1, P2sso

Stitch Key

▪ MC Turquoise

▪ C1 Violet Heather

▪ C2 Bright Milling Blue

▪ C3 Burnt Orange

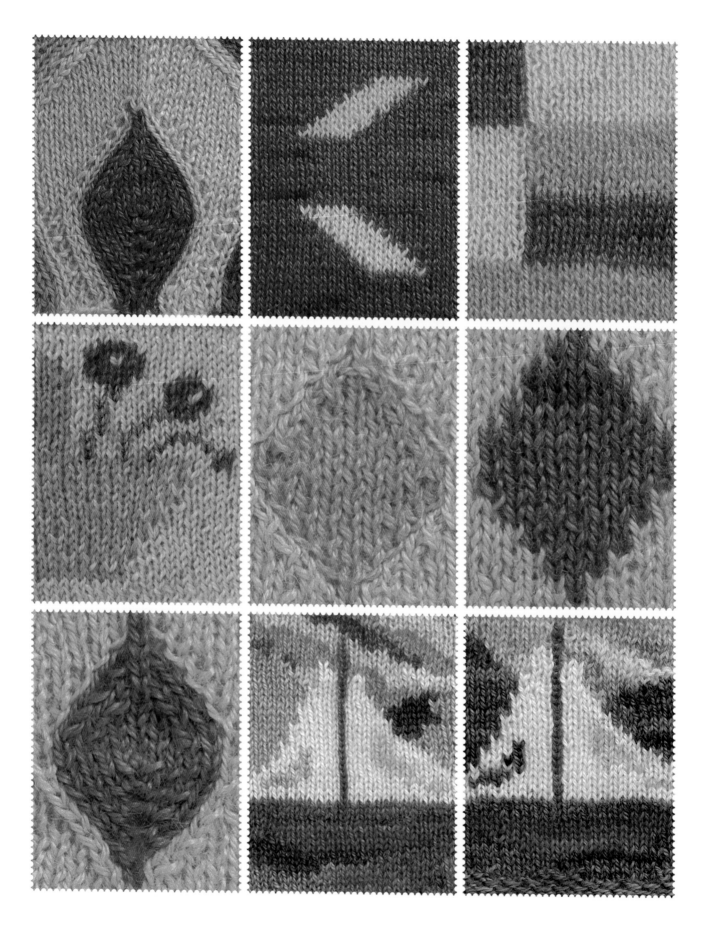

6 INTARSIA

Intarsia knitting features multiple colors, but unlike stranding, the yarn is never carried across the back of the fabric to be used elsewhere in the row. It is characterized by isolated areas of color that do not repeat, and it lends itself to pictures rather than repetitive patterns. The difference between stranded knitting and intarsia is clear when you compare the wrong sides of pieces done using these methods. With intarsia, no strands of yarn cross the back of the fabric, except where one color changes to another. At these points, the strands are interlocked, twisted together to prevent holes from forming at the transition between them, and then run up to the next row to be used again. Stranded fabric is thicker and less stretchy the more strands there are across the back, but intarsia creates a fabric as thin and flexible as plain stockinette. Intarsia is usually worked in stockinette, since the focus is on the image produced by the changing colors, but you can add areas of texture, if you wish.

{Intarsia Basics}

Intarsia has a misleading reputation for being difficult. Knitting intarsia is not difficult, but it does require close attention and a significant amount of time for weaving in ends, and it is not quick compared to some other knitting techniques. Taking care to maintain even tension when changing colors and while weaving in ends is crucial to fashioning perfect intarsia. The technical concepts behind the knitting itself are very simple:

» *Color design.* A colored design is represented by a chart, which can be colored or may use symbols substituted for each color.

» *Yarn supply.* You must have a separate supply of yarn for each occurrence of a color on any row. If there are three sections of a particular blue, for example, you need three separate supplies of blue yarn.

» *Getting started.* It's usual, but not required, to cast on with a single color. On each row, work across, knitting each stitch in the appropriate color based on the chart (See Using Charts, page 304.)

» *Flat knitting.* Intarsia is usually worked flat (rather than circularly), because once the stitches are knit, the yarn is abandoned at the left-hand edge of each colored area on each knit row, and must be picked up at the same point and knit back across the same area on the following purl row.

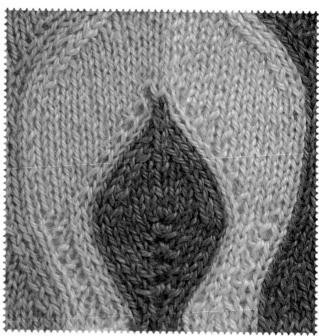

right side

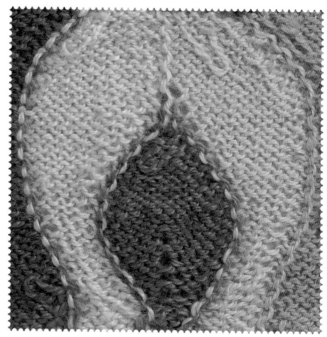

wrong side

INTARSIA SAMPLE SWATCH. Compare the front and back of this shaped intarsia with the photos of stranded knitting on page 148.

{Yarn Management}

How you deal with the many strands of yarn that intarsia requires depends a great deal on your personality. Some knitters prefer to keep everything very neat, to have a place for each ball or bobbin of yarn, and to straighten things out every time they change colors. Others don't mind the tangling and restore order only when it becomes impossible to pull enough yarn loose to keep knitting. Still others absolutely hate having to stop and deal with the yarn (they'd rather be knitting!) and use cut strands of yarn that can easily be pulled free from the snarl. You probably already know which group you fit into. If not, you'll discover it very quickly when you begin working.

Keeping Things in Order

If you like to keep things neat at all times or you expect to straighten them out periodically, before you begin knitting you'll need to prepare enough separate supplies of each yarn to make all of the color changes on the busiest row. For colors that you plan to use in large areas throughout the piece, you may prefer to wind the yarn into center-pull balls. For small- to medium-sized areas, winding a bobbin or making a yarn butterfly probably works best.

When using several center-pull balls, you can help prevent tangling by working while seated at a table with the yarns on it. Place the balls in the order they will be used inside a box that will hold them tightly, to prevent them from shifting position (A). You can also put small jars inside the box, with a ball of yarn in each one, to keep them weighted and in place. This has the added benefit of creating a placeholder when a ball of yarn runs out or gets too small to hold its own spot. When you get to the end of a knit row and turn back to work on the purl side, the yarns will twist to cross each other from one side to the other (B). When you finish the purl row, turn the knitting in the opposite direction, which untwists all the yarns. If you accidentally turn the knitting the wrong way, the additional twist is immediately noticeable and you can untwist before you begin knitting the next row. Each time you interlock the yarns, they twist, but they untwist when you work the interlock on the following row. If the order of the colors changes or if you introduce new colors, stop and untwist the yarns before working the next row, taking only one ball of yarn out of the box at a time.

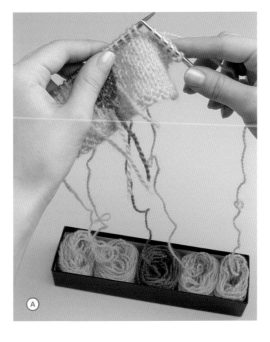

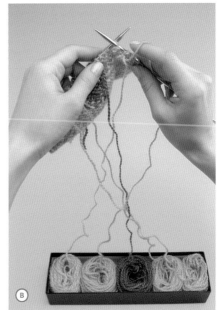

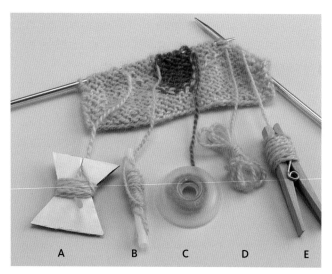

A   B   C   D   E

Making a yarn "butterfly"

▲ *Bundling up.* There are numerous ways to organize your short- to medium-length yarn supplies into little bundles. Cardboard or plastic butterflies, which you can buy or make yourself, have a narrow waist for winding the yarn and a notch to secure it (A). Short lengths of plastic drinking straws with a notch cut at one end serve the same purpose (B). Round plastic bobbins snap closed to secure the yarn when it's not in use (C). Wind butterflies of yarn around your fingers and secure them with a half hitch (D, and at right). Clothespins are also useful; wind the yarn around the hinge-point and secure it by catching it in the jaws (E).

To prevent tangling, these small supplies of yarn must be secured close to the back of the fabric when not in use. Unfortunately, this can make it uncomfortably heavy to hold while knitting. To reduce the weight, leave a strand long enough to rest in your lap, but expect them to become twisted around each other.

Going to lengths. If you hate to stop knitting to deal with the yarn, try working with arm's lengths, especially when using more than two or three yarn supplies. When beginning a new supply of yarn for a new area of color, pull a long arm's length (up to 2 yards [1.8 m] long) from the ball and cut it. This way, there's no need to wind off yarn supplies before you begin knitting, and you can leave all these long strands trailing as you work. Usually the yarns don't tangle, but if they do become intertwined, pull out the strand you need. Because there are no bobbins or balls to prevent it from coming loose from the mass of other strands, it slips free easily. Knit with each until it runs out, then cut another length of the same color, splice it to the end of the original, and keep knitting. You may prefer to just knot the ends together when you need more yarn, and either leave them dangling on the back of the work forever or weave them in later. When you finish an area, cut the yarn, leaving a 4–5" (10–12 cm) tail, and set the remaining yarn aside to use later in the project. If you prefer a neater finish for the back of your work, however, splicing reduces the amount of effort required in the long run. (See Making Connections, facing page.)

AVOIDING COMPLETE CHAOS

If the yarn-management methods suggested here seem like too much trouble, you certainly aren't required to use them. I would, however, caution you against leaving all the center-pull balls in a jumble in your knitting bag or basket while you knit. Constant pulling on the working yarn and adjustments to tension will rearrange the balls as you work, twisting and braiding all the strands of yarn together. When this happens, you must unbraid them by hand or cut the strands of yarn and pull them out. Place the larger balls in ziplock plastic bags and then seal them to prevent unwinding while you straighten things out.

MAKING CONNECTIONS

Splicing means that there will be no ends at the join to deal with later. Untwist the ends of the yarn and pull the plies apart for about 4" (10 cm). Break off half of the plies on each end. If you are working with a single-ply yarn, untwist the ends and pull some of the fibers out to reduce the thickness. Overlap the ends and twist or wrap them around each other in the direction of the original twist. Wet this section of the yarn and rub it a little to help the fibers adhere to each other. Hold onto the spliced section while you knit the next few stitches. Once it has been knitted, it will not come apart.

Splicing works best on fuzzy yarns. For smooth yarns (especially those made from fibers like cotton, linen, or silk), the splice may look different from the rest of the yarn and be noticeable in your finished knitting, so it should be avoided.

Estimating How Much Yarn to Prepare

If you are winding balls or bobbins of yarn, especially if you're nearly out of the materials for your project, you probably want to allocate the yarn accurately to the supply for each area. How do you know how much you need? First, refer to your chart and count the number of stitches in this color in the section you plan to knit. Save time in large areas by multiplying the number of rows by the approximate number of stitches per row. You have two choices on how to use this information.

The precise approach. If you'd like to be mathematically precise, you need to work out the length of yarn required for each stitch and multiply by the number of stitches in each section. To estimate the number of inches (or centimeters) per stitch for your yarn at the gauge you are knitting, cast on 25 stitches in the yarn you're using (one color only) and knit one row. Right where the yarn

emerges from the last stitch, fasten a safety pin through the yarn. Work 4 more rows in stockinette stitch. Place another safety pin through the yarn where it emerges from the last stitch. Between the two safety pins there are 100 stitches (4 rows × 25 stitches). Unravel the knitting and measure the yarn between the two safety pins.

The quick-and-dirty method. If knitting and unraveling seems like too much trouble, you can get a less accurate but still usable estimate by wrapping yarn once around your needle 100 times. Space the wraps about the way that real stitches would be spaced and try to approximate the same tension as in actual knitting. Place safety pins at the beginning and end of the wraps. This is how much yarn you'll need for 100 stitches.

DOING THE MATH

To determine the length of an individual stitch, divide the length you got by either "the precise approach" or "the quick-and-dirty method" by 100. If the length is 68" (173 cm), then

68" ÷ 100 stitches = .68" per stitch
(173 cm ÷ 100 stitches = 1.73 cm per stitch)

To calculate how much yarn is needed for any one area, multiply this result by the number of stitches and add 10" (25 cm) for tails at the beginning and end of the area. If there are 75 stitches, then

.68" per stitch × 75 stitches = 51"
(1.73 cm per stitch × 75 stitches = 1.3 m)
51" for stitches + 10" for tails = 61"
(1.3 m for stitches + 25 cm for tails = 1.55 m)

{Interlocking Colors}

As you work across each row, work all the stitches in each color, creating an interlock each time you change colors.

▲ *To start a new yarn supply,* lay the end of the yarn between the needles with the tail hanging on the right side of the fabric. Bring the yarn used to knit the previous stitch over this strand and drop it to the left of it. Lift the new strand up to the right of the old one and begin knitting with it. While you work, leave the tail hanging on the right side of the fabric so you don't confuse it with one of the working yarn supplies; you can weave it in later.

▲ *To change between yarn supplies* that are already in use, form the interlock in the same manner: drop the old color to the left of the new color on the wrong side of the fabric, then pick up the new color under and to the right of the old one. Use this method regardless of whether you are working a knit row or a purl row and regardless of whether the color change is directly over the color change on the previous row or to the left or right of it.

As you start each new color, watch your tension. Pulling the yarn too firmly will collapse the last stitch you worked with this yarn, making it noticeably tighter than the stitches around it. Holding the yarn too loosely will leave that last stitch plus the first stitch on the new row too loose. Tighten up the old stitch until it's the proper size, work the new stitch with a medium tension, then work the second stitch firmly. If your stitches are a bit uneven at the color changes, you can adjust them later. All efforts you make to work the stitches consistently in the first place are valuable and will save you time.

If you are working an irregular area of the color or a diagonal that extends into a point, the first or last stitch may be distorted because the yarn from the previous row enters the stitch from the left rather than from the right or because the yarn exits the stitch going up to the next row in the wrong direction. Adjust the angle of the yarn by twisting the working yarn around the yarn in the adjacent color block a stitch or two before you begin using it on the next row.

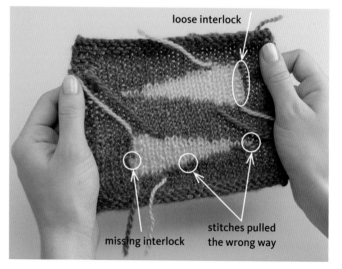

loose interlock

stitches pulled the wrong way

missing interlock

TENSION TROUBLES. This swatch has several defects caused by uneven tension, missing interlocks, and yarn entering or exiting a stitch from the wrong direction. (See pages 184–185 for ways to correct these problems after the knitting is completed.)

Ending a Color

When you are done with a strand of yarn, cut it to a reasonable length and save the extra to use later. Again, you may find it helpful to leave it dangling to the front of the fabric, so that you don't confuse it with the yarn supplies still in use. You may decide that it keeps the work neater to weave in the tails periodically as you complete sections of the garment. Making this effort as you knit also means you'll have less work to do after the knitting is finally completed.

Combining Stranding with Intarsia

It is generally not a good idea to combine stranded knitting with intarsia. Stranded knitting makes a thicker fabric than intarsia, and the strands pull the stitches closer together. In addition, it can be difficult to prevent distortion in the stitches where there is a transition between the two techniques.

▲ *Wrong side of combination.* To successfully combine the two techniques, never carry the background color across the back of the stranded section. At the edge of the stranded area, *both* of the yarns carried across that section must be interlocked with yarn in the surrounding background section, even if one of them is the same as the background color. Use one supply of the background color for the preceding section, separate supplies of each of the colors in the stranded section, and another supply of the background color following the stranded section. If there is a point where the dividing line between the two sections shifts suddenly, such as where the handle begins, it's usually best to cut the yarns. This prevents the stitches from being distorted, although you'll have more tails to weave in later.

▲ *When combining stranding and intarsia works.* In some situations, however, it makes sense to introduce a stranded section. For example, stranding is a good choice if you have a small area where two colors are used alternately within the overall intarsia design. In the mostly intarsia basket design above, the basket was best worked using stranding, with details on the handle and the flowers worked in duplicate stitch after the piece was completed. The chart for this design is shown on page 304.

Dealing with Isolated Stitches

Occasionally designs contain isolated single stitches, such as those on the basket handle, a vertical column of stitches, or a diagonal line of stitches. These are best worked in duplicate stitch after the piece is completed. If the stitches are near the beginning or end of another area of the same color, leave a tail of that color long enough to use for the duplicate stitch and work it while weaving in the ends. (For duplicate stitch, see page 296.)

{Handling All Those Ends}

Weaving in ends properly is the second key to good-looking intarsia. Ends that are woven too tightly, too loosely, or at the wrong angle distort the stitches and make them a different size than the stitches in the rest of the fabric. Stitches may also be distorted when the tail is woven in a different direction than the line of interlocks it completes. Trim each tail immediately as you finish sewing it so you don't accidentally cut one that has not yet been secured. Leaving all the beginning and ending tails dangling to the front of the piece will also help to prevent confusion.

▲ *Cross tails, if appropriate.* If one color starts where another color ends, there may be two tails adjacent to each other. Cross the two tails as you weave in the ends.

▲ *Examine right side before weaving in.* When you prepare to weave in an end, begin by adjusting the tension of the stitch it's attached to and checking the stitch from the right side of the fabric to see how it looks.

▲ *Fix holes.* If an interlock is missing at the beginning or end of a color, causing a hole, pull the tail through the interlock to correct the problem before weaving in the end.

Watch tension while weaving in. Weave in the end on the wrong side of the fabric, being careful not to change the tension of the stitch attached to this tail.

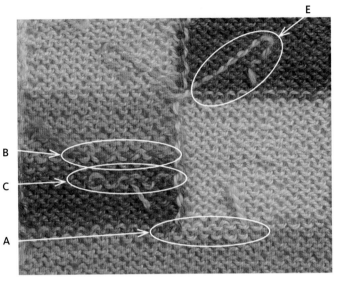

▲ *Duplicate stitch.* Weaving in duplicate stitch on the wrong side for at least the first stitch ensures that the stitches aren't distorted; but in some fabrics, contrasting colors may show through, or the row may be noticeably thicker. Duplicate stitch appears in yellow yarn at A.

▲ *Use the purl bumps.* Zigzagging horizontally under the purl bumps also prevents distortion (shown in red at B). Doubling back on the woven end, splitting the plies as you go, locks the yarn in place so the end can't pull loose (shown in orange at C). The end, however, may show through the fabric (especially if the end is dark and the fabric is light) and it may be noticeably thicker.

▲ *Split the difference.* Still another method, which avoids problems with show-through and thickness but still allows the fabric to stretch, is to use a darning needle with a sharp point and sew through the plies of the purl bumps (D and E), working diagonally away from the last stitch in the color so that it's not distorted on the front of the fabric. Try to continue in the same direction as the line of interlocks that the tail completes. To lock the tails in place, either work back over them in the opposite direction (C) or double back to form a fish hook (E).

{Repairing Mistakes}

Even if you maintain constant vigilance while you work, you may still discover errors and inconsistencies once the knitting is done, but don't panic. Here are some methods that disguise intarsia errors so well that no one but you will ever know there's a problem.

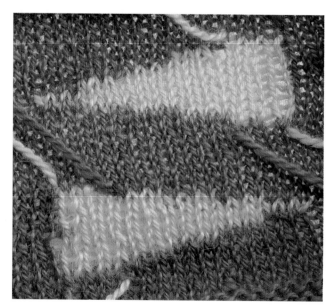

Taking a critical look.

Uneven stitches. Uneven stitches are inevitable, especially at color changes. Use the tip of a needle to coax yarn from a loose stitch into a tighter adjacent stitch of the same color. Blocking under tension also smoothes out most inconsistencies and creates smoother, flatter edges, making sewing up easier.

▲ *Tension uneven at vertical changes.* When there is a vertical color change, looser and tighter stitches alternate along the edge. On the back of the fabric, insert a knitting needle into each interlock, pulling down to shift the looseness out of the upper stitch into the interlock, then stretch the fabric vertically.

▲ *Missing interlock.* If an interlock is missing, causing a hole at the color change, cut a piece of yarn in the same color and sew it through on the back of the fabric to close the hole (shown here in yellow for clarity).

▲ *Tightening up.* Use this technique to adjust the tension at the color change if you've left loose stitches. Pull the excess yarn to the back of the fabric so that the stitches are the correct size on the front. Then weave in an additional piece of yarn (shown here in yellow) just beyond the edge of that color, catching the loose yarn at every interlock to stretch it across the back of the fabric. (See previous photo.)

Camouflage. Small mistakes in color can be camouflaged by working duplicate stitch in the correct color over the offending area. For a larger area in the wrong color, first consider whether there's some way of making it appear correct. After all, you may be the only one who knows it's wrong. If so, can you live with it? Would duplicate stitch in a different color over part of the area, or scattered occasionally across the area, make it look intentional? If neither of these options appeal to you, consider knitting an appliqué, a separate piece the size and shape of the area, and then sewing or crocheting it on. You could also crochet or embroider over the area, which would add textural interest while correcting the color. Yet another solution is to actually replace one color with another. Duplicate stitch the new color one stitch at a time and, as you work, remove the stitch in the old color that you just duplicated. A last-ditch solution is to unravel your work back to the mistake and reknit from there.

▲ *Fixing a distorted outlying point.* When the interlock enters a stitch from the wrong direction, one side of the stitch will pull in, making it look uneven. Correct this by using a piece of yarn to pull the interlock in the correct direction, then weave in both ends.

{Working in the Round}

While intarsia's natural habitat is flat knitting, there are several ways to integrate it into a circular environment. In the most practical method, you are still truly working a flat piece of knitting but are joining the beginning and end of each row as you work so you don't need to sew a seam later. Using a circular needle or a set of double-pointed needles, cast on and work any plain section at the beginning circularly. Place markers or safety pins in the first and last stitch of the round. Work the first round of the intarsia design, then follow the illustrated steps at right for joining rounds. I have illustrated two ways of joining rounds: with yarn overs and with wraps. If using a yarn over to join the rows at the beginning and end of round leaves a loose stitch, you may find that applying short-row wrap-and-turn techniques makes a slightly tighter join.

Knitting intarsia in the round

Joining Rounds with Yarn Overs

1] When you have completed the last stitch of the round, turn your work so the purl side is facing you. Yarn over and work back around on the purl side in your intarsia pattern.

2] Work until one stitch remains before the yarn over. This is the first marked stitch you come to. P2tog to join it to the yarn over.

3] Turn your work so that the knit side is facing you. Yarn over and work in intarsia on the knit side in your intarsia pattern.

4] Work until one stitch remains before the yarn over. Again, this will be the first marked stitch you come to. Work it together with the yarn over using ssk, which hides the yarn over on the purl side.

Turn and turn again. Continue this pattern of turning, working a yarn over at the beginning of each row, and joining the last stitch of the row to the yarn over with a P2tog on the purl side and an ssk on the knit side. The yarn over always falls between the two marked stitches and you always join a marked stitch to the yarn over using either ssk or P2tog. If you continue to need the stitch markers to stay oriented as you work, move them up closer to the needles periodically.

When you have completed your intarsia pattern, if the last row is on the knit side, simply resume working circularly. If the last row is on the purl side, turn at the end of row once more, working the yarn over at the beginning of the row. In either case, when you reach the last stitch of the round, ssk to join the final yarn over to the last stitch, but don't turn your work. Resume working circularly on the knit side.

Joining Rounds with Wraps

1] When you have worked the first row of your intarsia pattern on the knit side, continue to the end of the round. Leaving the yarn in back, slip the first stitch of the next round purlwise. Bring your yarn forward between the needles. Turn your work so the purl side faces you. Slip the same stitch to the right needle purlwise. Bring the yarn forward again and work the intarsia pattern all the way around on the purl side.

2] When you reach the last wrapped stitch, work the wrap together with the stitch in this manner: Insert the needle up through the wrap on the back of the fabric and through the stitch purlwise. Purl the stitch, then lift the wrap off over the new stitch to the front of the knitting. Leaving the yarn in front, slip the next stitch purlwise.

3] Take the yarn to the back, turn your work so the knit side faces you, slip the same stitch to the right needle purlwise, and take the yarn to the back again.

4] Work the intarsia pattern all the way around on the knit side. When you reach the wrapped stitch at the end of the round, insert your needle up through the wrap from the front, then through the stitch. Knit the stitch, then pass the wrap over it to the back of the knitting.

Repeat this process, working back and forth on the knit and purl sides, working the wrap together with the stitch at the end of each round and immediately slipping and wrapping the next stitch while turning.

{Shaping Intarsia}

One small annoyance of traditional intarsia is the jagged edge that marks the border between one color and another. If you want a smooth line with no stair steps, use an increase on one side of the color change and a decrease on the other to create a smooth diagonal. There must be an equal number of increases and decreases on each row so that the total number of stitches remains the same and the color can only shift one stitch to the left or right on each row. Although the increases and decreases do create smooth lines, the more of them there are, the more distorted the fabric will be. If the fabric is knit firmly, it may dimple and pucker, even after vigorous blocking; it's best to use as little shaping as possible and to create a soft, rather than a firm, fabric.

Examples of Shaped Intarsia

There are various approaches you can take to working shapes in intarsia.

A. In the dark gold diamond, the K2tog decreases at the right edge and the ssk decreases at the left edge outline at the bottom of the diamond. The increases inside the diamond are decorative eyelets, made by working K1-yo-K1 into the center stitch. The

top half of the diamond is decreased at the center using a raised double decrease, so the center stitch remains prominently on top. Shaping in yellow along the upper edge is minimized, as it is in the orange diamond (B), by twisting the Make 1 (M1) increases so they follow the edge of the diamond. Working the increase one stitch away from the edge would have created an outline of one stitch to mirror the bottom half of the diamond. Shaping the dark gold diamond in the center, rather than at the edges, causes it to be a bit puffy and changes the grain of the knitting.

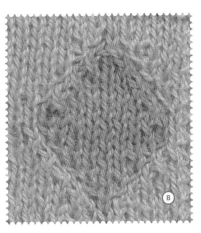

B. The shaping around the orange diamond was worked with an ssk on the right side and a K2tog on the left side of the bottom half, to make the decreases as unnoticeable as possible. M1 increases were worked in orange along these edges, twisting so that the diagonal strand of the increase follows the interior edge of the diamond. In the top half of this diamond, the decreases were reversed, with the K2tog at the left edge in orange and the ssk at the right edge. Again, the M1 increases in yellow were twisted so that they follow the outer edge of the diamond.

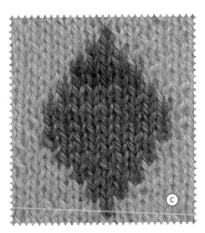

C. For comparison, the raspberry diamond was worked in traditional intarsia and shows the characteristic stair-step edges.

As you can see, the type of increase or decrease and its placement significantly affects the appearance of the knitting. The step-by-step instructions below produce a slightly different look from those illustrated. You can vary the position and type of increase and decrease to produce exactly the effect you want.

Techniques for Shaped Intarsia

Cast on and work a base row or two, using a separate yarn supply for each area of color. It's easiest to work all the shaping on right-side rows. These instructions make a stitch in each color travel parallel to each other up either side of the color change, which creates the neatest join. If you prefer, you can use the ssk decrease for the right slant and K2tog for the left slant to get rid of one of these edge stitches. To eliminate the edge stitch on the other side of the color change, work your increase immediately after you interlock the colors; however, maintaining consistent tension at the color change in this situation is tricky.

▲ *Left slant.* Work until 1 stitch remains before the color change, inc 1, K1 (A), interlock the yarns, ssk (B).

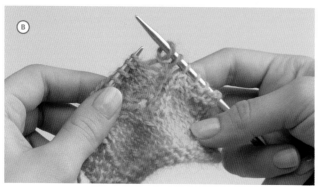

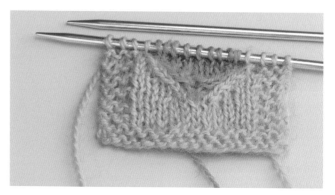

▲ *Right slant.* Work until 2 stitches remain before the color change, K2tog, interlock the yarns (A), K1, inc 1 (B), and continue across the row.

{Garter Stitch}

There are two approaches to working the interlocks if you are making a garter-stitch fabric rather than one knit in stockinette. One is to designate each face of the fabric as right side or wrong side, and to work the interlocks so they are visible only on the wrong side. The second is to make a reversible fabric, where the interlocks appear every other row on both sides. Both of these methods can also be worked with other pattern stitches where the first and last stitch of each color is always knitted.

In swatch A, the right side of nonreversible garter stitch intarsia shows perfect interlocks. On the wrong side, the interlocks are just as obvious as in stockinette intarsia. In swatch B, reversible garter stitch intarsia has interlocks that are slightly more noticeable, but it's the same on both sides.

▲ *Nonreversible garter stitch.* On the right-side rows, both yarns hang from the back of the fabric, so the interlock can be worked as usual. When knitting across on the wrong side, the new yarn hangs at the front of the fabric, where it was left on the previous row. To work the interlock, bring the new yarn (orange) between the needles to the back and set it down to the right of the old yarn. Bring the old yarn (apricot) between the needles to the front. This forces all the interlocks to the wrong side of the fabric, where they are quite noticeable, but they cannot be seen at all on the right side of the fabric. (Photo shows wrong side of fabric.)

Reversible fabric. Work the wrong-side interlock on every row. Using this technique, the interlocks alternate on both sides of the fabric. While this does not look as perfect on the right side as the nonreversible method described above, the vertical sections of the interlocks are hidden in the valley between the garter-stitch ridges unless the fabric is stretched from top to bottom.

{Inspiration for Design}

Inspiration for designing your own intarsia can come from any number of sources: nature, photographs, textiles, digital images, decorative objects, or your imagination. Once you have a design in mind, there are four preliminary steps to take before you can begin knitting.

Swatch. You need to know the stitches and rows per inch before you can chart the image, so select your needles, yarn, and colors; work up a gauge swatch; and measure it carefully. (See page 285.)

▲ *Plan color palette.* I worked up this swatch not only to plan the gauge, but also to get a general idea of how the colors would work together and in what order and proportion I would use them.

Measure. You also need the measurements of the area your image will cover in your knitting. For example, the front of a sweater that measures 44" (112 cm) around will be 22" (56 cm) wide, but the sides of this will be hidden under the arms. Decide whether you want your design to appear just in the center of the knitting, or if it will continue all the way to the side seams.

Calculate. Once you know how wide and tall the area will be, multiply the width by the stitches per inch (or cm) and multiply the height by the rows per inch (or cm) to determine the width in stitches and the height in rows. To chart the design, you'll need a grid with at least this many rows and columns.

Chart. Try whichever of the several approaches described below suits you best.

Charting Your Design

Here are several suggestions for getting your design onto the graph paper, ranging from low to high tech.

» *Direct draw.* Draw the design on the graph paper with colored pencils or markers. Fill in the squares completely with each color to get a better feel for how the finished product will look when knitted.

» *Backlit.* Lay the graph paper over the image and tape the two sheets to a window or lay them over a light box so the light shines through, making it easier to see the design, then color it in. The image must be the correct size in relation to your graph paper.

» *Trace onto a transparency.* Print or copy the graph paper onto a transparency and lay it directly over the image. Use water-soluble markers to draw your design so you can wash off areas to make changes. The ink from most ink-jet printers is also water soluble, so mark your design on the back of the transparency to prevent smearing.

» *Charting software.* Chart the pattern using charting software. Set the height and width of the cells to match the proportions of a knitted stitch. It may be possible to import an image directly into the chart.

» *Spreadsheet software.* Chart the pattern using spread-sheet software or a table in word-processing software. Both of these methods can be very time-consuming. You must first adjust the height and width of the cells to the correct proportion, then select each cell and fill it with a color. It may be quicker to type in a symbol.

» *Internet conversion.* Create a chart in a PDF file at the Web page *www.microrevolt.org/knitPro* using an image on your computer. Be sure to select one of the knit-ting options, which produces rectangular rather than square cells. "Landscape" is standard if you plan to knit your work from bottom to top. Use "portrait" for work-ing side to side.

» *Image editing software.* Programs such as Adobe Photoshop allow you to superimpose a transparent grid in a layer over an image and may also help you automatically reduce the number of colors.

KNITTER'S GRAPH PAPER

It's important to use knitter's graph paper when you draw out your design. This paper features cells that are wider than they are tall, to match the shape of the knitted stitches. If you use regular graph paper, your design will look perfect on paper, but the proportions will be too short and too wide in the knitted ver-sion. Large sheets of knitter's graph paper are available from machine- and hand-knitting suppliers and come in different gauges (such as 5, 5½, or 6 stitches per inch) so you can work at "life size." You can also make your own graph paper using your computer, by printing it from an Internet site, using a spreadsheet program, or making a table in a wordprocessing program.

Fearful Symmetry

If you need to reverse the design for the opposite section of the garment (the sleeves, or the left and right fronts, for example), charting it on a transparency allows you to flip the transparency over and read the chart from the opposite side. Most charting, image-editing software, and word-processing programs also allow you to flip an image horizontally before printing it out, to achieve the same results.

In many cases, especially if a design goes all the way to the edge of the fabric, it's a good idea to draw in the outline of the garment piece, including armholes and neck shaping, to help you visualize the placement of the design on the finished garment. This can be extremely helpful in staying oriented during the actual knitting. You may want to draw the outline first, then chart the design within it — or it may work best to add the outline after the image is charted.

Choosing Yarn

You can use any yarn you like to work intarsia, but the results will differ significantly depending on your choices.

Scale. If you use a fine yarn (for instance, fingering weight that knits up with a gauge of 8 stitches per inch), you can fit more detail into your design than you can with a bulky yarn at 4 stitches per inch.

Texture. The varying surface qualities of different yarns can dramatically influence the appearance of a design. Wool, cotton, and silk all reflect light differently, as do fuzzy yarns and smooth yarns. Using fuzzy or tex-tured wool yarns throughout causes color changes to be softer and less obvious. A smooth, tightly plied silk, on the other hand, results in a crisp, clean appearance, where every stitch can be clearly seen. Combining smooth and textured yarns and various fibers in one garment adds the dimensions of texture and finish to color and composition, with results that may range from fabulous to distracting. You also have the choice of solid versus variegated yarns. Variegated yarn can make it look like you're changing col-ors more frequently than you really are, bringing nuance and complexity to the design.

Two Takes on the Same Design

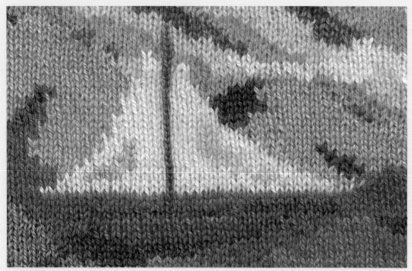

Design A

Design B

WHILE MOST INTARSIA IS WORKED IN STOCKINETTE STITCH, you can introduce a little variety by using textured stitch patterns in some areas. Reverse stockinette adds nubbly areas that have the same gauge as stockinette. Neither Seed Stitch in small areas nor scattered purl stitches affect the overall gauge of the project. On the other hand, garter-stitch areas are wider and shorter than the surrounding stockinette stitch. Twisted stitches and cables can be used to define architectural elements, such as columns or posts, but since cables pull in horizontally, you may need to increase a stitch or two where they begin and decrease again where they end. When combining textured stitches, it's best to create a loose fabric so that the knitting stretches to accommodate variations in gauge between pattern stitches.

Design A is executed in the colors shown on page 193. Design B uses multicolored yarns and various textural stitches to create a completely different look for the same design.

Finding Inspiration

Any image can be the basis for a design, and it can be as realistic or as abstract as you like. The sailboat (facing page) is an example of a design from my imagination. It started with a sketch, which was the basis for the chart. Abstract symbols, doodles, and arabesques can all be used this way. Photographs, from close-ups to landscapes, can easily be converted to charts. Textiles of all sorts are excellent sources of inspiration. And graphic art, from old masters to abstract contemporaries, can serve as starting points for intarsia designs.

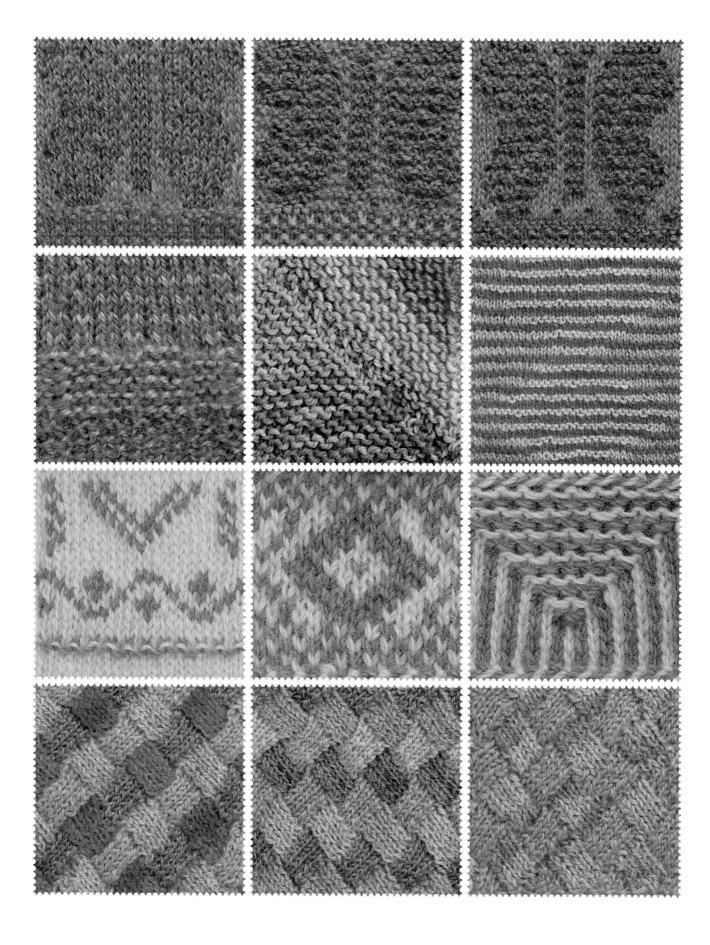

7 OTHER TECHNIQUES

The possibilities of color knitting aren't really infinite, but there are so many techniques to choose among and so many potential variations within them, that they might as well be! It's impossible to go into depth on every aspect of color knitting in the scope of a single book, or even to provide a complete reference to all the possible methods. In this chapter, however, I'd like to showcase a sampling of approaches I particularly enjoy using when I knit with more than one color. You'll find sections on helix, shadow, mosaic, twined, double, and modular knitting (including entrelac) — all guaranteed to broaden your knitting horizons.

{Helix Knitting}

Helix knitting produces perfect interlocking spirals of each color in single-row stripes. Once you start a color, there is no perceptible beginning or end of round, just an endless spiral of that color. You can work helix knitting with as few as two balls of yarn or as many balls as you have stitches on your needle. Helix knitting works on circular needles, on double-pointed needles, or on I-cord. (For Many-Color I-cord, see page 266.) The beauty of helix knitting is that while it's extremely simple, it's loaded with possibilities, especially when you add texture to the mix.

IN GEOMETRY, A HELIX is described as a three-dimensional curve that lies on a cylinder or cone. As you can see in this drawing of a double helix, the two spiral smoothly and continuously around each other.

Helix knitting must be done with at least two colors. Knit one full round with one color; then knit another round with the second. Unlike intarsia, when you switch colors, don't twist or tighten the yarn. As you alternate colors, you create a perfect peppermint-striped tube.

HELIX KNITTING RULES
» Always work circularly.
» Always use your yarns in the same order.
» Never twist the yarns when you change colors.
» Don't tighten the last stitch too much when you bring a yarn back into use.

Getting Started on Circular Needles

There are several ways to cast on and begin the helix, depending on whether you're working on circular needles or double-pointed needles, and whether you want to cast on with all your colors or just one.

1] Cast on enough stitches to fit comfortably around a circular needle. Do not join the beginning and end of this round.

2] Beginning with the first stitch you cast on (not the last stitch), knit across with a second color. Turn your work so that the working yarns are both in your right hand. The work is not yet joined into a round.

3] Drop the second color. Make sure the knitting isn't twisted around the needle. To join the beginning and end of the round, pick up the color you used to cast on, which is hanging there waiting, one row down. Knit one round with this first color.

4] Continue knitting around, alternating rounds of the two colors. At the cast on, there will be a corner hanging down where the beginning and end were joined on the third round. Tighten up the stitches at the corner and weave the ends in to hide this bump. The picture above shows the perfectly smooth transition of colors where the end of round meets the beginning of round.

SOLVING PROBLEMS ON CIRCULAR NEEDLES

Tight or loose stitches. Wherever you change colors, the stitches should look identical to the rest of your knitting. *If they're tight,* you're pulling the yarn too firmly when you change colors. Instead, adjust the tension just enough so that the stitches are all the same size. *If they are too loose,* firm up a bit when you start a new color.

Twisted yarns distort the stitches where you change colors and are very noticeable. When you change colors, drop the working yarn to the right of the new yarn and pick up the new yarn to the left. This is the opposite of how you interlock the yarns in intarsia and, in fact, prevents the interlock from forming.

Making a Smooth Start on Circular Needles

If you are using more than two colors or you want to avoid the annoying corner that forms at the bottom of your knitting even with just two colors, cast on an equal number of stitches in each of your colors, leaving all the balls of yarn attached (see photo on following page). When you're done casting on, use the last color to knit across the first. Continue around, changing colors each time you come to a new yarn hanging from the needle. For example, assume you have four yarns and want to cast on 80 stitches:

1] Divide the number of cast-on stitches by the number of yarns you're using (80 ÷ 4 = 20). If your result includes a fraction, simply adjust by one stitch in a few colors to make the total come out right.

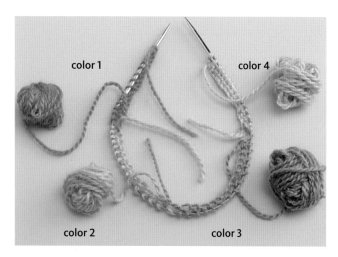

2] Cast on 20 stitches with color 1 and leave the yarn attached, add 20 more stitches with color 2, add 20 more with color 3, and finally 20 with color 4.

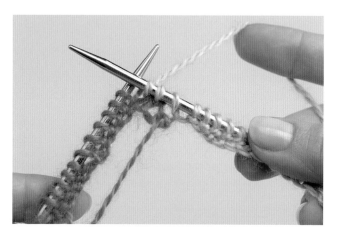

3] Continuing to use color 4, knit across color 1. This joins the beginning and end of the round and starts your first round of knitting.

4] When you reach the end of color 1, its yarn will be waiting for you. Abandon color 4, pick up color 1 and knit with it to the end of the next color. Continue working around, knitting to the end of each color and switching to the yarn waiting there.

Note: When you get back to the beginning of the round, do not change yarns. In fact, there's no yarn attached at that point. Continue knitting with the current yarn until you get to the point where another yarn is attached.

Getting Started on Double-Pointed Needles

By far, the simplest way to begin helix knitting on double-pointed needles is to cast on with one color, join the beginning and end of the round, and work at least one round before starting the other colors. Once you have this base, divide your number of stitches by the number of additional yarns you plan to add. Work a section in each of the additional yarns. You may find it most convenient to end a color when you get to the end of a needle. When you return to the beginning of the round, the original yarn will be waiting for you. Continue working around, knitting to the end of each color and switching to the yarn waiting there. You can use this same method to begin with a solid color on a circular needle.

In this example, we'll assume you need 60 stitches total and you are working with 3 yarns.

1] Using double-pointed needles and one color of yarn, cast on 60 stitches. Divide the number of stitches by the number of yarns you plan to add (60 ÷ 3 = 20). Arrange your stitches so there are 20 on each of three needles. Join the beginning and end of the round, and work at least one round.

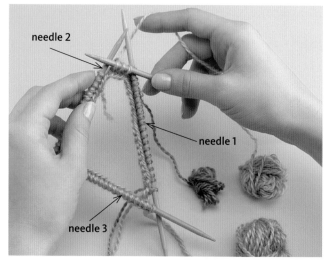

2] Using the first new color (shown in green), knit across the first 20 stitches. This will bring you to the end of Needle 1. Using the second new color (shown in celery), knit across the next 20 stitches, to the end of Needle 2.

3] Using the third new color, knit across the next 20 stitches. This will bring you to the end of Needle 3 and back to the beginning of the round. Pick up the original color and knit across Needle 1 with it.

4] Continue working across each needle and picking up a new color before you start the next needle. If you set your knitting down and need to find the proper place to begin, look for the point where there are two yarns attached. Begin knitting with the lower yarn.

SOLVING PROBLEMS ON DOUBLE-POINTED NEEDLES

Tight stitches can be more of a problem when working on double-pointed needles than on circular needles. I suspect this is caused by our habit of working the first few stitches of each needle firmly to prevent loose stitches wherever two needles meet. You must break this habit in helix knitting, or the stitches will compress into an unyielding column resembling a seam. When you start a new color, don't pull on that yarn. Instead, adjust the tension so the last stitch in that color looks the same size as all the others. If this is difficult for you, slip your empty needle through this stitch, then knit across the next needle. When you come to this stitch on the next round (as shown below), slip the needle out of it.

Making a Smooth Start on Double-Pointed Needles

If you prefer to begin with all your colors at the cast on, you can cast on about an equal number of stitches in each color, putting one or two colors on each needle. In this case, you join the knitting into a round by working just the first 2 or 3 stitches of one needle with the yarn attached to another. Once all the needles are connected, work around changing colors each time you come to a new yarn. When you reach the end of a round, continue with the current yarn until you come to a ball you can use. For example, assume a total of 60 stitches, three yarns, and a set of four double-pointed needles, and divide the total stitches by the number of yarns (60 ÷ 3 = 20).

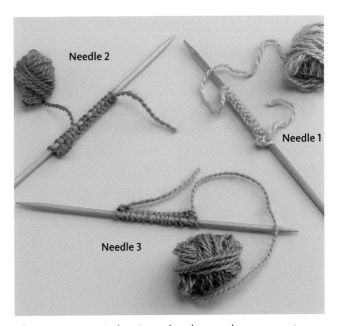

Needle 2

Needle 1

Needle 3

1] Cast on 20 stitches in each color, on three separate needles.

2] Hold Needle 1 with the yarn attached at the tip in your right hand. Hold Needle 2 with the yarn attached at the far end. Knit just 2 or 3 stitches from Needle 2 onto Needle 1.

3] Hold Needle 2 in your right hand. (Needle 1 will dangle annoyingly from its other end, but just ignore it.) Hold Needle 3 in your left hand, with the yarn attached at its far end. Knit 2 or 3 stitches from Needle 3 onto Needle 2.

4] Hold Needle 3 in your right hand and Needle 1 in your left hand. Knit 2 or 3 stitches from Needle 1 onto Needle 3.

5] *Change yarns.* Your knitting is now joined into a round and you can begin working with any of the three yarns. Each time you reach another ball of yarn (in this example, it always happens at the end of a needle), change yarns. When you set your knitting down and then try to start again, begin working where two yarns are attached at the same point. If there are no places where this occurs, then start again with any of the yarns.

THINKING DIAGONALLY

Circular knitting, even in just one color, makes a very gradual spiral. The more colors you work in helix knitting, the greater the angle of the spiral. When the project is as large as a sweater, multiple yarns won't make a noticeable difference; in narrower pieces like mittens or socks, the slant can be quite apparent.

Working Helix in Pattern Stitches

When working circularly with a single color, patterns worked on a particular number of stitches repeat seamlessly, with the knits and purls automatically aligning themselves over the proper stitches on every round. When you introduce a second yarn in helix knitting, however, the stitch count sometimes works differently (see Guidelines for Stitch Counts on facing page).

If you are using more than two balls of yarn, whenever you have an odd number of colors, the rules for a single ball apply. When you work with an even number of colors, the same rules apply as for just two colors.

STARTING FROM THE BOTTOM, purple and lavender alternate in K2, P2 ribbing, purple and green alternate in Seed Stitch, and purple and lavender alternate in broken garter. At the top, purple is used in one round, while lavender and green are alternated in stranded knitting on the other rounds.

Combining Helix and Stranded Knitting

One of the easiest and most effective ways to combine helix and stranded knitting is to knit one round with a single color, then alternate two other colors on the next round. Over an even number of stitches, the two colors line up on subsequent rounds. With an odd number of stitches, they appear in a checkerboard (see photo on facing page). You can also work two different colors on both of the two rounds.

Increasing and Decreasing in Helix Knitting

You'll need to be able to shape your helix to make garments. Decreases work just the same as in other knitting and look fine in helix knitting, but increases can be a bit trickier. Some increases distort the stripes and can be very noticeable: knitting into the front and back of the stitch will leave a bump, like a purled stitch, of the color below. The Make 1 (M1) increase (either using the working yarn or picking up the strand from the row below) is usually less noticeable. You may need to experiment to find the best increase for each particular project.

Creating Borders and Binding Off

Borders for helix knitting can be worked in a single color or in all the colors of your helix. To begin with a solid border, cast on all your stitches, work your border, then introduce the additional colors evenly spaced around your knitting. To finish with a solid border, work all the way around with a single color and cut the other yarns, leaving tails to weave in later. Make your border and bind off as usual. If you work all the colors all the way to the end, you can bind off in one color or in sections of each color, following the established helix pattern.

For mittens knit using the helix method, see page 231.

Guidelines for Stitch Counts

Stitch Pattern	With 1 Ball of Yarn (or any odd number of yarns)	With 2 Balls of Yarn (or any even number of yarns)
K1, P1 ribbing; K2, P2 ribbing; or any other pattern that is *identical* on every round.	Use a multiple of the pattern repeat. *Examples:* • For K1, P1 ribbing, this is a multiple of 2. • For K2, P2 ribbing, this is a multiple of 4.	Same as for one ball of yarn.
Seed Stitch, broken-garter stitch, or any other pattern where the knits and purls *alternate* on every round.	Use a multiple of the pattern repeat, plus half a repeat. *Examples:* • For Seed Stitch, based on a repeat of K1, P1, use a multiple of 2 stitches plus 1, which gives you an odd number of stitches. • For broken-garter stitch, when alternating K3, P3, use a multiple of 6 stitches (the full pattern repeat) plus 3 (half of the repeat).	Use a multiple of the full pattern repeat. *Examples:* • For Seed Stitch, use a multiple of the 2-stitch pattern repeat, which is always an even number. • For broken-garter stitch, use a multiple of the full pattern repeat; so when working a repeat of K3, P3, use a multiple of 6.

{Shadow Knitting}

Shadow knitting, or illusion knitting, is based on two-row stripes, where the design emerges from the background thanks to purled stitches that raise it from the surface of the fabric. Consider charting and knitting your design sideways for sweaters, because when looked at straight on, the design will not be visible. To see it, people would need to either kneel at your feet and look up at you, or gaze down at you from a balcony. If the design is worked sideways, anyone standing to your left or right is able to see it, or you can show it off in profile. Let's begin by charting a design and then try knitting it.

OPTICAL ILLUSION. Head-on, shadow knitting just looks striped (below). From an angle, the pattern appears (above).

Charts for Shadow Knitting

There are several ways to chart shadow knitting, depending on whether the chart is in color or in black and white. To make it as consistent with standard knitting charts as possible, these examples have colored squares to indicate the color of the stripes, and purl symbols (–) to show where to knit on the wrong-side rows, because these stitches will appear as purls on the right side of the fabric.

Designing Your Own Charts

To design your own, start with a small, simple motif, because patterns expand a great deal both in width and length when converted to shadow knitting. Follow the steps below to develop the chart.

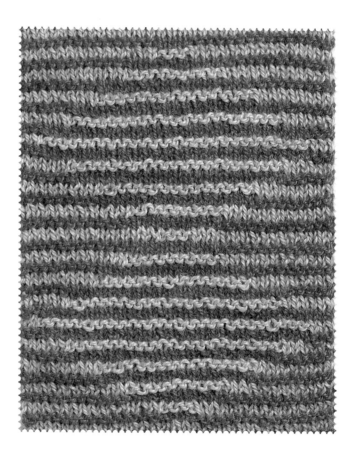

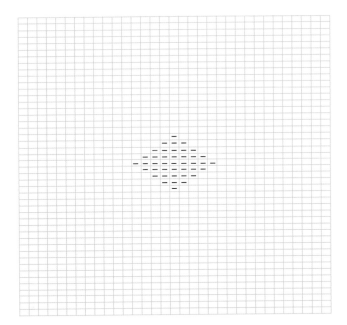

1] Chart out a small simple pattern. Avoid single-stitch elements because they don't show up well.

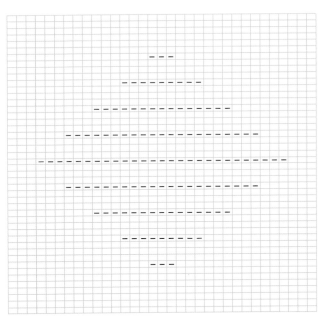

3] Spread it horizontally, making it three times as wide.

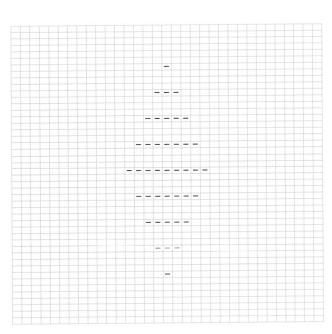

2] Chart it out again putting 3 blank rows between every row of your original chart.

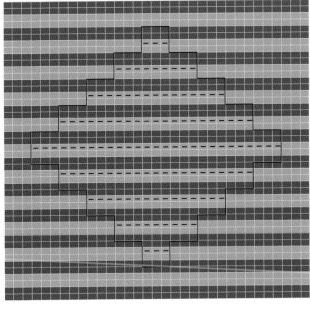

4] Draw a line around the charted pattern to mark the area of the contrasting design. Draw it immediately to the right and left of charted stitches, but mark it 2 rows above and 2 rows below these stitches. Now add the colors of your two-row stripes. Notice that the dashes always fall on the second row of the contrasting color, shown here in light green.

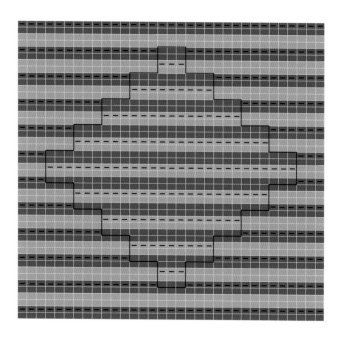

5] In the areas outside the lines, fill dashes to indicate knit stitches on the wrong-side rows of the background color. These will appear as purl stitches on the right side.

NOTE: If you find it difficult to see the dashes or if your chart is in black and white, you may want to use other symbols, for example, a B for purl stitches in the background color and a C for purl stitches in the contrast color.

Knitting from Your Chart

Working in shadow knitting can be confusing at first, so here are some tips that may help:

» Always work two rows of each color.

» Always knit the first, right-side row of each color.

» Work the pattern on the wrong side rows: purl unless there's a dash on the chart that indicates you should knit.

Now let's try knitting from the chart we made (at left). Using blue, cast on 33 stitches. Now start at the bottom right corner of the chart and follow it row by row. Right-side rows are read right-to-left and wrong-side rows are read left-to-right. The instructions below match the chart.

ROW 1 (RS): With blue, knit.
ROW 2 (WS): With blue, knit.
ROW 3 (RS): With light green, knit.
ROW 4 (WS): With light green, purl.
ROW 5 (RS): With blue, knit.
ROW 6 (WS): With blue, K15, P3, K15.
ROW 7 (RS): With light green, knit.
ROW 8 (WS): With light green, P15, K3, P15.
ROW 9 (RS): With blue, knit.
ROW 10 (WS): With blue, K12, P9, K12.

Continue in this fashion until you reach the last row of the chart.

TIPS FOR SUCCESSFUL DESIGNS

» Use smaller needles than usual to produce firmer fabric.

» Use two colors with lots of contrast.

» Use smooth, solid-colored yarn.

Check your design as you work, to be sure it's visible. Small elements may disappear, so you may want to eliminate the knit stitches in the background color around them to make them more visible.

{Mosaic Knitting}

Mosaic knitting, invented by Barbara Walker, is a method of working with multiple colors in which the knitter uses only one color at a time, knitting the stitches in one color while slipping the stitches that will be worked on future rows in the other color. Because only one yarn is used at a time, more complicated textures combining knitted and purled stitches are easier to execute.

For each row of the chart:

RIGHT SIDE: Using the color designated in the first stitch on the chart, work from right to left, working the stitches in that color and slipping the rest.

WRONG SIDE: Using the same color, proceed across, working the stitches on your needle that are the color you are currently using and slipping the ones in the other color. On this row, there's no need to read the chart: just follow the colors on your needle.

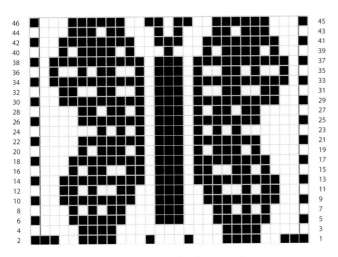

MOSAIC KNITTING RULES

» Always slip purlwise to prevent twisting.
» Always hold the yarn on the wrong side of the fabric. This means that you hold the yarn behind your work on the first row and in front on the second row.

Reading Mosaic Knitting Charts

Charts for mosaic knitting are read differently from standard knitting charts. Cast on using background color, and unless you used the long-tail cast on, work at least one row before beginning the chart. Start from the bottom right corner of the chart, with a right-side row, just like a standard knitting chart. The black squares represent the foreground color, and the white squares the background. The red lines mark the pattern repeat. The color in the first square is the one you actually work; you slip the other stitches all the way across. Each horizontal row on the chart represents two rows of knitting. The numbers on the chart reflect this: For example, the bottom row is Row 1 starting from the right and Row 2 starting from the left. You must work two rows (across and back again) in each color. Here's how it works:

Butterfly Sample Three Ways

As shown in these swatches, mosaic knitting can be worked in stockinette, garter stitch, or a combination of the two, but the proportions of the knitting are different, because garter stitch is shorter and wider than stockinette.

▶ *For stockinette stitch,* knit the stitches on the first row and purl the stitches on the second row of each pair.

▶ *For garter stitch,* knit the stitches on all rows, remembering to move your yarn to the wrong side whenever you slip stitches on the wrong side.

▶ *For a combination of stockinette and garter,* work the stitches in one color in stockinette (purling on the wrong side) and the stitches in the other color in garter stitch (knitting on the wrong side). To provide visual consistency on the combination swatch

shown here, I used garter stitch for any stitches in the background color that fell within the wings of the butterfly, as well as for all the contrasting stitches.

Working Borders in Mosaic Knitting

The borders on the butterfly swatches were each worked in a different mosaic pattern stitch: mosaic rib on the stockinette swatch, mosaic Seed Stitch on the garter stitch swatch, and mosaic beads on the combination swatch. Standard mosaic charts are black and white, but in the charts for these borders, the color changes are indicated by the colors of the squares. All the stitches on the first row of a color are always knitted or slipped, never purled. A purl symbol in the square indicates that it is knitted on the second (wrong-side) row.

▲ *Mosaic rib (odd-number of stitches).* If you wish, break the rule and purl on the right-side rows in mosaic rib as well as on the wrong side, to produce a true K1, P1 ribbing. This works because each column of stitches is always the same color. Cast on in the color of the purl ribs (shown in purple in the chart) and purl these stitches on all the right-side rows in addition to knitting them on the wrong-side rows.

▲ *Mosaic Seed Stitch (odd-number of stitches).* To integrate the cast on with this border, cast on using the third color. If you use the long-tail cast on, begin working Row 1 of the pattern immediately. If you use another cast on, knit one row in the cast-on color before beginning Row 1. A ridge of garter stitch or two rows of stockinette stitch provide a transition above the border pattern before the main mosaic pattern begins.

▲ *Mosaic beads (odd-number of stitches).* Notice that this is not a true mosaic stitch, because the main color is used for four consecutive rows in order to place a garter-stitch ridge between each occurrence of the color pattern.

Working Mosaic Knitting Circularly

In some ways, working the mosaic technique is easier in circular knitting than in flat knitting. The yarn is always held behind the fabric while slipping because the right side is always facing you. Just as you work two rows in each color in flat knitting, work two rounds in the same color for each row of the chart, but read from right to left both times. Even if it doesn't fit into the pattern repeat, always work the first stitch of each round with the working yarn. If you're making a garment like a sweater, you may want to add one stitch at the opposite "seam" so that you can work a stitch in the main color at the beginning of the round and at the halfway point for symmetry.

With circular knitting, it's easy to work stockinette by knitting every round. To work garter stitch, knit the first round of a color and purl the second. To work a combination of the two, knit all the rounds in one color and alternate knit and purl rounds in the second color.

Solving Problems with Mosaic Stitch

Tension can be an issue in mosaic knitting. The large proportion of slipped stitches pulls the fabric tighter, and if the slipped stitches are aligned from bottom to top of the design, columns of them may become puckered. Maintaining even tension at the beginnings and ends of rows can also be challenging, because there's a tendency for the edges to be looser where colors are changed. As you knit, after slipping a group of stitches, take care to spread them out smoothly across the right needle before you knit the next stitch. When you change colors at the beginning of a right-side row, pull the yarn gently to remove any looseness in the row below before knitting the first stitch.

DESIGNING YOUR OWN MOSAIC STITCH PATTERNS

The rules governing mosaic knitting place certain restrictions on what you can design, so patterns tend to be squared or diagonal.

» The working color on a given row should be used on at least half of the stitches.

» The stitches slipped on each row must be those worked in the other color on the previous pair of rows.

» Traditionally, you should avoid slipping more than three consecutive stitches because it can make the fabric pucker; however, I feel that slipping four or even five stitches presents no problem.

Mosaic patterns are generally more successful when the fabric is fairly firm — the pattern is less visible if the knitting is too loose. As with all knitting techniques, it pays to experiment with needle size to discover what is optimum for your yarn and your specific design.

Shaping in mosaic knitting can be worked in either color at the edges of the knitting. Take care to maintain your pattern as the knitting gets wider or narrower. Decreases or increases spaced across the row are most easily worked on a plain row but can be integrated into the mosaic pattern with a little care; however, it will change the number of stitches in the pattern repeat.

{Twined Knitting}

Twined knitting is the translation coined by Robin Orm Hansen for the Scandinavian two-strand circular knitting technique known in Swedish as *tvåändssticking,* in Danish as *trebinding,* and in Norwegian as *tveband.* It is, from the Swedish, literally "two-end knitting," because the two strands are the two ends of one center-pull ball of yarn. The strands are used alternately and are twisted between every stitch. Twined knitting produces a smooth, tight, durable fabric unlike that created by other methods of knitting and is known for its elegant monochrome textured patterns, as well as two-color patterns.

Traditionally, the yarn used in twined knitting is a 2-ply Z-twist, spun and plied in the opposite direction from the S-twist yarn that is the current standard for commercial yarns. If you must use an S-twist yarn, look for one that is loosely plied, because the constant twisting of twined knitting will add twist to it. If you can purchase or spin Z-twist yarn, opt for a tight ply, because twining will remove some of the twist.

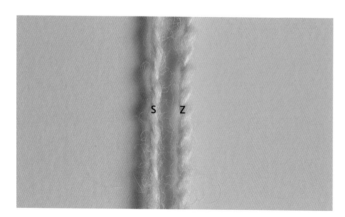

MIND YOUR S's AND Z's. Note the difference in the ways these 2-ply yarns twist.

Twining with Color

There are two basic approaches to working with color while twining. When two colors are used in about equal amounts in a pattern stitch, just two strands are used: one of each color. If there is significantly more background color than pattern color, it's best to use three strands: two in the background color and a third, as needed, for the pattern color.

Casting On for Twined Knitting

Any cast on can be used for twined knitting, but a firm one works best as the base for the firm twined fabric. A twined variation of the long-tail cast on produces a fine striped edge. For this, you need three strands: the two ends of one center-pull ball, plus a contrasting strand. For best results, work this cast on firmly.

1] Knot the three ends together around the needle in either an overhand knot or a slip knot. Do not include the knot in your stitch count because you will unravel it later. You'll do a 2-handed variation on the long-tail cast on that makes it easier to manage the three strands. Prop the needle against you or hold it under your arm or between your legs (this doesn't work with a circular needle!), and hold one of the strands from the center-pull ball in your left hand. Manipulate the two other strands with your right hand. Holding the needle against your palm, bring your left thumb up under the strand from the back.

2] Slip the needle into it parallel to your thumb.

3] Pick up the lower of the right-hand strands, bring it to the front and wrap it around the needle.

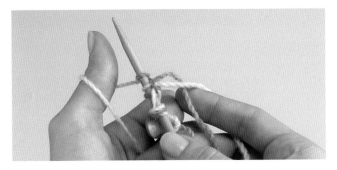

4] Lift the thumb loop off the point of the needle over the wrapped strand, pull your thumb out and tighten the loop.

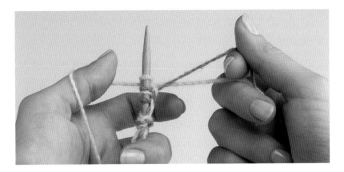

5] Repeat steps 2 and 3, each time bringing the lower strand on the right to the front, until you've cast on enough stitches. Stop periodically and unwind the right-hand yarns, which will become firmly twisted. When you're done, remove the initial knot from the needle.

Assuming that you'll be working circularly, you must now transfer the stitches to a circular needle or a set of double-pointed needles. To save time, just work the first row onto the appropriate needle(s), then join the beginning and end of the round and begin working circularly.

USING A CENTER-PULL BALL

When working with two colors in twined knitting, wind a center-pull ball with one inside the other. Tradition dictates that the dark color should be on the outside to keep the light color clean. The two strands of yarn twist around each other while you work — there's no way to avoid it. If you place the yarn in a basket with a rounded bottom or on a turntable, you can spin it occasionally to do the untwisting, or when the strands of yarn become too tightly twisted to work, secure them around the ball with a couple of half hitches or by spearing it with a needle and securing the yarn to it, and let the ball dangle to unwind itself. If your knitting is small, you may find it easier to hold the knitting up and let it untwist instead of untwisting the yarns.

When you use three strands, they frequently become tightly braided and you'll need to stop often to untangle them. You may find it more pleasant and efficient to create small supplies of the three strands as for intarsia, rather than working from large center-pull balls.

Basic Twined Knitting Stitches

When working twined knitting, knits and purls are made exactly as usual, but the yarn must be twisted, always in the same direction, between each stitch. How you hold the yarn has a significant effect on how comfortably and efficiently you can manage the twist.

▲ *Knitting.* Hold both strands of yarn in the right hand since the constant twisting of strands is nearly impossible when they are held in the left hand. Hold one strand between your thumb and index finger and the other one between your middle and ring finger. Always change strands before you knit a stitch and always bring the strand to be used over the other strand. As shown here, when white is knit, the white yarn is taken over the blue (A). When blue is knit, the blue yarn is taken over the white (B). Stop frequently and untwist either the yarn or the knitting (whichever is smaller and more convenient).

▲ *Purling.* When purling an entire round, hold both strands of yarn in the right hand, and keep both in front of the fabric at all times. Alternate colors and twist the two strands on every stitch in the same direction as when you were knitting. Counterintuitively, to do this you must bring the strand for the next stitch *under* the other strand each time. As shown here, when white is purled, the white yarn is taken *under* the blue (C). When blue is purled, the blue yarn is taken *under* the white (D). Purling around alternating colors results in a diagonally striped ridge. (This is the first half of the Horizontal Braid described on page 252.) To purl isolated stitches, twist the two yarns, bring the yarn forward, purl the stitch, and take the yarn to the back.

Working Twined Stitch Variations

Knitting and purling variations add greater texture, affecting the surface and appearance of twined knitting. These can be used as the basis for pattern stitches.

▲ *Deep Purling.* To make more pronounced relief in the fabric, work purl stitches by purling both strands together (A). You may also twist the deep purl stitches by wrapping the yarn around the needle in the opposite direction, or by working into the back of the stitch on the next round. This produces tighter, deeper stitches. Columns of deep purl stitches make excellent "seams."

▲ *Deep Knitting.* Another variation can be produced by bringing the strand not in use to the front before knitting a stitch, then taking it to the back again (B). If several of these are worked consecutively, take the yarn to the back, twist the yarns, and bring the other yarn to the front before knitting the next stitch — you must keep changing the strand in front for each stitch. When working in two colors, alternating between the colors and alternating regular knits with deep knits makes a horizontal line of the color brought to the front. (See small inset of sampler on page 214.)

Twined Knitting Pattern Stitches

Pattern stitches in twined knitting are created using the basic and deep knit and purl stitches. These are worked in two colors for complex combinations of color and texture.

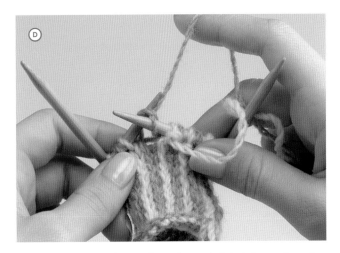

▲ *Crook Stitch.* The scalloped Crook Stitch is produced by alternately purling with one strand (C) and knitting with the other while keeping the purled yarn in front of the fabric all the time (D). You may work a minimum of three stitches (P1, K1, P1) or as much as a whole round. Crook Stitch is typically used at points in a garment that should be narrower, like the wrist of a mitten, because it pulls the fabric in horizontally. When worked in two colors, a scalloped line of the purled color is raised above the surface of the knitting. (See sampler on page 214.)

Chain Path. Chain Path is two rounds of Crook Stitch, where the second round is worked one stitch offset from the first. When worked in two colors, it produces a raised chain of the purl color. A variation of chain path is the O Stitch. This tiny raised stitch is really just a very short Chain Path. On the first round, work P1, K1, P1. On the second round, bring the yarn to be purled forward, K1, P1, K1, take the purled yarn to the back. Groups of O Stitches can be arranged to form diamonds, chevrons, and other patterns.

Increasing and Decreasing in Twined Knitting

Decreases can be worked as in any other type of knitting. Working with two strands, however, provides an opportunity for a different type of increase.

▲ *Increasing in twined knitting.* Knit into the stitch with one strand (A), then twist the strands and knit into the stitch again with the other strand (B).

Effects with Two-Color Twining

As noted above, work with two strands of two different colors when they are used in about equal amounts on every round. When working alternate stitches, twist the two yarns between every stitch. When several stitches are worked in the same color, twist the strands after every stitch or every other stitch to maintain the twined character of the fabric while carrying the color not in use across the back.

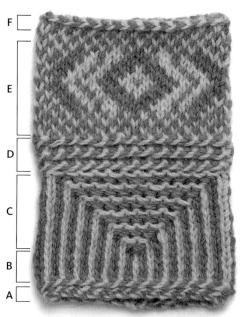

The Z-twist yarn used in these twined knitting examples is 2-Ply Worsted Weight from Black Water Abbey Yarns.

The swatch shown above illustrates a variety of the effects that can be produced when working with just two strands — one blue and the other white. A decorative edge at the bottom of this two-strand sampler (A) is the result of casting on using the Two-Color Long-Tail Cast On (see page 246), followed by a purled round alternating the two colors. Alternating the two colors in knitting on an even number of stitches produces the vertical stripes that appear just above this (B). On one side of the tube, crook stitch creates the effect of a mitered square (C): starting from the center stitch, working progressively more stitches on each round, and continuing to alternate colors. On the other side, deep knit stitches produce the same mitered square, but with much less texture (G). Above this, knit rounds and purl rounds alternate to make three garter-stitch ridges (D). The diagonals of the twisted strands in the ridges look like candy stripes. Decreasing one stitch and continuing to alternate colors on an odd number of stitches produces the tiny checkerboard known as *salt and pepper,* which serves as a the background for a simple diamond-and-chevron pattern (E). Turning the swatch around and binding off in knit on the inside places the characteristic striped purl ridge along the upper edge and reduces curling (F).

Effects with Three-Color Twining

Three strands are best when one color serves as the background and another appears less frequently. It's important to twine all three, bringing the strand for the next stitch in front of the other two before knitting or purling with it. When colors aren't used in sequence, twist a strand around just one of the others to bring it into the correct position. For isolated motifs, use a separate piece of the contrasting yarn, carrying it up from row to row. Work V-shaped motifs by knitting the center of a piece of yarn at the point of the V and using each of the ends for one side of the V.

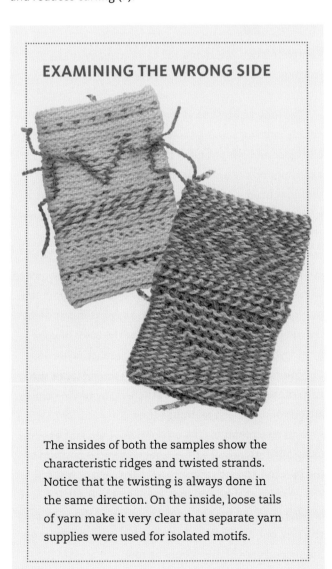

EXAMINING THE WRONG SIDE

The insides of both the samples show the characteristic ridges and twisted strands. Notice that the twisting is always done in the same direction. On the inside, loose tails of yarn make it very clear that separate yarn supplies were used for isolated motifs.

The plain white background of the sampler above was worked with two strands of white twined throughout. Contrasting blue was used in the twined cast on (A), chain path (B), and crook stitch (C). The wavy line and diamonds are a continuous pattern (D), worked using all three strands of yarn all the way around. The three isolated patterns above are each knit from a separate piece of blue yarn (E). The striped ridge at the top (F) is the natural result of twining the three strands while working one stitch in succession with each of the three yarns. This purled ridge was actually worked by turning and knitting around on the inside of the tube.

{Double Knitting}

Double knitting allows you to knit two layers of fabric at the same time, using two balls of yarn. Assuming that the two yarns are different colors, switching yarns between the front and back layers of the fabric creates reversing color patterns. Double knitting tends to be looser than regular knitting because both layers of fabric share space on the needle, so use a needle 2–3 sizes smaller than usual. If you are a firm knitter, however, you may find that you like the results you get on normal-sized needles.

A WARM, REVERSIBLE FABRIC. Double knitting creates a two-layer fabric with the color pattern reversed on back and front sides.

Casting On for Double Knitting

There are numerous ways to cast on for double knitting, but all methods result in double the normal number of stitches to allow enough for both layers.

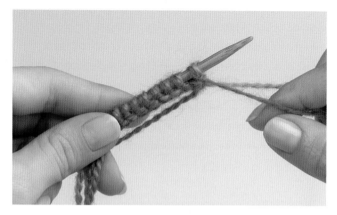

Completed two-color long-tail cast on, ready to start knitting.

The long-tail cast on is the easiest method, but for double knitting you use three strands. Take two strands of one color and one strand of the other and make an over-hand knot or a slip knot on your needle. Don't include this knot in your stitch count because you will remove it when the cast on is completed. Put two different-colored strands over your index finger and the remaining strand over your thumb. Work the long-tail cast on, using both strands on your index finger in every stitch, until you have worked enough doubled stitches for one side of your fabric. Try to keep the two colors in the same order all across the needle. The first strand should be the color of your front layer, the second the color of your back layer, and the colors should alternate across. On the first row, work each of the strands as a single stitch. If any of the colors are out of order, just rearrange them.

You may prefer to cast on normally, then knit one row using both strands of yarn — again, keep the position of the two colors consistent as you make each new stitch. You can also cast on and then knit into the front and back of each stitch on the first row. This doubles the number of stitches, but all will be the same color; you'll begin using the second yarn on the following row.

Knitting Two Layers at the Same Time

It may be a bit daunting at first to work with both yarns, and both layers, at once, but just take it one step at a time and you'll very quickly become adept.

1] To get started, knit the first stitch with the front color, then bring both yarns forward.

2] Purl the second stitch with the back color, then take both yarns to the back.

To reverse colors, give the two strands a twist, so they trade places on your finger, before working the next pair of stitches.

Managing Your Yarn

When working with two yarns at the same time, it's easy to accidentally work with the wrong one and to unintentionally twist the two strands. It can also be difficult to maintain consistent tension, so one layer of your fabric may be noticeably looser than the other. Holding on to both yarns all the time can help with all these problems.

If you hold your yarn in your right hand (see photos at left), hold the yarn you use to knit the front layer in front of your index finger and the yarn you use to purl the back layer behind your index finger. Maintain tension on them by holding them against your palm, all the time. When the yarns are in back, pinch the front yarn between the thumb and index finger to knit with it. When the yarns are in front, tuck the index finger under the back yarn to purl with it. Working this way, you don't have to let go of the yarns, so you can maintain constant tension.

When you need to swap yarns, give them a twist and then reposition the two yarns for the next stitch. Of course, if you can knit with either hand, it's also possible to hold one yarn in each hand, always remembering that you must move both strands forward before purling and backwards before knitting.

Working from Charts

Double knitting charts show only one side of the fabric. For each square on the chart, you will actually work two stitches, one from the front layer and one from the back layer.

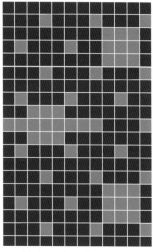

Double knit chart for circular knitting (shown on page 216)

In the Round

ROUND 1. In the lavender-and-blue chart above, the first row is all purple. This means that the front layer is blue, but it also means that the back layer is lavender. To work it, hold both strands of yarn in back and knit the first stitch on your needle with the blue yarn. If you cast on with two colors, the first stitch should be blue. Bring both strands of yarn forward and purl the second stitch with the lavender yarn. If you cast on with two colors, this stitch should be lavender. Return both strands of yarn to the back of the work. Repeat this for every square in the chart, until you get to the end of the round.

ROUND 2. The second row of the chart indicates that there is a lavender stitch, followed by three blue stitches, and this is repeated around. Twist the two strands to switch colors and knit the first stitch with the lavender yarn, bring both yarns forward, and purl the second stitch with the blue yarn. The second square is blue, so take the yarns to the back and knit the next stitch with blue, purling the stitch following it with lavender. Continue around, knitting the stitch in the color shown and purling the following stitch in the opposite color. Work every round of your knitting the same way.

FLAT VERSUS CIRCULAR DOUBLE KNITTING

Double knitting is far easier to work in the round than flat, because the chart shows only one side of the knitting. In the example, the background color is blue and the pattern is lavender. Working circularly allows you to make a front layer that matches the colors on the chart, while the colors on the side away from you are reversed. If you are working flat, when you turn to work the opposite side, the background in your knitting is lavender with a blue pattern, the opposite of your chart, and you'll be working from left to right instead of right to left, which can be very disorienting. You may find it easier to reverse the colors mentally on the wrong-side rows if you use a black and white chart.

Working flat also requires that you anchor both yarns at the end of each row. To do this, purl the final stitch of the row using both yarns, then slip this stitch knitwise at the beginning of the following row, or work the final stitch with a single strand and then twist the two yarns together before beginning the next row.

ROW 1. Work exactly the same as for circular knitting, but when you reach the end of the row, anchor the yarn as described above.

ROW 2. Turn your work and reverse the reading of the chart. Read Row 2 from left to right. If you're working from the colored

Chart for flat knitting, including edge stitches to center the pattern. Knitting is shown on page 219.

chart, you'll also have to reverse colors. That is, if the stitch is lavender, knit the blue stitch first, then purl with lavender. If you're working from the black and white chart, just determine which color is your background and work that stitch first for the white squares. Work the contrast color first for the marked squares. Remember to anchor your yarns at the end of the row.

Decreases in Double Knitting

1] Work to the point where you are ready to decrease. Slip the first 3 stitches off the needle: 2 from the front layer with 1 stitch from the back layer in between.

2] Return the back stitch to the needle, then replace the 2 front stitches. Now, K2tog or ssk with the front yarn (working the front 2 stitches together).

3] P2tog or ssp with the back yarn (working the back two stitches together).

Increases in Double Knitting

It's simplest to use the make 1 (M1) increase using the working yarn. Make 1 first with the front yarn (A), then with the back yarn (B), then continue across or around. If you must use a different increase — one made using another stitch — rearrange the new stitches after increasing, so that the new stitch in the front yarn is immediately to the right of the new stitch in the back yarn.

Binding Off Double Knitting

You have several options for binding off, depending on how stretchy you want the edge and whether you want a two-color edge.

▲ *Simple bind off.* The simplest bind off is to use only the front yarn, knit the first front stitch, and then bind off working K2tog into each front-and-back pair of stitches all the way around. This makes a firm single-color edge and leaves contrasting purl bumps on the opposite side of the knitting.

▲ *Alternating bind off.* Knit the front stitches with the front yarn and purl the back stitches with the back yarn as you bind off. If you choose this option, work firmly so the edge doesn't flare. It will make a bind-off chain alternating the two colors, centered along the edge.

For a very stretchy, seamless edge, work Kitchener stitch (see page 298) to join the front layer to the back layer. This is best done after at least one plain row so that any disruption of the pattern stitch isn't obvious.

{Modular Knitting}

A module can be any shape at all: a square, rectangle, triangle, circle, or part of a circle. In modular knitting, these shapes are assembled to make a larger piece of knitted fabric. The modules can all be the same — for example, a sweater made completely of strips the same width or an afghan made of squares — or a variety of shapes and sizes can be combined. In entrelac, the fabric is formed of rectangles, placed on alternating diagonals to form a basket weave, with triangles inset to make straight edges. Modular knitting offers a universe of possibilities. The rest of this chapter is intended to give you a taste!

Making modules can be as simple as knitting squares or strips in different colors and joining them together, but you can also make more complex compositions by integrating triangles and other shapes. For instructions on making mitered squares, triangles, circles, and octagons, see Putting Geometry to Work, page 125. These are just a few of the possible shapes — experiment to come up with your own modules. Keep things simple by using a single color for each module, use a variegated or self-striping yarn so that it looks like you changed colors, or go ahead and change colors yourself to make stripes within your modules.

Joining Modules

Making a garment from many modules means you have to join them together somehow. Luckily, there are lots of options. Wait until all your modules are made, arrange them to your satisfaction, then sew or crochet them together. Or, if you'd rather be knitting, pick up stitches along the edges of the pieces to be joined and then use the three-needle bind off to make a decorative join. Reduce the number of seams to begin with by picking up stitches along the edge of a module and knitting the next one onto it. If your modules are strips, attach the edge of each new strip to the previous one as you knit. (See chapter 8 for more on this topic.)

You can also avoid seams altogether by making a fabric that looks like separate modules but is actually worked continuously in short rows. There are advantages and disadvantages to each approach. On the one hand, working

individual modules is easy and highly portable, but joining them all together in the end can be very time-consuming. On the other hand, an entire project worked by attaching the modules as you go becomes less portable and more bulky as it grows. Short-row modules make seaming unnecessary, but can be confusing to work, especially in a distracting environment. You'll find several books on modular knitting recommended in the bibliography, with expert advice on working, joining, and designing.

Scarf and hat based on short-row triangles

Designing with Modules

To design a garment in small modules or in modules of varying sizes, it's best to overlay the geometric pattern of the separate elements on a schematic. You'll find some ideas for working garments in large modules in chapter 4 (see pages 131–132), and basic garment schematics in chapter 9 (see pages 280–283). Draw lines on the schematic to represent the edges of your modules, then color in the grain of the knitting and any colored stripes you envision in each module. You can also color and cut out modules from paper and arrange them like a puzzle until you come up with a plan that pleases you. Shaping around necklines and armholes can be pieced together using strategically placed triangles.

Miniature sample for Shawl

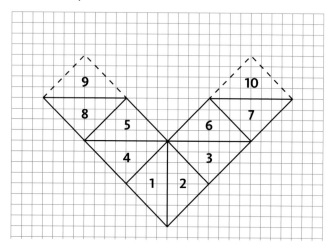

Work a Small Sample

If you plan to connect the modules as you go, knitting a small sample to test the joining techniques and to get a feel for the finished fabric can be extremely helpful. This shawl is an example of a piece worked in large modules using a self-striping yarn, but the concept was worked out in miniature using self-striping sock yarn.

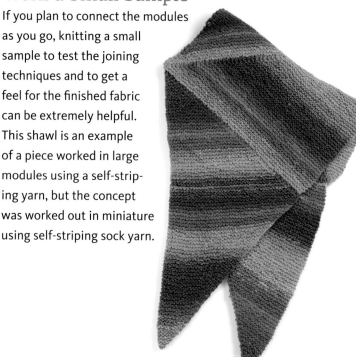

{Entrelac}

Entrelac is a form of modular knitting in which rectangles are worked one at a time, knitted onto each other in a basket-weave pattern. Every rectangle can be a different color, although it's easier to work an entire row of rectangles in one color. Entrelac is an excellent way to integrate lots of colors into a consistent fabric, using just one at a time, and it works extraordinarily well for variegated and self-striping yarns. The rectangles in entrelac can be made tiny (just 4 stitches wide) or as large as you like.

Getting Started in Entrelac

Entrelac is built upon a base of foundation triangles at the cast-on edge, then rows of rectangles are filled in between the foundation triangles. On every other row of rectangles, a triangle is required at both ends to make the edge of the fabric even. Entrelac is finished off with a row of triangles across the top that also serve to bind off the knitting.

▲ *Foundation triangles.* To get started, you first create a series of triangles across the bottom. Decide how many stitches there should be in each rectangle and how many rectangles you want across the fabric. For example, to make 5 rectangles, each 6 stitches wide, you need 30 stitches. Cast on that number of stitches very, very loosely — the knitted cast on is a good choice.

ROW 1 (WS): P2, turn.

ROW 2: K2, turn.

ROW 3: P3, turn.

ROW 4: K3, turn.

Continue in this way, working 1 additional stitch on each purl row and knitting the same number of stitches on the returning knit row, until you've purled a row with the full number of stitches. For example, if your rectangles will be 6 stitches wide, work until you have purled 6, then do not turn your work. You've completed the first triangle. Leave these stitches on the right needle and begin again at Row 1 to make the second triangle. Repeat until you've made triangles all the way across the cast on.

Entrelac hat

▲ *Right-edge triangle.* Next, cut the yarn, knot a new color onto the tail, and make a triangle at the right edge, as preparation for the first row of rectangles.

ROW 1 (RS): K2, turn.

ROW 2: P2, turn.

ROW 3: Knit into front and back of stitch, ssk (joining the current triangle to the next one on the left needle), turn.

ROW 4: Purl across the triangle, turn.

ROW 5: Knit into front and back of stitch, knit until one stitch remains of triangle, ssk, turn.

Repeat Rows 4–5 until all stitches of the triangle below have been used. Do not turn after the final Row 5 has been completed.

▲ *Right-side rectangles.* Now you can continue across the row, filling in rectangles in the spaces between the triangles.

ROW 1 (RS): Pick up and knit the stitches for your rectangle along the second side of this same triangle (A), turn. In this example, this is 6 stitches.

ROW 2: Purl to beginning of this rectangle (the stitches you just picked up), turn.

ROW 3: Knit until 1 stitch remains of this rectangle, ssk (joining it to the next triangle) (B), turn.

Repeat Rows 2–3 until all of the stitches of the triangle below have been worked. Do not turn after the last row. All the stitches for this rectangle should now be on the right needle. Once again, in this example, this is 6 stitches. Begin again with Row 1 to make the next rectangle. Continue making rectangles across the row until you have attached a rectangle to the last triangle.

▲ *Left-edge triangle.* You must now make a triangle at the end of the row to fill in the edge of the fabric.

ROW 1 (RS): Pick up and knit the stitches for your triangle along the second side of the last triangle, turn. In our example, that's 6 stitches.

ROW 2: P2tog, purl to the end of the current triangle (the stitches you just picked up), turn.

ROW 3: Knit across the current triangle, turn.

Repeat Rows 2–3 until only 2 stitches remain of the current triangle. Purl these two together but do not turn. You will have just 1 stitch on the right needle (shown above).

ROW 1 (WS): Along the edge of the triangle you just made, pick up and purl one less stitch than you need for your rectangle. Including the single stitch remaining from the edge triangle, you should once again have the correct number of stitches for your rectangle. In our example, this is 6 stitches. Turn.

ROW 2: Knit across the current rectangle, turn.

ROW 3: Purl until one stitch remains of the current rectangle, P2tog (joining it to the next rectangle from the row below), turn.

▲ *Wrong-side rectangles.* You are now ready to begin working the second row of rectangles on the wrong side of the fabric. Cut the yarn, knot a new color onto the tail, and get ready to make a second row of rectangles, this time working across on the wrong side of the fabric.

Repeat Rows 2–3 until all the stitches from the rectangle below have been worked.

When you complete Row 3 for the last time, do not turn. Instead, begin the next rectangle by picking up and purling as many stitches as you need along the edge of the rectangle below (in our example, this is 6 stitches) and work Rows 2–3 until the rectangle is completed. Repeat until rectangles have been completed all the way across.

Putting It All Together

Continue working in this fashion. Begin the rows of right-side rectangles with a right-edge triangle, followed by right-side rectangles across the row, and ending with a left-edge triangle. Then work a row of wrong-side rectangles back across the wrong side of the fabric. Change colors each time you begin a new row of rectangles.

▲ *Bind-off triangles.* When the knitting is long enough, complete a row of right-side triangles, then work a row of bind-off triangles. These triangles fill in the spaces between the rectangles and bind off the stitches at the same time so that the edge of the fabric is straight. They must be worked from the wrong side of the fabric. Change colors before beginning the first triangle.

ROW 1 (WS): Along the side of the left-edge triangle, pick up and purl as many stitches as you need for your triangle. Including the one stitch remaining from the triangle at the end of the previous row, you will have one more stitch than is normal for your rectangle. (For our example, this is 7 stitches.) Turn.

ROW 2: Knit across the current triangle (all the stitches you picked up, plus the one left from the edge triangle), turn.

ROW 3: P2tog, purl until 1 stitch remains of the current triangle, P2tog (joining to the rectangle below), turn.

Repeat Rows 2–3 until 3 stitches remain of the current triangle, ending with a knit row. On the next purl row, P2tog twice, turn. Knit across the remaining 2 stitches, turn. P3tog and begin the next triangle, picking up stitches as described in Row 1. Repeat until all the stitches have been bound off.

3-color entrelac

4-color entrelac

Entrelac with alternating rows of
solid and variegated yarns

Changing Colors

Making entire rows of rectangles in a single color is probably the least complicated option with the greatest impact.
For a more complex appearance, change colors when you
begin a new rectangle while working across the row. For
example, you can alternate the colors of the rectangles
across each row (as shown in 4-color entrelac above), or
change colors at random. If you change colors after every
rectangle or triangle, you'll need to cut the yarn and knot
the ends together. Be forewarned! If you do this, you'll
have a huge number of ends to weave in, although you can
deal with them as you work by weaving both tails from
each knot along the row as you pick up the next module.
(See Weaving In as You Go, pages 156–57.)

Adding Stitch Patterns to Entrelac

Up until now, we've been discussing stockinette entrelac,
but there's no reason you can't introduce textured or
colored patterns in each rect-
angle. In garter stitch, the
rectangles turn into squares
and the fabric lies much flatter. To make garter stitch
entrelac, knit all the wrong-
side rows instead of purling,
and any time there is a P2tog
or a P3tog to be worked,
substitute K2tog and K3tog.
When you pick up stitches

Garter stitch entrelac

along the edge of the rectangles or triangles from the
wrong side, however, you still need to purl them up.

Seed Stitch has the same fabric-flattening effect as
garter. You can also introduce just the occasional ridge by
knitting across on the wrong side or add bobbles, cables,
or other embellishments to some rectangles. Color patterns using intarsia, stranding, or slipped stitches are
another option. Entrelac gives you the flexibility of working a completely different technique in each rectangle.

MANAGING MULTIPLE YARNS

» To avoid creating ends that must be
woven in, consider using three balls of yarn
and working a whole row of rectangles with
each. Use each of the three colors repeatedly
in the same order. When you reach the end of
the row, leave the yarn attached — it will be
waiting for you at that edge when you need it
again — just carry it loosely up the side.

» You can also make entrelac all with one ball
of yarn, never cutting it, so there are no ends to
weave in. This is an especially effective way to
use variegated and self-striping yarns.

Working Entrelac Circularly

Entrelac can also be worked circularly, with no need for edge triangles. Begin by casting on very, very loosely and working a row of foundation triangles. Cut the yarn and join the beginning and end of the round by tying the tails of yarn together, with the knit side facing out (A).

Using a different color, begin a round of right-side rectangles by picking up and knitting as many stitches as you need for your rectangle along the edge of the triangle immediately to the right of the beginning of round. Work the first right-side rectangle, joining it to the foundation triangle on the left side of the beginning of round (B).

Continue, placing a rectangle between each pair of triangles all the way around. Cut the yarn after the last rectangle is completed and knot it to the starting tail of the same color.

Turn to the wrong side and purl up as many stitches as you need along the side of the first rectangle. Then follow the instructions for a wrong-side rectangle. Make wrong-side rectangles all the way around. Continue to alternate rounds of right- and wrong-side rectangles until the knitting is as long as you want it. End with a round of right-side rectangles, then turn to the wrong side and work a round of bind-off triangles, picking up one more stitch than the number normally required for each of your rectangles.

> ### SOME INSIDER TIPS ON KNITTING ENTRELAC
>
> *Turn and turn again.* Some knitters find the constant turning to work the short rows of each triangle and rectangle painfully tedious. There are two ways to mitigate the tedium. The simplest is always to work entrelac on a circular needle (even when working a flat fabric), and to rotate the needle at the end of every row without dropping the working yarn. The other is to learn to knit backward, so that you can comfortably work from left to right as well as from right to left across the row without turning at all. (See pages 298–99.)
>
> *Picking up.* When picking up stitches along the edges of entrelac modules, knit or purl them up through the center of the edge stitch, rather than a whole stitch in from the edge. The resulting fabric is thinner, without heavy ridges between rectangles, and you produce more area with each rectangle you knit. Pick up and purl may be an unfamiliar technique. Hold the fabric with the wrong side facing you, insert the tip of your needle from behind the fabric, and purl out a stitch to the back. (See photo page 225, top right.)

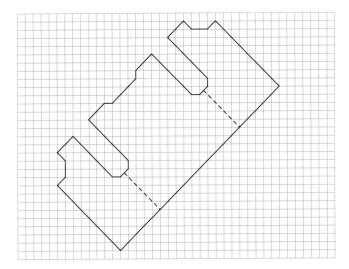

Shaping in Entrelac

Because all the rows of knitting are on the diagonal and the edges are much tighter than the center of the fabric, there is no way to determine gauge unless you knit a swatch and measure. When designing a project, it's easiest to plan it based on complete modules (that is, whole rectangles in width and whole rows of rectangles in height). For garments like sweaters, use graph paper with large squares and draw the outline of the garment on the diagonal. Use edge triangles wherever you need a straight vertical edge. Omit them when you need a diagonal, such as for underarm or neck shaping.

You can also achieve some shaping by changing the size of the modules. For example, work the crown of a hat by making the rows of rectangles with progressively fewer stitches to shape the crown. (See page 223.) Do this by picking up one fewer stitch along the edge of the rectangle below, then work as usual until two stitches remain of the rectangle below. At the end of the next decrease row, which is the final row of the rectangle, work a double decrease. On the wrong side, work P3tog to get rid of the extra stitch. On the right side, work slip 1, K2tog, psso.

In garments, panels of entrelac can be integrated with conventional knitting and the shaping done in the plain sections. Knit the entrelac panels first, then pick up stitches along any of the edges. Plain stockinette, worked above or below the entrelac, requires significantly more stitches to achieve the same width. Use a stockinette stitch swatch to determine your gauge, measure your panel of entrelac, and multiply its width by the stockinette gauge to determine the number of stitches you need to pick up. The best way to pick up along the edge of the bind-off triangles and the edge triangles (thereby producing the neatest transition with no gaps), is to pick up and knit one stitch directly into the top of every column of stitches and under every chain stitch between those columns all along the edge. Using this method, you will pick up more stitches than you need. Decrease to the correct number on the following row. Along the cast-on edge, it's more difficult to pick up enough stitches, so loosely pick up as many as you can, neatly and consistently, then increase to the correct number on the following row.

HELIX MITTENS

These mittens were knit in a worsted-weight yarn using size US 4 (3.5 mm) needles. You may also work them in sport- or DK-weight yarn, using US 2 (2.75 mm) needles, or size needed to create a firm fabric. For the lighter-weight yarn, begin by casting on 6 stitches and then follow the instructions as written. For further information about Helix Knitting, see page 198.

Measurements

These mittens are custom knit to fit any size hand. While working them, you will need to try them on to determine sizing as you go. If you are knitting them for someone else who's not available for fittings, please refer to the chart below for suggested sizing.

	Small (primary or preschool)	Medium (child or small adult)	Large (adult)
Hand circumference	7" (18 cm)	8" (20 cm)	9" (23 cm)
Fingertip to thumb opening	3½" (9 cm)	4¼" (11 cm)	4¾" (12 cm)
Hand length (to top of cuff)	6" (15 cm)	7" (18 cm)	8" (20 cm)
Cuff length	2" (5 cm)	2¼" (6 cm)	2½" (6.5 cm)
Thumb length	2" (5 cm)	2¼" (6 cm)	2½" (6.5 cm) or more

Yarn

The mittens shown were knit in Kid Hollow semi-worsted, 50% wool/50% mohair, 4 oz (113 g)/ 180 yd (164.5 m), one skein of each of the following: C1: Chamas Green; C2: Raspberries.

You may use two colors of any sport-, DK- or worsted-weight yarn. You'll also need a small amount (about 18" [46 cm]) of waste yarn in a third color, cut into two pieces

Needles   Set of double-pointed needles in a size that will create a firm fabric. Recommended sizes are US 4 (3.5 mm) for worsted weight yarn, or US 2 (2.75 mm) for sport or DK

Gauge   No gauge is given because you can knit these in a variety of yarns, varying the size needle as necessary. Just make sure that the fabric is fairly firm so that the mittens will be warm and hold their shape.

Knitting the Mittens

Using MC, cast on 4 stitches.

SETUP ROUND   Knit into the front and back of each stitch. *You now have 8 stitches.* Pull the needle out of the stitches. Half will pop to the front and half to the back (you may need to use the tip of your needle to encourage them to do so). Insert the needle again into just the front stitches. Insert a second needle into the back stitches. Slip half of the stitches from one needle onto a third needle. Mark the beginning/end of the round and the halfway point.

Shaping the Mitten

ROUND 1 (INCREASE ROUND) Using C1, *knit into the front and back of the first stitch, knit until 2 stitches remain before marker, knit into front and back of next stitch, K1; repeat once more from *.

ROUND 2 Knit around.

NEXT ROUNDS Repeat Rounds 1 and 2 until the mitten tip is wide enough to fit over the four fingers of the hand. At the beginning of the next round, knit into the front and back of the first stitch. *You will have an odd number of stitches.* **Do not increase anywhere else on this round.**

Working the Helix Pattern

ROUND 1 Using C2, *K1, P1; repeat from * around, ending K1.

ROUND 2 Using C1, knit around.

ROUND 3 Using C2, *P1, K1; repeat from * around, ending P1.

ROUND 4 Using C1, knit around.

REPEAT ROUNDS 1–4 until hand of mitten is long enough to reach to the crease where the thumb meets the hand. End with Round 1 or Round 3.

Thumb Opening

For Left Mitten, use waste yarn and knit across as follows:

For Small, knit across about ¾" (2 cm) of stitches

For Medium, knit across about 1" (2.5 cm) of stitches

For Large, knit across about 1.25" (3 cm) of stitches

Note the number of stitches you just knit. Slip these stitches back to the left needle, leave the waste yarn dangling, then using C1, knit to the end of the round.

For Right Mitten, work until the same number of stitches you knit in waste yarn for Left Mitten remains at the end of the round. Using waste yarn, knit across these stitches. Slip these stitches back to the left needle. Use C1 to knit to end of round.

Completing the Hand

Continue to work in Helix Pattern until mitten is long enough to fit comfortably from the fingertips to the wrist bone. Cut C2 yarn, leaving a tail to weave in later.

Using C1, K2tog, knit to end of round.

NEXT ROUNDS (RIBBING)   *K1, P1; repeat from * to end of round until cuff is 2½" (6.25 cm) long, or desired length. Bind off loosely in ribbing.

Working the Thumb

SETUP ROUND   Remove waste yarn, which will leave active stitches or loops of yarn across the top and bottom of the opening. Slip one needle into the stitches across the top of the opening. Slip two needles into the stitches across the bottom of the opening.

ROUND 1   Using C1, knit around, picking up 2 stitches at the gap at each end of the opening.

ROUND 2   Knit around decreasing 2 stitches, one at each end of the opening. If desired, slip stitches between needles so that there are approximately the same number on each needle.

NEXT ROUNDS   Continue knitting each round until thumb is long enough to fit comfortably.

NEXT ROUND   K2tog to end of round. If you have an odd number of stitches, knit the last stitch.

Cut the yarn and pull the tail through the remaining stitches.

Finishing

Weave in ends on inside. You may discover small holes on either side at the base of the thumb. Use the beginning and ending tails from the thumb to close up these holes as you weave them in.

FINISHING TOUCHES

8

While the knitted fabric itself is the main event in most garments, the details are great places to play with color as well. Cast ons, bind offs, borders, and edgings contribute more than you'd expect to the finished look of the knitting and provide an opportunity to embellish with color at the edges of the fabric. They can be plain or quite fancy. After the base fabric is completed, you can also add knitted surface ornaments, not to mention fringes, pom-poms, and tassels. You'll find complete directions for all of the techniques discussed, either within this chapter or in the Appendix.

{Perfect Finishing}

Joining pieces, by sewing, knitting, or crocheting them together, adding borders, coping with tails of yarn, and blocking are all part of finishing. How you handle the edges of your knitting is also crucial to faultless finishing.

Creating Neat Edges

Edge stitches are a key ingredient in neatly finished seams and borders. They are especially important when you're adding a contrasting border, joining two pieces of different colors, or trying to match stripes perfectly at a seam. In knitting, there are always several ways (if not more!) to accomplish anything, so if you don't like the way something looks, experiment to see if you can improve on it. Use these tips to make the cleanest edges possible, and your seaming and picking up will be much neater and easier.

» *Edge stitches.* If you plan to seam or add finishing treatment to the edge of the fabric, don't slip the edge stitches. Slipped selvedges may look neater, but they are more difficult to deal with later.

» *Consistent edge.* If the fabric is mostly stockinette stitch, keep 1 or 2 stitches at the edge in stockinette.

» *Designs with simple pattern stitches.* In garter stitch, seed stitch, or any other pattern stitch where the first and last stitch of every row is knitted, work the edge stitches in either stockinette or in garter. For shaped edges, like armholes and neck openings, however, stockinette stitch works better.

» *Designs with complex pattern stitches.* When the body is done in a more complex pattern stitch, leave 1 or 2 stitches in stockinette at each edge.

▲ *Increasing and decreasing.* Always work any increases or decreases a stitch or two away from the edge, keeping the edge stitches intact. I prefer to work an ssk decrease at the beginning of a row and a K2tog at the end of a row to follow the slant of the shaping, making it easy to follow the parallel columns of stitches along the edge when picking up or seaming. Some knitters prefer to do the opposite, placing ssk at the end of the row and K2tog at the beginning, because they feel the stitches are less noticeable this way.

Mastering Joins

Knitted pieces can be joined by sewing together, knitting together, or crocheting together. When sewing multicolor pieces together, the goal is for any pattern to match perfectly and for the seam to be almost unnoticeable. Knitting or crocheting the pieces together offers the benefit of joining and embellishing at the same time.

Mattress stitch. To join pieces of knitted fabric together, use mattress stitch. For a neat seam in stockinette, always sew a whole stitch in from the edge and take care to exactly match any design elements, like stripes. (See photo facing page, bottom.) You have several options with garter-stitch edges. For a very flat, bulk-free seam, sew through the tiny bumps at the end of each ridge. For a neater but slightly bulkier seam, sew through the "smiles" or "frowns" of the ridges closest to the edge.

Three-needle bind off. Knitting two pieces together while binding off is efficient and makes a very neat join. It's most often used to join the shoulders of garments and is usually worked on the inside where it doesn't show, but it can embellish the outside as well. Like the normal single-layer bind off, it has a chain along the knit side and a ridge along the purl side. Be careful to control the direction your chains travel in, and the position of the ridge, especially if they are worked in a contrasting color. (See Three-Needle Bind-Off, page 243.)

bind off

▲ *Joining a top to a side.* Here, the top of one piece is joined to the side of another. To do this, pick up stitches along the side of the piece so you have live stitches to use for the three-needle bind off. In the example shown, the pattern was worked up to the final garter stitch ridge in the light color, then stitches were picked up along the edge of the other piece and the bind off was worked in that same color, forming the final ridge of the pattern. This method of joining is particularly useful for attaching sleeves to the armhole of a garment. Make sure you pick up the same number of stitches around the armhole as there are in the top of the sleeve.

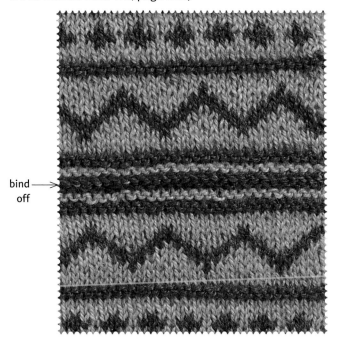

bind off

▲ *Joining the top edges.* This bind off is integrated with the ridges that separate motifs in the Fair Isle patterns and is used to join as well as bind off at the tops of the two pieces of knitting. A purl ridge that falls on the opposite side of the chain from the bind off's own purl ridge balances it nicely.

▲ *A symmetrical three-needle bind off.* Any two edges may be joined using the technique just described, if you pick up stitches along both of them, as demonstrated here. This also shows a symmetrical variation of the three-needle bind off. Instead of knitting every stitch, the bind-off was worked with alternating knits and purls, making a zigzag chain that lies flat on the face of the fabric.

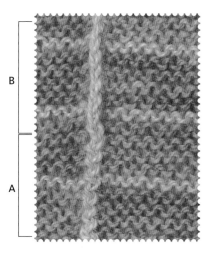

▲ *Crocheted seams.* A single-crochet seam places a chain of contrasting color along the seam line. This can look similar to the three-needle bind off. Alternately working through a stitch on one side of the seam and then on the other side of the seam creates the zigzag effect (A). Working through both layers at once (B) makes a straight chain of stitches but has a tendency to flop to one side.

Joining by Knitting On

If you are making a garment, or anything else, in strips, you can attach each strip to its neighbor as you knit so that seaming isn't necessary. There are numerous ways to do this. Some require no preparation, some call for a slipped stitch at the beginning of every row to make picking up stitches easier, and others use stitches picked up all along the edge of one strip to join it to the next. Leave about a 4" (10 cm) tail at both the cast on and the bind off and use this to close the tiny gap that forms at the top and bottom between strips. You can make each strip any width you like and you can change colors within each strip to make blocks of color.

▲ *Joining garter-stitch strips.* Knit the first strip and bind off. If you usually slip the first stitch or make a selvedge or edge stitch of some sort, don't do it on these strips. For the next strip, cast on the desired number of stitches. Make sure both strips are facing the same way (the cast-on tails may hang down from either the left or the right corners, but both should be the same). Insert the right needle into the stitch (one strand from the edge) just below the first ridge on the strip and knit up a stitch. *Turn and knit across on the wrong side. Turn and knit on the right side until 2 stitches remain (A), ssk (B), knit up a stitch below the next ridge. Repeat from * until the current strip is the same length as the previous strip. Bind off. This makes a join where the two colors alternate along the seam.

▲ *Joining garter-stitch strips with a contrast ridge.* Cast on for the first strip using the loop, knitted, or cable cast on. Knit until the first strip is as long as you like, then bind off. With whichever you consider the right side facing you, use a contrasting color to pick up and knit 1 stitch for each ridge on the strip. Knit 1 row (wrong side). Cut the yarn, leaving a tail to be woven in later. With the right side facing you, cast on the stitches for the next strip at the beginning of this needle, using the same cast on as for the first strip.

*Knit the new stitches until 1 remains, ssk (working the last stitch of the new strip together with the first contrasting stitch). Turn, knit on the wrong side. Turn. Repeat from * until the new strip is the same length as the previous strip. Bind off, taking care that you are working in the same direction as the bind off on the previous strip. If you worked the joining ridge in the same color as the new strip, there's no need to cut the yarn in between. If you change colors in the course of your strip, you may want to work a garter stitch ridge between colors to match the contrasting ridge between strips.

MAKING THE STRIPS MATCH
Because you can't use the long-tail cast on at the beginning of a row, you won't be able to use it here. This is why several other options for casting on were recommended for the first strip, so all the stripes will match.

▲ *Joining stockinette-stitch strips.* Work the first strip in stockinette, casting on 1 stitch more than the desired width. On the knit rows, keep the yarn in back, slip the first stitch purlwise, then knit the rest of the row. On the purl side, keep the yarn in front, slip the first stitch purlwise, then purl the rest of the row. Work to the desired length and bind off. Cast on for the second strip. With the right side facing you, *slip 1 purlwise, knit until 1 stitch remains, slip 1 knitwise (A), with the right side of both strips facing you, insert the right needle into the first slipped stitch on the old strip (B), pick up and knit a stitch, pass the slipped stitch over. Turn to wrong side, slip 1 purlwise, purl to the end of the row. Turn to right side. Repeat from * until new strip is the same length as the previous strip. Bind off, taking care that you are working in the same direction as the bind off on the previous strip.

Note: It's important to insert the needle directly into the stitch as you pick up and knit each new stitch, to make a neat join.

▲ *Joining stockinette strips with a contrast ridge.* Cast on 1 stitch more than the desired width, using the loop, knitted, or cable cast on. On the right-side rows, slip 1 purlwise with yarn in back and knit across. On the wrong-side rows, purl. Work until strip is desired length, then bind off. Using a contrasting color and with the right side facing you, pick up and knit 1 stitch for each slipped stitch along the right edge of the strip, inserting the needle a whole stitch (two strands) in from the edge. The slipped stitch will disappear entirely behind the new stitches. Knit 1 row. Cut the yarn, leaving a tail to be woven in later. With the right side facing you, cast on the stitches for the next strip at the beginning of this needle. *Slip 1 purlwise, with yarn in back, knit the new stitches until 1 remains, ssk (working the last stitch of the new strip together with the first contrasting stitch; see photo). Turn to wrong side. Purl across. Turn to right side. Repeat from * until the new strip is the same length as the previous strip. Bind off, taking care that you are working in the same direction as the bind off on the previous strip.

Sometimes this join is a bit uneven, with smaller and larger stitches alternating up the column. If this annoys you, be careful not to pull the yarn tightly on the first stitch of the purl rows. Another option is to slip the first purl stitch. This results in a straight column of evenly tensioned slipped stitches, twice as tall as the adjacent stitches. If you do this at the join, then for consistency you may want to slip the first stitch on the purl rows when you work the first strip.

Working Neat Borders

Neatness is crucial when you make contrasting borders. Sometimes a good solution is to pick up for the border with the same color as the knitting attached to it, then switch to the border color on the next row. This is no help, however, if the edge is multicolor. For the most consistent-looking edge, always pick up stitches by knitting up a stitch using the working yarn. In stockinette stitch, always insert the needle a whole stitch from the edge. In garter stitch, work either a whole stitch or a half stitch from the edge — choose based on how it looks and how easy (or difficult) the method is in each particular piece of knitting.

If you're dealing with stripes, you may have many loose ends to cope with along the edge. Wait to weave them in until after the border is completed. Doing so earlier can make it difficult to pick up along the edge. The width of the border is also critical: Each pattern stitch has its own proportion of stitches to rows.

GARTER-STITCH BORDER ON GARTER STITCH. **Pick up one stitch for every ridge.**

To add a ribbed border to stockinette, pick up about 3 stitches for every 4 rows. For other situations — when adding a fancier border, when the garment was knit in a pattern stitch, or both — make a sample of your border and measure it to determine the number of stitches per inch or centimeter. Measure the edge that the border must fit, and multiply the gauge by that length. This is the number of stitches you need to pick up, which may be modified somewhat to suit your pattern stitch.

If you prefer to test out a border rather than calculate the correct number of stitches, pick up and knit about 20 stitches along the edge where the border will go. You can see if it flares out or pulls in and can adjust accordingly.

► *Picking up along a concave edge.* Concave borders, such as for armholes and necklines, need to be shorter than the edges they complete so they don't flare. One way to make them shorter is to pick up fewer stitches than you would along a straight edge,

but with contrasting borders it's very noticeable if there are spaces between stitches along the picked-up edge. To make a neat transition, pick up 1 stitch in the top stitch of each column and 1 stitch at the end of every row along the edge, then decrease to the number of stitches you actually need on the first row of the border. When the border is completed, bind off firmly to prevent flaring.

► *Picking up along a convex edge.* Convex borders, such as for a shirttail, need to be shaped, starting smaller at the beginning and getting wider as you work. Multicolor borders, whether in ribbing, garter stitch, or some other pattern, can spice up a plain project or harmonize with a complex one.

Dealing with Ends

Ends, of course, should be woven in neatly on the back of the garment. Unfortunately, if you've used a lot of colors, you'll end up with a huge number of ends, and weaving them in can be extraordinarily tedious. If they are concentrated at one point in the fabric (along an outer edge, or along a seam line) they can also be very bulky and affect the way the right side looks. Here are a few ideas for dealing with ends. (See also Handling All Those Ends, page 182.)

▲ *French braid.* If the ends are clustered along a seam line, as with stripes and entrelac, start at one end of the seam and braid them together, picking up additional ends as you come to them. Begin at the outer edge of the fabric and work toward the center so that no ends will be left dangling beyond the edge. You may need to trim some of the ends to prevent the braid from becoming too thick.

Braids on the outside. Tails of yarn can also become decorative braids. As you're knitting, leave tails at least 4" (10 cm) long, so you can work with them easily. Pull through to the outside of the fabric, and braid them in groups of three. If you have an extra strand and no other tails nearby, simply double up one of the strands in a three-strand braid. This technique is very effective for hiding the jog at the beginning and end of round in stripes worked circularly, and you can embellish the braids with small beads or bells. If there's fringe nearby, you could also incorporate the tail into it.

Glass cozy with decorative braided fringe

Binding the Edges

Binding an edge combines functionality with decoration. I describe just two ways to construct a bound edge, but these are open to many variations. You can make them in solid colors, stripes, or pattern stitches, with a crisp folded edge, or in the form of a rolled cord. In a garment constructed of large modules, binding can enclose ends wherever you pick up stitches to begin a new module. Before you work any of these options, though, secure all the ends that will be encased in the binding, either by knotting them together or by hand- or machine-sewing along the edge stitches. Make sure you catch every strand of yarn so it can't unravel. Once secured, trim the ends to a little less than the anticipated width of the binding. Leave them as long as possible, but avoid any unnecessary bulk inside the binding.

Double-Width Border

The first and simplest option is to pick up stitches along the edge as if you were adding a regular ribbing or border. Work any stitch you like. Plain stockinette or a simple ribbing are the most common, but you could use a decorative pattern stitch or colorwork. Try to avoid creating a very thick fabric, though, because it will be even thicker when the binding is doubled over with yarn ends inside.

When the border is as wide as you like, knit across on the wrong side. This will make a ridge, which forms a neat fold line for the outer edge of the binding. Work this inner section in any color or pattern you like — it doesn't have to be the same as the outside. It's best, however, to work in stockinette to make a thin smooth fabric. To ensure that the outer layer doesn't bulge, switch to a smaller needle or evenly decrease a few stitches on the first row after the turning ridge so that the inner layer is smaller than the outer layer.

▲ *Sewing down a double-width binding.* When you've worked the inner layer until it's the same length as the outer layer, you have three options: You can bind off, then sew the border down on the inside (A). You can sew the live stitches down without binding off, sliding them off the point of the needle as you work (B). Or, as you bind off, each time you insert the needle into a stitch to knit it, pick up a loop on the back of the fabric and knit it together with the stitch (C). The first option is thickest, because it involves a bind off plus sewing down. The second is least bulky, since there's no bound-off edge. The third falls in between. In all cases, be careful to work loosely when binding off and sewing so that the binding stretches as much as the fabric it's attached to.

▲ *Natural rolled edge.* A variation on this binding is to make a border without a turning ridge, which creates a rolled edge. Using reverse stockinette takes advantage of the fabric's natural tendency to curl. When very narrow, it appears to be cording. In this case, if you have lots of ends, be sure to make it big enough so the ends will fit inside.

Working a Two-Layer Binding

▲ *Preparing for a two-layer binding.* Achieve almost the same effect without any sewing by knitting both layers of the binding at the same time. Using a circular needle and the working yarn, with the right side of the fabric facing you, pick up and knit stitches along the edge to be bound. With a second circular needle and the same working yarn still attached, turn to the wrong side and pick up and knit the same number of stitches across the back of the fabric (above). This is most neatly accomplished by picking up under the strand between each stitch on the first needle. Cast on 1 extra stitch at the end of the needle, then turn your work so that the right side is facing you. Abandon the second needle for the time being, pick up both ends of the first needle, and work across it with the same ball of yarn still attached. This will leave all the stitches for the back of the fabric on the second needle and all the stitches for the

front on the original needle. At the end of this first needle, cast on 1 stitch. Continue your binding by turning and working all the back stitches onto their own needle, then turning again and working all the front stitches onto their own needle.

When the binding is the desired depth, you have two options: use the three-needle bind off to attach the two layers together and finish off the edge, or knit the two layers together without binding off and continue to make a single layer fabric.

▲ *Three-needle bind off.* With the ends of the circular needles parallel, use an empty needle to knit together one stitch from the front needle and one from the back needle; repeat for the next stitch on both needles (A). Pass the first stitch on the right needle over the second to bind it off (B). Continue in this manner until all stitches are bound off.

Merging to a Single Layer

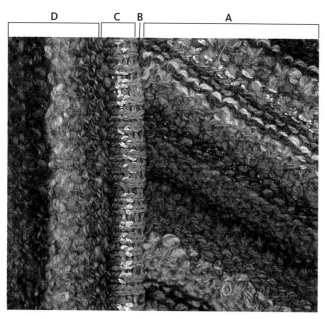

Merging to a single layer is very helpful if you plan to make buttonholes in the band or if the binding is at the edge of a new section you are adding to the garment. For example, I made the back of a vest by working the diagonal center panel first (A). I picked up along the edge of the center panel (B) and then knit outward using the two-layer binding technique (C), so the ends are encased on both the inside and the outside. I then knit the two layers of the binding together to form a single layer, and continued working to form the side panels (D).

Blocking Methods

In much colorwork, blocking is necessary. Stranded knitting and intarsia both should be wet and stretched while drying to even out the stitches and flatten the surface. To show them to full advantage, pattern stitches such as those in chapters 3 and 4 frequently need to be blocked and stretched. Use your own judgment on how much tension to exert to make the stitches look their best. Lace, almost always, needs stern blocking to open up the eyelets.

In all of these cases, the best method of blocking is to soak or wash the finished object gently, roll it in a towel to remove excess moisture, and then stretch and pin it out to dry. Blocking wires can make the process of pinning out much easier, with more consistent results, since they hold the entire edge even with just a few pins. Sock, mitten, and glove blockers exist, but can be hard to find or may not be the right size. You can cut your own out of sturdy cardboard, stiff plastic (the sides of gallon milk jugs work well) or bend coat hangers to fit the exact shape and size of your garment.

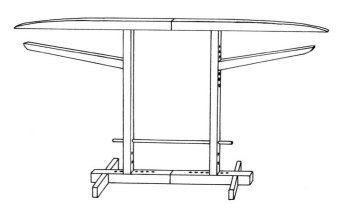

Woolly board for blocking drop-shoulder sweaters

{Decorative Cast Ons}

Casting on is sometimes a complete afterthought, but the beginning edge of whatever you're making provides an opportunity for embellishment, either subtle or striking. For example, multicolor cast ons can be integrated with the pattern stitch — this level of detail produces a very professional, custom-made look. The crocheted cast on can easily be removed (allowing you to make decisions about the bottom border later) or worked in a contrasting yarn as an embellishment. If you're planning to add fringe, use the knitted cast on; its loose loops make fringing easy.

Two-Color Cable Cast On

Using two colors of yarn, make a slip knot with both strands and place it on the left needle. Work the cable cast on, making the first stitch between the two strands of the slip knot and then knitting each color alternately, as described below.

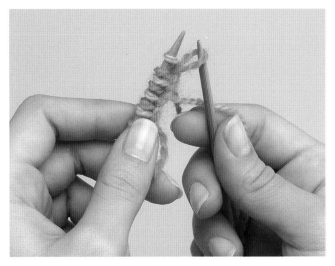

2] Knit out a new stitch, alternating colors and taking care to twist the strands in the same direction between every stitch.

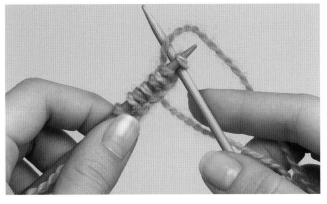

1] Insert the needle between the first two stitches on the left-hand needle.

▲ *The result.* The cable cast on produces a double twisted-rope effect across the bottom of the fabric.

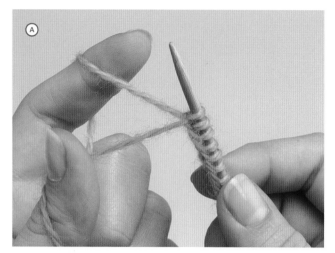

▲ *Two-Color Long-Tail Cast On.* Using two colors of yarn, make a slip knot with both strands and place it on the needle. Work the long-tail cast on as usual, with one color for the thumb strand and the other over the index finger. Don't include the slip knot in your stitch count. At the end of the first row, unravel the slip knot. The color on your thumb appears in a very thin line across the bottom edge of the fabric, and the color on your index finger forms the stitches on the needle (A).

▲ *Alternating Two-Color Long-Tail Cast On.* A variation on the previous cast on is to alternate colors as you cast on. Between each stitch, give the two colors a half twist and swap their positions on the thumb and forefinger. Always twist the two strands in the same direction between stitches. Stitch colors alternately across the needle, creating a peppermint-stipe effect across the bottom edge on the right side of the fabric. On the wrong side (C), this cast on forms a chevron of alternating colors along the edge (B), making this the perfect way to start K1, P1 corrugated ribbing.

▲ *Long-Tail Cast On with Multiple Thumb Strands.* For an easy-to-work but high-impact cast on, simply replace the single thumb strand of the long-tail cast on with multiple strands. First, make a slip knot with all the strands. Then work the cast on as usual, with one strand over the index finger and all others over the thumb. Place the stitches as close together on the needle as you can and tension the thumb strands just enough to make a neat edge. This is the cast on used for the top edge of the glass cozy (page 241).

Crocheted Cast On

This is a provisional cast on (sometimes called an open cast on) designed to be easy to remove, leaving live stitches that can be picked up on a needle so you can knit down from the original cast on edge. If you haven't decided what the borders will look like, or you want to be sure you have enough yarn, use this cast on, then go back and add the borders later.

If your corrugated ribbing has a tendency to curl, this cast on allows you to add it last, working a firm bind off to subdue the curling. It also makes an excellent decorative cast on, leaving a chain of contrasting color across the bottom of the fabric, visually similar to a bind-off chain. When using the crocheted cast on as a decorative element, cast on as many stitches as you need in a contrasting color, then cut the yarn and pull it through the loop on your crochet hook to secure the end.

{Decorative Bind Offs}

Just like casting on, binding off offers an opportunity for one more flourish of color.

▲ *Binding off with contrast.* To make a contrasting chain on the right side, change to the contrasting color, then bind off in knitting on the right side or in purl on the wrong side. To make a finished ridge in a contrasting color at the edge of the fabric (shown above), change to the contrasting yarn, knit across on the right side, then bind off in knitting on the wrong side.

Binding Off in Pattern

When you're working a color pattern up to the very edge of the knitting, you may want to continue the pattern into the bound-off edge. If you knit each stitch in the color from the row below, when you pass the stitch over to bind off, the color shifts to the left. To align the color in the bind off with the color in the fabric below, switch to the new color one stitch early as you work across.

▲ *Binding off in K1, P1 corrugated ribbing.* Work the opposite color of the row below throughout the bind off (A). In this way, the bound-off stitches match the ribs directly beneath them (B).

Binding Off with I-Cord

You can use I-cord to add polished, versatile edgings to many knit items. The I-cord edging on the coaster below produces a cord along the bound-off edge of a piece, and since it is not terribly stretchy, it can be used to support the fabric. See at right for how to do it.

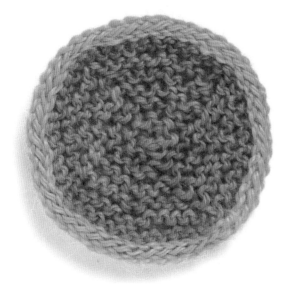

I-cord bind off.

Decorative I-cord loop bind off (for instructions, see page 250)

1] End with a right-side row. At the beginning of the next row (wrong side), cast on 3–6 stitches for the cord. *Knit until 1 stitch remains of the cord, slip 1 knitwise, knit 1, pass slipped stitch over (this works the last stitch of the cord together with the first stitch to be bound off).

2] Slip all the stitches back to the left needle purlwise. Do not turn.

3] Repeat from * until all stitches across the row have been used and only the cord stitches remain. Cut yarn and pull end through all stitches. This is usually most successful with 3–4 stitches for the I-cord. For a quicker join, substitute K2tog tbl for the cumbersome skp.

Decorative I-Cord Loops

Looped I-cord makes a more decorative finish (see photo, page 249). Although the stitches to be bound off may be on any kind of needle, it's easier if they are on a circular needle (here, referred to as "main" needle). You will also need 2 double-pointed needles (dpn) to work the I-cord loops.

1] K3 from the main needle onto a dpn.

2] Using a second dpn, work I-cord until loop is desired length. (*Note:* Be sure to make note of how many rows of I-cord you work, so that you can make all of the loops the same length.)

3] Bring yarn to front of work. Rotate the dpn so yarn hangs from the right-hand side of the stitches and hold double-pointed needle in front of main needle. Using an empty dpn, [slip 1 knitwise from front needle, slip 1 purlwise from back needle].

4] Repeat twice. Set aside the empty needle.

5] Using the main needle and working with the stitches on the dpn, lift the second stitch off over the first, binding it off; slip the first stitch back to the main needle. Repeat twice to bind off two more stitches. The dpn will be empty.

If you are working across a flat piece of knitting, repeat Steps 1–5 until 3 stitches remain to be bound off. Work the last loop 1 row shorter than the others. Use Kitchener stitch to join to the last 3 stitches. If you are working circularly, continue until no stitches remain on the main needle. Work the last loop 1 row shorter than the rest, then sew the last three stitches down behind the beginning of the first loop.

You can also work this trim using narrower or wider I-cord. Just bind off the same number of stitches from the main needle as you have in the I-cord when you join the end of each loop.

Edgings

Edgings are worked (as their name implies) along the edge of the fabric and are joined to the fabric at the end of every other row, using one of the techniques described in Joining by Knitting On, page 238. They are particularly useful when worked as a bind off if you don't want an inelastic chain across the top of the fabric. Edgings can add color, texture, and ornament. Openwork edgings are frequently worked on lace knitting, and books on knitted lace are a wonderful source of instructions. You can, of course, always work any edging in a different color (or colors) from the main body of the knitting. Try one of these basic garter stitch edgings. You can work them as narrow or as wide as you like.

First, pick up stitches along the edge. If the base fabric is stockinette, pick up 4 stitches for every 5 rows to make the edging the correct length. For garter stitch, pick up one stitch for each ridge. For other pattern stitches, knit a sample of garter stitch and measure the ridges (not rows) per inch, measure the length of the edge, then multiply the two to calculate how many stitches to pick up.

Edgings may also be used to bind off. When applied to the top of garter stitch, Seed Stitch, or similar patterns, the proportion of these edgings is perfect. When applied to stockinette, however, they are just a bit too wide for the top of the fabric. You can adjust for this by using smaller needles.

▲ *Garter-stitch edging.* With the wrong side facing you, cast on as many stitches as desired for the width of the edging at the beginning of the row. *Slip 1 knitwise with yarn in back, knit until 1 stitch of border remains, K2tog working the last edging stitch together with the stitch to be bound off. Turn to the right side. Knit until 1 stitch remains, purl 1. Turn to the wrong side. Repeat from * until all the stitches have been bound off. If you are working a flat piece of knitting, bind off the edging stitches. If you're working a circular piece of knitting, sew them neatly to the cast on at the beginning of the edging.

▲ *Two-color garter-stitch edging.* With the wrong side facing you, cast on as many stitches as desired for the width of edging at the beginning of the row. *Sl1 knitwise, knit until 1 stitch of border remains, K2tog, working the last edging stitch together with the stitch to be bound off. Bring the working yarn to the front, turn. Change colors (once you get started, the yarn should already be hanging there). Knit until 1 stitch remains, P1. Repeat from *.

{Creative Embellishments}

Sometimes a project just needs a little something extra, either to balance an over-the-top design or to enhance a very plain one. Embellishments such as horizontal braids, vertical stripes, I-cord, ruffles, and woven strands, not to mention pom-poms, tassels, cords, and straps, can all fulfill this role. Some are worked while the knitting is in progress; some require preparation during knitting, but are added afterwards; and some are surface ornaments that can be applied at the very end.

Creating Horizontal Braids

Knitted braids aren't really braided: they are actually the strands on the back of color patterns oriented to look like braids or chevrons. They can be worked from the wrong side of the fabric in knitting (so that the strands fall on the right side), or worked on the right side by purling. In either case, an entire two-color row or round is worked changing colors on every stitch and twisting the yarn in the same direction between each stitch. This twists the two strands quite a bit, but you should resist the urge to untwist them. The second step of the process is to work around alternating colors again, but twisting in the opposite direction, which serves to untwist the yarns. Make sure you knit each stitch with the same color on both rounds so the strands line up correctly to form the "braid." The strands slant diagonally in one direction on the first round and the opposite direction on the second round, forming a chevron. Work just 2 rows or rounds to make a single row of chevrons, or work more rows, alternating the direction of the twist to make a herringbone or zigzag pattern.

Working Vertical Stripes and Plaid

Horizontal stripes are easy to make in knitting, but vertical stripes involve working slipped stitches, intarsia, or stranded knitting. You can, however, add vertical stripes after the knitting is completed. If you just want vertical stripes, work a piece of knitting that's mostly stockinette, with a column of purled stitches wherever you will add a stripe. If you work horizontal stripes on the base fabric, you'll end up with plaid.

▲ *Crocheting a vertical stripe.* After the base fabric is completed, use a crochet hook to crochet a chain of the contrasting color in the purled channels. To begin, make a slip knot and hold the yarn behind the fabric. Insert the crochet hook through the bottom purl stitch and into the slip knot. Pull the slip knot through to the front of the fabric. Insert the hook into the next stitch, hook up a loop of the yarn (still behind the fabric) and pull it through the loop already on the hook. Repeat this until you get to the top of the column. Cut the yarn and pull the end through the fabric and through the top loop to secure it. The contrasting chain nestles into the column of purled stitches and is even with the surface of the stockinette stitch on either side.

Making the Most of I-Cord

I-cord applied by knitting, sewing, and lacing.

stitch of the cord together with the picked up stitch). Knit up a stitch through the edge of the fabric. Repeat from * until you've applied I-cord all along the edge. Cut the yarn and pull the end through all the stitches.

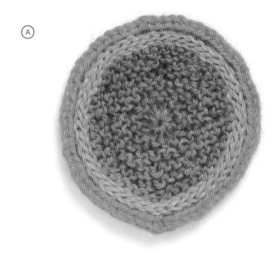

Ⓐ

I-cord is such a versatile little tube. Not only can it be used when binding off (see Binding Off with I-cord, page 249), it can also stand on its own as a cord and be used as a surface embellishment on the knitted fabric, as shown on this swatch. Used this way it's called applied I-cord. There are various techniques for attaching the I-cord, including knitting, sewing, and lacing it on.

Ⓑ

▲ *I-cord on the edge.* Using a double-pointed needle, cast on 3 to 6 stitches. With the right side of the fabric facing you and the needle in your right hand, pick up and knit a stitch through the edge of the fabric. *Do not turn. Slip the stitches to the other end of the needle and shift it to your left hand. Pull the yarn across the back of these stitches and knit until two stitches remain, skp (this works the last

▲ *Multiple rows of I-cord.* You can apply row after row of I-cord along the edge of any piece of knitting (A), and if you need a buttonhole, it's easy to work I-cord for a few rows without knitting up any stitches (B). When the cord for the buttonhole is long enough, start attaching it again, leaving a slit for the button to pass through.

▲ *I-cord for button loops.* If you'd prefer decorative button loops, they too are easily achieved in I-cord. Mark the positions of your buttonholes with safety pins or split markers. When you reach these points, work plain I-cord until it's long enough to go around your button (A). Pick up and knit the next stitch in the same place you knitted up the stitch at the beginning of the loop — this prevents a gap (B).

I-cord as Surface Decoration

I-cord can either be knitted onto the surface of the fabric or sewn on. For free-form shapes, tight curves, or acute angles, it's best to knit the I-cord, arrange it on the fabric the way you want it, and sew it on.

"frown"

"smile"

▲ *Horizontal applications.* You can knit straight lines and slight curves of I-cord directly onto the fabric by planning ahead and working purls in the base fabric where you want the I-cord to be. For horizontal lines, purl a row where you want the I-cord. When you're ready to add the embellishment, fold the knitting so the purl stitches make an edge, and apply your I-cord in the convenient purled bumps. Pick either the "smile" or the "frown" of the purl stitch, but be consistent.

TROUBLESHOOTING APPLIED I-CORD

» If your I-cord is just a bit too long for the edge or the surface it's attached to, use a smaller double-pointed needle or skip a row in the base fabric occasionally when knitting up a stitch. If the I-cord is too short, use a larger needle.

» If you need to turn a corner, pick up and knit a stitch twice in the same stitch immediately before and immediately after the corner.

▲ *Vertical applications.* A column of purled stitches makes it easy to accurately place the I-cord. First, pick up and knit stitches through the fabric, holding the working yarn behind your knitting (A). Next, work an I-cord bind off (B). (For instructions, see page 249.)

▶ *Zigzags and curves.* As you knit the base fabric, work purls where you want the I-cord to be (as outlined in photo below). You can pick up all the stitches before you start, or knit the I-cord onto the purl bumps as you go. Keep in mind that diagonal lines are longer than straight lines across the same number of stitches. If your I-cord is too tight, pick up additional stitches, use a larger needle, or work some plain rows of I-cord between pickups to compensate.

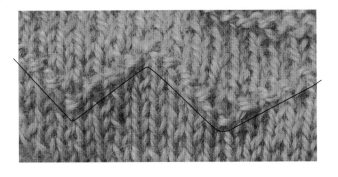

Lacing I-cord

I-cord can also be laced through holes in the fabric either through eyelets or cables.

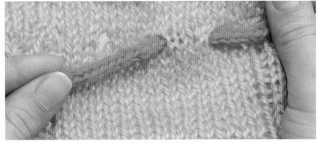

▲ *I-cord through eyelets.* Work eyelets wherever you like by making a yo, then K2tog. Use an even number of eyelets (after all, what goes in must come out!), and secure the I-cord at both ends, either by sewing or knotting it to something. I-cord woven through eyelets can be used to lash pieces of knitting together rather than sewing.

▲ *I-cord through cables.* Cables create natural gaps wherever they cross: lace I-cord through these to give the impression of a two-color cable.

For a More Frivolous Touch: Ruffles

Ruffles, although they can take considerable time to knit, are simple constructions. Three factors affect their appearance: fullness, depth, and pattern stitch. Ruffles can be made when casting on or binding off, and they can be applied to the surface of the fabric.

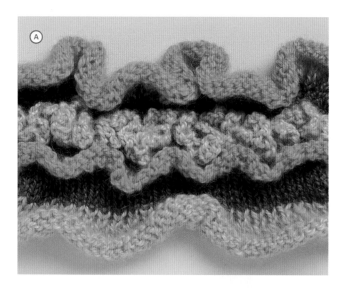

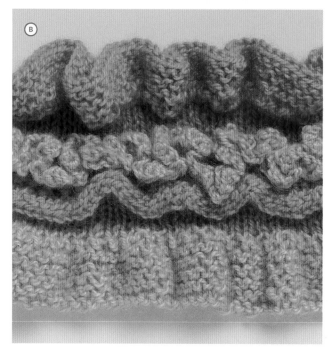

How full a ruffle is depends on the proportion between the width of the ruffle and the fabric it's attached to. Ruffles need to be at least twice as wide as the fabric, but frequently three or four times as wide looks better. Compare the ruffles on the swatches at the left. The ruffles at the edges of each swatch are twice as wide as the base fabric. Look at the pairs of narrow ruffles at the centers of each swatch: The bottom ones are also twice as wide as the base fabric. The top ones are four times as wide, so they ruffle twice as much.

Depth depends on how many rows you knit. A narrow ruffle takes much less time and yarn to knit than a deeper one. In both these swatches, the cast-on (bottom) ruffles are 1½" (3.75 cm) wide, the bind-off (top) ruffles are 1" (2.5 cm). The narrow ruffles in the center are only three rows deep (about ½" [1.25 cm]).

Curling depends on the pattern stitch. Ruffles knit in stockinette curl at the edges because of stockinette stitch's natural tendency to curl. Ruffles knit in garter stitch, or any other noncurling pattern, remain flat. The two sets of ruffles in the photos are identical, except ruffle swatch A was worked in stockinette stitch and ruffle swatch B in garter stitch. The wider stockinette stitch ruffles curl noticeably, while the garter stitch ruffles exhibit a very restrained ripple. The difference is not as apparent in the narrow ruffles.

Working a cast-on ruffle. Cast on two to four times as many stitches as you need. A loose cast on works better than a tight one. The knitted cast on and the long-tail cast on are both good choices. Work in stockinette for a curly ruffle or in garter for a ripple until the ruffle is as deep as you want it. Decrease quickly down to the correct number of stitches; for example, if you cast on twice as many as you needed, K2tog all the way across. If you cast on more stitches, you may need to work the decreases over 2 rows. No matter how many stitches you are working with, squeeze them tightly together on your needle and work firmly for a few rows so they ruffle properly.

Working a bind-off ruffle. On the last row, increase to two to four times the number of stitches on your needle. Depending on the type of increase, you may not be able to add that many stitches in one row, so you can spread them out over two rows if necessary. Yarn overs worked between every stitch or working K1, yo, K1 in every stitch may produce the best results with the least amount of effort. Yarn overs make the ruffle lacy. If you want a solid ruffle, it may be best to use the make 1 (M1) increase using the working yarn. Working a yarn over and then working into the back of it on the next row to twist it produces exactly the same increase as an M1 and is much easier to knit into. Bind off when the ruffle is as deep as you want it. The standard bind off is stiff and unyielding and prevents the fabric from ruffling to its full potential. To allow your ruffle full freedom of expression, work a yarn over between every stitch while binding off. To do this, knit the first stitch, *yo, pass the knitted stitch off over the yarn over, K1, pass the yarn over off over the knitted stitch. Repeat from * until all the stitches have been bound off.

▲ *Adding a ruffle to completed fabric.* Work a purl ridge wherever you want to add the ruffle. Fold the fabric at the ridge, pick up and knit one stitch in each purl stitch. Work into either the "smiles" or the "frowns," but be consistent. In the above photo, the knitter slips the left needle into the stitch, picking it up, then knits it with the right needle. Once the stitches are on your needle, work exactly as described for a bind-off ruffle.

Adding Weaving to Knitting

Some of the pattern stitches included in chapter 3 imitate woven fabric, using strands of the working yarn carried across the face of the fabric. True weaving is worked with at least one other yarn passed in and out of knitted stitches in the background yarn. Horizontal weaving is most efficiently done while you knit. Vertical weaving is best done after the background fabric has been completed. Only the most basic weaving is shown here. You can vary the woven pattern by using doubled strands of yarn or by working the woven pattern so it makes diagonals or herringbones.

Horizontal weaving. In this example, the background stitches (C1-light pink) are knitted or purled on every row, but the contrasting yarn (C2-dark pink) is just woven in and out between these stitches. For a garter-stitch fabric, knit the background stitches on Row 2 rather than purling. Begin by casting on an odd number of stitches using C1 and purl 1 row (WS).

ROW 1: K1 with C1, holding C2 in front of work, *move C2 to back between needle points (A), K1 with C1, move C2 to front again, K1 with C1 (B); repeat from *.

ROW 2: Bring C2 around edge of fabric to front, P1 with C1, *move C2 to back between needle points, P1 with C1, move C2 to front between needle points, P1 with C1; repeat from *.
Repeat Rows 1–2.

▲ *Adjusting the tension.* At the end of each row, adjust the tension of the woven yarn. You may hold the contrast color so that it falls either above or below the main color as you work, but be consistent because changing position in the middle of the piece will be quite noticeable. If you can hold the woven yarn in your left hand and knit with your right hand, this weaving goes almost as quickly as plain knitting.

▲ *Vertical weaving.* Knit the base fabric in garter stitch, Seed Stitch, ribbing, or with horizontal weaving as described above. If the base fabric has knitted stripes or yarn woven in horizontally, vertical weaving creates a plaid fabric. After you've bound off the fabric, block it to its final dimensions. This not only makes weaving easier by preventing curling, but it ensures that your woven strands are the correct length, because it is impossible to stretch the fabric after the weaving is completed. Thread a yarn or tapestry needle with contrasting yarn and sew it in and out through the fabric.

VERTICAL WEAVING TIPS

» Loosely spun yarns are not appropriate for weaving because constant abrasion during weaving damages and weakens them.

» Keep the lengths of yarn short enough that you can work with them easily, but long enough to reach the edge of the fabric and leave a tail for fringe or weaving in.

» On ribbing, weave in and out of the stitches in the purled columns.

» On garter stitch and Seed Stitch, weave under the bumps of purl stitches.

» Weave the loose ends in on the back of the fabric (see pages 182–183), or cut a separate piece of yarn for each row of weaving and knot the ends into fringes.

» For a reversible fabric, weave strands on both sides.

{Finishing Off with Fringe}

You can incorporate fringe into your work as you knit, or you can apply it afterwards. Here are a few methods I particularly like to use.

Fringing as You Go

Choose a noncurling pattern stitch like garter stitch, Seed Stitch, or ribbing, because you won't be able to add borders at the sides. Plan for a tail at the cast on that's at least as long as you want your fringe to be, then cast on enough stitches for the width of what you're making (a placemat or coaster, for example) or for the length (a scarf; see Reversible Scarves, page 38). Cut the working yarn, and knot a new strand of yarn onto this tail (A). Be sure to leave enough yarn on both the old and new working yarns to make the fringe as long as you want it. Continue to work each row, leaving tails at both ends for fringe and knotting them onto the tail from the previous row. Change colors every row, either following a pattern or at random, or make wider stripes of one color by using it on repeated rows and cutting the yarn at the end of every row. When your project is finished, bind off loosely, neaten up any knots that need it, and trim the ends neatly (B).

Applying Fringe to Completed Items

Plan ahead for fringe by using a loose cast on, like the knitted cast on. To work a bind off specifically for fringe, either work very loosely on large needles or work a yarn over between each stitch as you bind off. I-cord makes a very neat, unfraying fringe. If you like, you can make longer I-cords, braid them together, and tie the braids with a separate piece of yarn.

▲ *Fringe variations.* In swatch A, single strands of variegated yarn are knotted (1), twisted (2), braided (3), and left plain (4). In swatch B, double strands of the same variegated yarn are attached alternately with solid colors ranging from burgundy to light pink. In swatch C, the edge is embellished with multicolor fringes spaced 3 stitches apart, each with five different strands of yarn.

▶ *Cutting the fringe.* Cut each strand of yarn twice as long as you want the finished fringe, because it will be folded in half when it's attached. Cutting numerous strands of yarn the same length can be a tedious process, so use a book or a piece of cardboard the right width to make it easier. Wrap the yarn around and around, then cut all the strands along one side.

▲ *Attaching the fringe.* Pull the folded lengths of yarn through the edge of the fabric using your fingers or a crochet hook (A). Tuck the ends through the folded loop and tighten (B).

▶ *Knotted fringe.* Divide each fringe in half and knot it together with its neighbor, then knot it back together with its original partner. This can be done loosely, creating a net of fringe, or tightly.

▲ *Twisted fringe.* Untwist two or more strands of the fringe until their plies are parallel (A), then twist both strands together in the opposite direction (B). Knot the end (C). If you are working with single-ply yarn, twist each strand more tightly, then twist two or more of the strands together in the opposite direction and knot the end.

Braided fringe. Knots are usually too bulky when all strands of a braid are used, so just tie one strand around the braid to secure it.

Working I-cord Fringe

▲ *I-cord fringe at the cast on.* Cast on 3 stitches on double-pointed needles and work the first I-cord until it's the proper length for your fringe. (See page 266.) Cut the yarn and slip the I-cord onto the needle you plan to use for your project. Make one cord for every 2 stitches you need to cast on and accumulate them on the extra needle. These cords can all be different colors. Slip the last onto the needle with the others, but don't cut the yarn unless you need to change to a different color. Make sure all of the cords are facing the same way. On the right side, work across all the cords as follows: K2, *K2tog, K1, repeat from *, end K1. The decreases join each cord to its neighbors and create a neat, even beginning for the knitting. Count your stitches and adjust to the correct number, if necessary, by increasing or decreasing a stitch on the following row.

▲ *I-cord fringe at the bind off.* On the last row, increase evenly spaced across the row so you have 50 percent more stitches than when you started. Make sure you have a multiple of 3 stitches. Knit the first 3 stitches onto a double-pointed needle and work I-cord on them with another double-pointed needle until it's the correct length. Cut the yarn and pull through all 3 stitches to secure. Repeat on the next 3 stitches until all have been used. Change colors whenever you like. You can also add I-cord fringe anywhere you like by picking up 3 stitches at that point and working the cord. The photo above shows an I-cord fringe in progress, with more stitches to be bound off on the left needle, but the ends have all been neatly hidden inside the I-cords.

TIDYING UP

» At the tip of each I-cord, use a yarn or tapestry needle to pull the tail through to the inside to hide it.

» At the back of each cord, the knitting may be loose. Adjust the tension as you weave in each tail to tighten the loose stitches and to close the gap across the back, then weave the tail into the wrong side of the fabric or pull it through to the inside of the cord.

{Pom-poms and Tassels}

Pom-poms and tassels can accent finished knit items with an attractive flourish. You can make multicolor pom-poms by changing colors as you wrap. Wrapping colors side by side results in a pom-pom with solid areas of each color. Wrapping the colors in several thin layers results in blended stripes of the colors throughout. Holding multiple strands of different colors and wrapping them together results in even further blending of the colors.

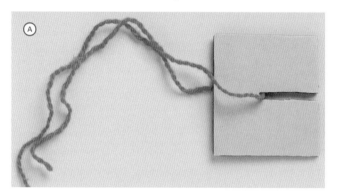

▲ *Making a pom-pom.* Buy a pom-pom–making tool or use a piece of cardboard as a base. Cut a square of stiff cardboard a little larger in dimension than the diameter of the pom-pom you want to make. You may want to double the cardboard to make it stronger. Cut a slit down the center of the cardboard, stopping just past the center point. Cut a length of yarn and drape it through the slit (A). Wrap yarn around the cardboard, changing colors. Use more wraps for a larger pom-pom, fewer for a smaller one. Cut the yarn. Tie the piece of yarn hanging in the slit tightly around the wrapped yarn (B). Cut the wrapped yarn along both edges of the cardboard. Remove the cardboard, shake out the pom-pom, and trim any uneven ends.

▲ *Making a tassel.* Cut a stiff piece of cardboard into a rectangle a little longer than you want the tassel and about 4" (10cm) wide. Wrap yarn lengthwise around the cardboard about 50 times, changing colors as desired. Cut the yarn even with the edge of the cardboard. Pull a doubled piece of yarn between the cardboard and the wrapped yarn, slide it up to one edge of the cardboard, and tie tightly around the wrapped yarn (A). Cut the wrapped yarn at the opposite end (B). Wrap another piece of yarn tightly around the tassel two or three times near the top and tie tightly. (See photo of tassel on following page.) Use a yarn needle to pull the ends of this tie through to the inside of the tassel. Shake out the tassel and trim evenly. *Note:* For a tassel with the center in one color and the outer layer in another, wrap about 20 times in the center of the card, then cover this completely (on top and on both sides) with the outer yarn.

▲ *Attaching pom-poms and tassels to surfaces.* To fasten a pom-pom or tassel to the surface of the fabric, like the center of a hat, pull the two ties through to the back of the fabric 1 or 2 stitches apart.

▲ *Attaching pom-poms and tassels to corners.* For an attachment to the edge or a corner of the fabric, pull one of the ties through from the front to the back, at least one row or stitch in from the edge.

When you are happy with the location, tie the two ends securely to each other on the wrong side, weave in on the back of the fabric, and trim.

{Multicolor Cords and Straps}

Cords or straps worked in more than one color can be striking embellishments. All of the knitted cords described below are best worked firmly on smaller needles to reduce stretching.

▲ *Twisted cord.* Twisted cords are quick to make. Decide how long the cord will be, add one-third to this measurement, then double the result. Cut at least two pieces of yarn in different colors to this length. Knot the yarns together at both ends. Have a friend hold the end, or hook it over a doorknob. Keeping the yarns stretched and taut, twist them very tightly. Pinch the twisted yarn at the center, then fold it in half, keeping it stretched out. Slowly release a few inches at a time, starting from the folded end, allowing the cord to twist back on itself. Knot both ends to prevent untwisting.

▲ *Braided cord.* Cut three strands of yarn about 50 percent longer than the desired cord. For a thicker braid, double or triple the yarn. Knot all the strands together at one end and attach them to something (like a hook or a doorknob) so that you can pull gently on the braid while you work. Arrange your colors neatly with one on the right, one in the middle, and one on the left. Bring the right strand over the middle, then the left strand over the middle, and so on. Tie a single strand around the braid to secure it.

▲ *Cast on–bind off cord.* Cast on enough stitches for the length of your cord, then change colors and bind off immediately on the next row. Be careful to bind off with your tension the same as it was for your cast on, or your cord will curve. Using the cable cast on results in a twisted cord because this cast on forms a spiral. The long-tail cast on makes a nice flat cord with no twist. Avoid cast ons that are naturally loose, like the loop or knitted cast ons, because they produce a loose, messy cord.

▲ *Cast on–bind off strap.* Knitted straps always stretch, but if you work them sideways, you can control the stretch somewhat with a firm cast on and bind off. For example, firmly cast on enough stitches for the length of your strap using the long-tail cast on. Change colors and knit one row (right side), then work in ribbing or any other noncurling pattern until the strap is almost the desired width. On the next right-side row, change back to the original color and knit across. Bind off on the wrong side in knitting (shown here). Adjust the tension of your bind off as you work to match the tension of your cast on. The right side of the strap has a ridge of contrast color along both edges.

▲ *Knit-weave strap.* This lovely, flat little strap is a recent invention of my own. It looks woven, but is made with two colors in a technique that combines I-cord and slipped stitches. It does have a tendency to twist slightly when not under tension. Use regular, not double-pointed, needles to prevent confusion over which direction to knit.

Using both colors, one over the thumb and the other over the index finger, cast on 3 stitches with the long-tail cast on. Using the thumb color, slip 1 knitwise, K2. Turn the knitting clockwise to begin the next row. *Using the other color, pull the yarn across the back, slip 1 knitwise, K2. Turn clockwise to begin the next row; repeat from *. The two yarns will become twisted around each other so you'll need to stop periodically and unwind them. When the strap is long enough, bind off with the same color you worked on the last row.

I-cord Plain and Fancy

I-cord is a narrow knitted cord, so versatile it can be put to many uses. Making I-cord in several colors is no more difficult than working it in one color and produces a gratifyingly interesting candy-stripe cord. If your I-cord normally has a gap across the back because you're a loose knitter, this won't be a problem when you're working with more colors. Three I-cords can be braided together to make a wider strap. To work basic I-cord, using two double-pointed needles, cast on a few stitches, usually 3 or 4. *Knit across. Slide stitches to other end of needle without turning. Shift the needle to your left hand. Pull yarn firmly across back. Repeat from * until cord measures desired length. To finish, cut yarn and pull through all stitches.

▲ *Two-color I-cord.* Using two double-pointed needles, cast on as many stitches as you like (3–8 work best) in first color. Slide the stitches to the other end of the needle, as shown by arrow above, and knit all the stitches with second color. Do not turn. Slide the stitches to the right end of the needle and switch the needle to your left hand. Pull first color across the back, keeping it below the other strand of yarn. Be careful not to pull it too tight. Knit all the stitches. Repeat this, alternating colors until the cord is as long as you like. Cut both yarns and pull both through all the stitches to secure.

▲ *Many-color I-cord.* Using a pair of double-pointed needles, cast on as many stitches as you like (3–8 work best) in the first color and knit across the right side repeatedly, making 1 row of each color. Knot the tails of all the yarns together loosely to keep the yarn organized. Pull the color you need (the first time, this will be the cast-on color) gently across the back of the cord under the other working yarns and knit across. Make sure the knotted ends are in front of the working yarn before you begin knitting with it. This will be easier when the cord is a little longer. Continue to work each color in succession until the cord is the desired length. Cut all the yarns and pull the one that would be used next through all the stitches to secure them. Because of the spiral effect of using so many colors, the ends of this cord are diagonal.

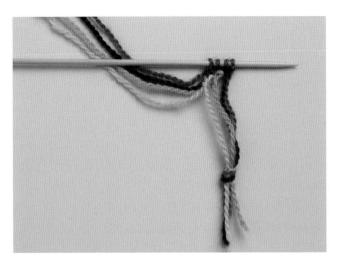

▲ *I-cord started with a straight end.* This I-cord can have as many stitches as you have balls of yarn. Make a slip knot with the first color and place it on a double-pointed needle. *Make a slip knot with the next color and place it on an empty double-pointed needle, then, using the same needle and the same color, knit across the first needle. The first time you do this, there will only be one stitch. Slide these stitches to the other end of the needle and switch it to the left hand. Repeat from * until you've used all your colors. You will have as many stitches as your have colors. Knot the cut ends together to keep them tidy and begin working circularly as described above for Many-Color I-cord.

▲ *I-cord finished with a straight end.* Knit using the next color in your sequence until 1 stitch remains, then slip the last stitch. Slide the stitches to the other end of the needle and switch it to the left hand. The slipped stitch will be a different color from the rest. On the next row, using the next color in your sequence, knit 1 stitch less and slip the remaining stitches. Repeat, working one stitch less on each row until you have worked the last color, knitting just 1 stitch and slipping all the rest. Cut all the yarns. Find the end attached to the last full row you knitted, pull it across the back under all the other loose ends, and pull it through the stitches.

RUFFLES SOCKS

Ruffles adorn these cozy socks for big and little girls.

Measurements (all Child sizes)			
	Small	Medium	Large
Fits US Shoe Size	2–7	8–12	13–6
Fits Foot Length	3½"–5½"	5¾"–7"	7½"–9½"
	(9–14 cm)	(15–18 cm)	(19–24 cm)

Yarn   Plymouth Happy Feet, 90% superwash merino wool/10% nylon, 192 yd (176 m)/ 1.75 oz (50 g), color #09, 2 skeins

For contrasting toes and ruffles, about 150 yards of Cherry Tree Hill Supersock Solids, 100% superwash merino wool (420 yds (384 m)/4 oz (113 g) per skein), Tangerine

Needles   One 5-needle set of US 2 7"- or 8"-long (2.75 mm) double-pointed needles, *or size needed to achieve correct gauge*

Gauge   32 stitches = 4" (10 cm) in stockinette stitch

Chinese Waves Pattern Stitch
(MULTIPLE OF 2 STITCHES)
ROUND 1   *P1, slip 1 purlwise wyif; repeat from * around.
ROUND 2   Knit.
ROUND 3   *Slip 1 purlwise wyif, P1; repeat from * around.
ROUND 4   Knit.

Ruffles Socks

Stitch Key

	Knit
−	Purl
⊻	Slip purlwise, with yarn in front

Working the Leg

	Small	Medium	Large
SETUP ROUND Cast on	40 sts	48 sts	56 sts
Arrange stitches as follows:			
Needles 1 and 3	10 sts	12 sts	14 sts
Needle 2	20 sts	24 sts	28 sts
Join beginning and end of round, being careful not to twist knitting.			
ROUNDS 1–10: Work circularly in Chinese Waves Pattern Stitch.			
ROUNDS 11–13: Knit.			
ROUND 14: Purl.			

	Small	Medium	Large
ROUNDS 15–20: Knit.			
ROUND 21 Purl.			
ROUNDS 22–27: Knit.			
ROUND 28: Purl.			
NEXT ROUNDS: Work in stockinette until measurement from cast on is	4" (10 cm)	4½" (11 cm)	4¾" (12 cm)

Working the Heel Flap

Using Needle 3, continue knitting across Needle 1 until 1 stitch remains, P1. Stitches are now evenly divided between two needles. Turn and begin working back across the needle you just finished, as follows:

WRONG-SIDE ROW Slip 1, K2, purl across until 3 stitches remain, K2, P1.

RIGHT-SIDE ROW Slip 1, knit across until 1 stitch remains, P1.

	Small	Medium	Large
Repeat these two rows until there are the following number of garter ridges along edge of heel flap:	10	12	14

End with a wrong-side row.

Shaping the Heel

	Small	Medium	Large
ROW 1 (RS): K___, ssk, K1, turn.	12 sts	14 sts	16 sts
ROW 2 (WS): Slip 1, P5, P2tog, P1, turn.			
ROW 3: Slip 1 purlwise, knit until 1 stitch remains before the gap formed by the last turning, ssk, K1, turn.			
ROW 4: Slip 1 purlwise, purl until 1 stitch remains before the gap, P2tog, P1, turn.			
Repeat Rows 3 and 4 until all the stitches of the heel flap have been worked. On the last two rows, you will be unable to work the final K1 or P1. Simply turn and work back on the other side. On this needle, *you now have*	12 sts	14 sts	16 sts

	Small	Medium	Large

This is the Bottom Needle; the needle you have not been using is the Top Needle. Knit across the Bottom Needle on the right side.

Picking Up Stitches

	Small	Medium	Large
Using an empty needle, knit up 1 stitch in each of the slipped-edge stitches along the right edge of the heel flap. (You are already at a corner of the heel flap, just keep on going around the corner to the left.) For a neat cabled edge, knit through just the outer half of the stitch. On this needle (now called First Side Needle), *you now have*	10 sts	12 sts	14 sts

Using another empty needle, knit across the Top Needle.

	Small	Medium	Large
Using another empty needle, knit up 1 stitch in each of the slipped-edge stitches along the left edge of the heel flap. On this needle (now called Second Side Needle), *you now have*	10 sts	12 sts	14 sts

Knit half of the stitches from the Bottom Needle onto the Second Side Needle and slip the remaining stitches to the First Side Needle. Your sock is now on three needles again. The beginning of the round is now the center bottom of the foot.

Decreasing for the Gusset

Begin working circularly again.

ROUND 1: Knit.

ROUND 2

FIRST SIDE NEEDLE: Knit until 2 stitches remain, K2tog.

TOP NEEDLE: Knit across.

SECOND SIDE NEEDLE: Ssk, knit to the end of the needle.

	Small	Medium	Large
NEXT ROUNDS Repeat Rounds 1 and 2 until you have	40 sts	48 sts	56 sts

	Small	Medium	Large
Work even in stockinette stitch (knit each round) until the foot of the sock measures ___ less than the desired length.	1" (2.5 cm)	1⅜" (3.5 cm)	1⅝" (4 cm)

Shaping the Toe

Change to contrast color, if desired.

Note: The beginning of round is at the center bottom of foot (between the two Side Needles).

ROUND 1

FIRST SIDE NEEDLE: Knit across until 3 stitches remain, K2tog, K1.

TOP NEEDLE: K1, ssk, knit across until 3 stitches remain, K2tog, K1.

SECOND SIDE NEEDLE: K1, ssk, knit to end of needle.

ROUND 2: Knit.

	Small	Medium	Large
NEXT ROUNDS: Repeat Rounds 1 and 2	5 times	6 times	7 times
You now have	20 sts	24 sts	28 sts
NEXT ROUNDS: Repeat Round 1	2 times	3 times	4 times
You now have	12 sts	12 sts	12 sts

Closing the Toe

Using the Second Side Needle, knit all the stitches from the First Side Needle. Your stitches should now be evenly divided, with the bottom stitches on one needle, and the remaining stitches on the Top Needle. Cut yarn, leaving an 8" (20 cm) tail. Use a tapestry or yarn needle to weave toe of sock together (see Kitchener Stitch, page 298 for instructions).

Making the Ruffles

Make a ruffle in each purl round at the top of the sock, as follows.

	Small	Medium	Large
SETUP ROUND: Fold top of sock to inside along purl round. Beginning at center back of sock, using an empty double-pointed needle, and working along folded edge of sock, knit up one stitch in each purl stitch, until the needle holds	10 sts	12 sts	14 sts

Repeat for 3 more needles, which should take you all the way around the sock.

ROUNDS 1 AND 2:   *K1, yo; repeat from * around.

BIND-OFF ROUND: K1 *yo, pass stitch over, K1, pass stitch over; repeat from * around until all stitches have been bound off.

Cut yarn, leaving an 8" (20 cm) end. Using a yarn needle, join last bound-off stitch to first bound-off stitch, then weave end down through ruffle to the sock. Pull ends of yarn to inside. Weave in ends on inside.

I-Cord Coasters

Mix and match colors and use your choice of I-cord embellishment on these quick-to-knit coasters.

Measurements   About 3" (7.5 cm) in diameter, not including I-cord borders

Yarn   Kid Hollow semi-worsted, 50% wool/50% mohair, 4 oz (113 g)/180 yd (164.5 m), one skein of each of the following: MC: Tangerine ; C1: Wild Strawberry; C2: UVA Orange; C3: Eosine Red

Needles   One set of US 7 (4.5 mm) double-pointed needles, *or size needed to achieve correct gauge*

Gauge   20 stitches = 4" (10 cm) in garter stitch

Knitting the Base

SETUP ROUND: Using MC, cast on 8 stitches and divide among 3 needles. Join beginning and end of round, being careful not to twist.

ROUND 1:   *K1, M1; repeat from * around (16 stitches).

ROUND 2:   Purl.

ROUND 3:   *K2, M1; repeat from * around (24 stitches).

ROUND 4:   Purl.

ROUND 5:   *K3, M1; repeat from * around (32 stitches).

ROUND 6:   Purl.

ROUND 7:   *K4, M1; repeat from * around (40 stitches).

ROUND 8:   Purl.

ROUND 9:   *K5, M1; repeat from * around (48 stitches).

ROUND 10:   Purl.

Cut yarn. Select one of the trim options below.

I-Cord Border

Tie C1 to end of MC. Turn to wrong side. Using C1, cast on 3 stitches at beginning of needle. Work I-cord Bind Off (see page 249 for instructions) until all stitches have been bound off.

Cut yarn, leaving a 6" (15 cm) tail. Sew end of I-cord to beginning of I-cord, then bury the end inside the cord.

Looped Border

Tie C2 to end of main color. Work Decorative Overlapping Loops, making each 10 rows long (see page 250 for instructions). If you find all the double-pointed needles unwieldy, slip the coaster onto a circular needle.

Multicord Border

Using C1, work I-cord Bind-off (see page 249 for instructions), then, using C3, work a second row of Applied I-cord (see page 249 for instructions). As you work the second row of I-cord, work into the same stitch again every fourth row, to insure that the new I-cord is long enough to go around the outer edge.

Finishing

Pull any ends near the I-cord inside it to hide them. Weave the tail at the cast on around the small hole at the center and tighten to close up the hole. Weave in any remaining ends on the wrong side.

Multicord Border

I-cord Border

Looped Border

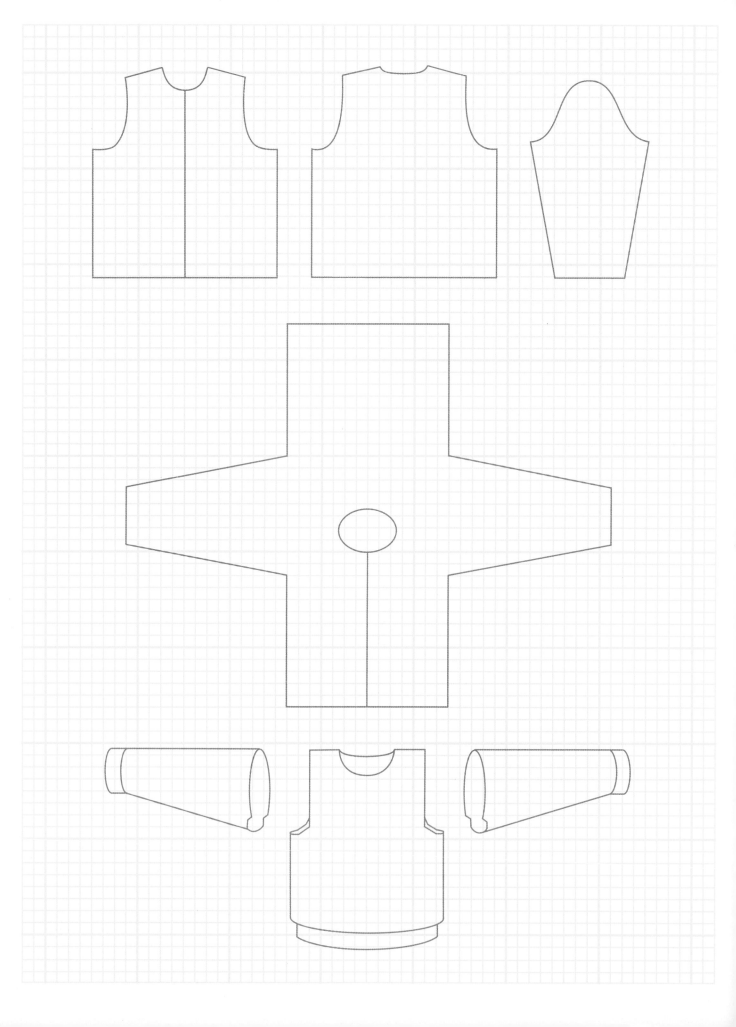

9 DESIGN WORKSHOP

You've experimented with color combinations; put color theory to work; and tried stripes, stranding, and intarsia. You may even have delved into the esoteric mysteries of double knitting, twined knitting, or entrelac. You've discovered a few tips and tricks you didn't already know and now you're excited about all the possible ways to put color to work in your next project. Now put these techniques into practice: find a project that uses a technique you're interested in, modify instructions for a project so that you can use techniques in this book, or design a project from scratch.

If you chose the first option, just refer to the related chapter in this book to clarify the instructions and check for tips to make the knitting easier and improve the finished product. If you're planning to change a garment design, some modifications are more difficult to incorporate than others, so you need to consider their effects on the entire garment. If you set out to design the perfect project from start to finish, you need to consider everything from the basic shape and size to the finishing details and embellishments.

{Modifying Existing Patterns}

If you're going to change a project to add some colorwork, begin with a little planning and make some important decisions before you start. First, review what you plan to do and analyze how significant the changes will be.

Consider This

For instance, do you want to add stripes, blocks of color, sections of intarsia, or make contrasting borders? Does the project already have a pattern stitch worked in one color, but you want to add more colors? These are all things that change the way the garment looks, but don't change the nature of the fabric. You can make these changes without any worries, as long as you're using the same type and weight of yarn that the original instructions call for and are working at the same gauge. (For more information, see Fabric Qualities, page 284.)

Other changes — such as introducing stranded, twined, or mosaic knitting, or changing the structure of a pattern stitch — alter the qualities of the fabric, so approach them with caution. You will be most successful if the resulting fabric is the same thickness and has the same amount of stretch as the original design. It may also be important for it to have the same amount of curl. A scarf or shawl, for example, should usually be made in a pattern stitch that doesn't curl, while a sweater or hat can be made from a fabric that may or may not curl. The proportion of rows to stitches may also change when the structure of the fabric changes. If the original design has diagonal shaping (along a V-neck or raglan sleeves, for example), these may no longer be at the correct angle. The best way to check for potential problems is to knit one swatch according to the original pattern directions and another with the changes you plan to make. Compare their thickness, stretch, gauge in both stitches and rows, and amount of curl. If they are very similar, you can probably make the changes successfully. If not, you may want to reconsider.

If you plan to modify just a section of the garment, for example, by adding a band of a pattern stitch or Fair Isle, it's important to consider the transition on either side of the patterned area. Stranded knitting tends to pull in, so that section of the fabric will be narrower. Pattern stitches, when only a narrow band is worked, may stretch or compress to match the plain areas above or below, or they may be wider or narrower. Adjust the number of stitches by increasing or decreasing before and after the patterned band, or change needle size in the patterned section to control the width. It may be possible, if the fabric is stretchy, to even up the width by blocking. Work out the details, including blocking, on a swatch. If the transition to and from your patterned area is a bit messy, you could work 1 or 2 rows in stockinette or reverse stockinette to make a neat boundary.

{Designing from Scratch}

To create a successful design of your own, begin by making a series of important decisions about what you want to make, including its construction, size, fabric, finishing, and embellishments.

Concept. Once you've decided what you're going to make, whether it's a hat, scarf, socks, mittens, sweater, vest, or shawl, figure out how big it should be. Make a sketch or drawing of your idea. You only need a simple schematic diagram, showing the basic shape with measurements. Sweaters are the most complex of these constructions and are almost always intended to fit a particular person, so they demand more preplanning than many of the others. You can figure out the appropriate measurements by measuring the body it should fit and then adding ease (see Easy Does It at right), by measuring a similar garment that fits, from a sewing pattern (allowing additional ease for the thicker hand-knit fabric), from sweater design software, or from the Craft Yarn Council of America guidelines (see Appendix).

If the garment is constructed in stages, decide the order you'll knit it in. For example, hats can be knit from the top down, increasing as you work, or from the bottom up, decreasing to shape the crown. Sweaters — the most structurally complicated garments — can be made in many ways.

EASY DOES IT

Ease is the difference between the measurement of a body and the garment that fits it comfortably. The amount of ease required depends on how thick the fabric is and how tightly you want it to fit. A skin-tight, stretchy garment may actually measure smaller than the body because it's designed to stretch when worn. Because of the thickness of the fabric, a bulky sweater must have more ease to fit comfortably than a thinner sweater.

After you choose the structure and shape of your project, consider the finishing details:

» *Seams.* Will they be decorative or invisible?
» *Shoulders.* Will the shoulders be sewn, or joined with three-needle bind off?
» *Sleeves.* Will you pick up stitches and knit them down, or will they be knit separately and attached later?

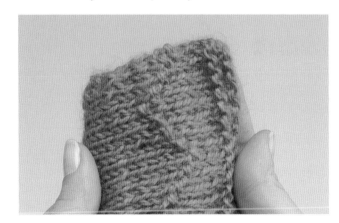

▲ *Embellishments.* Do you need to prepare for them? Perhaps include a row of purled stitches as a base for a ruffle or I-cord?

{Sweater Architecture}

Your approach to sweater construction affects the final result, and your choice is in part dependent on the sweater style you have in mind. You can work circularly from the top down or the bottom up. You can also work flat, either sideways (from cuff to cuff) or working each part of the sweater separately.

Dropped Shoulder

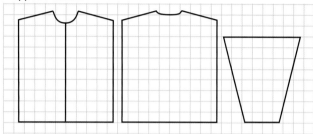

Square Shoulder

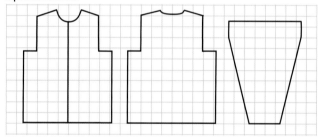

Set-In Sleeve

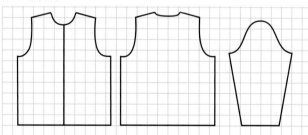

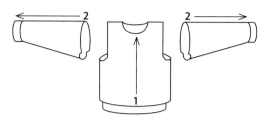

drop shoulder with underarm shaping

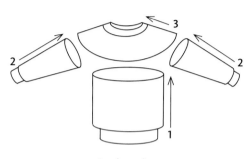

circular yoke

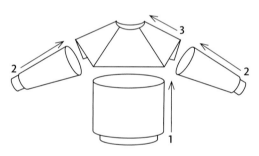

raglan sleeves

▲ *Flat sweaters.* If you are knitting a sweater flat, you can work the pieces in any order, then join them together and add the borders. Although sweaters are traditionally knit from bottom to top, the individual parts may be knit in any direction you like. Flat knitting is best for intarsia designs, pattern stitches that are difficult to work circularly, and for yarns or fibers that tend to stretch, because seams help support the garment amd tailored shaping makes it fit better.

▲ *Circular sweaters* require that you work the sections of a garment in a particular order, either from the bottom up or from the top down. The drawings here represent three possible circular structures, including the order of construction. Circular design lends itself best to stranded knitting, pattern stitches most easily worked in the round, and yarns with good elasticity, like wool. Some sweaters knit in the round are constructed like traditional Fair Isle and Scandinavian stranded sweaters. These are worked circularly and then cut after the body is completed to make openings at the front, armholes, and neck. (For more information about this technique, see Demystifying Steeks on page 162.)

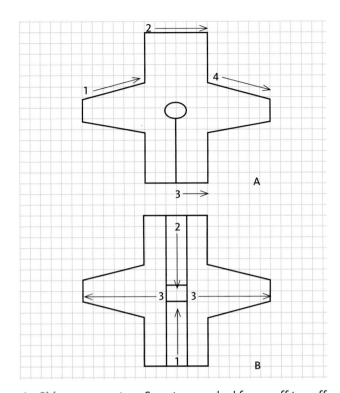

Exercise your options. The garment shapes presented here are the most basic. For example, almost all the necklines are simple, round-neck openings. Other options include boat necks, V-necks, lower scoop necks, and asymmetrical neck openings. Sleeves can be long, short, belled, puffed, or nonexistent, to mention just a few possibilities. There are excellent resources available for those who want to design their own garments. (For suggested books on knitting design, see page 312.) More and more sweater design software is also becoming available, which allows you to enter your measurements; choose the neckline, ease, shape, and other details; and then produce instructions, schematics, or both. These programs do not take the qualities of the fabric — such as stretch, drape, and thickness — into account, so you as the designer must still exercise some judgment.

▲ *Sideways sweaters.* Sweaters worked from cuff to cuff (sideways) are usually knitted flat, all in one piece (A). To reduce the bulk you have to handle while working the second sleeve of a large sweater, make both halves separately from the cuff to the center and then join them at the center back. For a seamless join, use Kitchener stitch at the point where a plain row would naturally fall. You can also make a firm seam at this point to help prevent a heavy sweater from stretching out of shape. Leave the center front open for a cardigan, or for a pullover, join it as you do at the back. Sideways sweaters can also be constructed from the center out, by working center front and back panels vertically, then picking up stitches on either side and working out to the cuffs (B) (see also chapter 4, page 131). This same shape can be worked from front to back or back to front, casting on to shape the sleeves when you reach the underarm, then binding off again to work the rest of the body. The sideways structure is best for loose, unfitted garments, in yarns with good elasticity, like wool. There are few seams to support these garments, so they often stretch and become oversized even if not originally designed that way. Any color technique that is convenient in flat knitting, such as intarsia, works for a sideways sweater.

{Fabric Qualities}

Ask yourself what kind of fabric will work best for the project you have in mind. For a shawl or baby blanket, it could be soft and stretchy; for a structured bag, it could be tight and stiff, so that it holds its shape. For a placemat or a scarf that must lie flat, it may be important that it not curl. You could choose warm wool for winter or cool cotton for summer. Select soft fibers to wear against the skin and coarser fibers for outerwear or rugs. Think about whether the fabric needs to be different in different sections of the project: the strap versus the bag, the collar versus the sweater, or the ribbing versus the body. You can limit yourself to just one pattern stitch or employ several different patterns. The qualities of the fabric you create are dependent upon three things: the yarn itself, the pattern stitch and color technique, and how tightly you knit.

▲ *Yarn.* Yarns are made of all sorts of fibers: wool, mohair, and other animal fibers; silk; cotton, flax, and other plant fibers; and petroleum products, such as acrylic and nylon. Each of these fibers behaves differently.

Yarn comes in a variety of thicknesses and is prepared in a variety of ways, can be spun or unspun, and plied or not plied. Different yarns look and behave differently, depending on fiber content and structure. For a garment that's not too heavy and holds its shape well, look for a springy wool or wool-blend yarn. For a fabric that's silky and drapes beautifully, try cotton, silk, rayon, unbrushed mohair, or similar nonstretchy yarns. To create crisp, clear stitches, use a yarn that is either a single ply or has 3 or more plies; avoid loosely twisted 2-ply yarns, which don't show textured stitches well.

Pattern stitches. Your choice of pattern stitch and color technique affects the texture, elasticity, and thickness of the fabric. For example, slipped stitches or strands running across the back tend to pull the fabric tighter, reduce the amount of stretch, and increase the thickness, while knitting into the stitch below makes the fabric wider, looser, and loftier. To make your project as successful as possible, think about how the fabric ought to behave.

Gauge. The size of your knitting needles and how tightly you knit also influences the stretch, thickness, and flexibility of the fabric. Start with the size you think will work best, based on your own experience or the recommendation on the yarn's label. If the fabric is too tight, try larger needles. If it's too loose, use smaller needles. The fabric's appearance also should influence your decision on needle size. If the fabric feels nice, but the pattern stitch looks too loose or uneven, then you'll need to work it more tightly. If you work it tightly enough for the pattern to look its best, the fabric may be stiffer and thicker than you'd like. In a case like this you need to compromise, find a different yarn, or try a different pattern stitch.

Swatches. Even if you conscientiously select what you think is the best yarn for a project, it may not behave the way you expect, so it's absolutely necessary to knit samples to test for the best combination of yarn, pattern, and needles. An 8" (20 cm) square sample swatch usually gives you a good idea of how the fabric will behave. Once you have a swatch that satisfies you, there are still a few more things you should do before you can trust your gauge measurement.

» Wash and dry the swatch the same way the garment will be cleaned, measuring before and after to check for shrinkage or growth.

» If you plan to block and stretch the fabric, then you should also do this to the swatch before you measure it.

» Remember gravity. Knitting stretches. Heavy, loose knitting stretches more. A thick cotton sweater, knit loosely, is longer when worn than it is while lying flat and well-behaved for measurement. Hang your swatch by the upper edge for a few days, perhaps with a little weight (such as a row of clothespins) attached to the bottom. Measure it before and after to see how much stretch to allow for.

MEASURING GAUGE ACCURATELY

The stitches may be distorted at the ends of rows and at the top and bottom, so measure across the center of the swatch, avoiding all the edges. Measure both stitches and rows over at least 4" (10 cm) to get an accurate figure, then divide the number of stitches or rows by the length you measured to find the exact number of stitches or rows per inch (or centimeter). When there are multiple pattern stitches, or plain stockinette areas interspersed with patterns, measure each of them individually and record them separately if the gauge varies.

Swatching gives you a chance to learn the pattern stitch, audition the colors, make adjustments, and determine whether you love or hate working the pattern. It's always a bad idea to spend tens or hundreds of hours doing something you hate, so it's best to know that you'll enjoy the work before making a commitment to a lengthy relationship. If there will be multiple pattern areas, test the transitions between them. You may need to increase or decrease the number of stitches to keep the fabric the same width, or the first row of one pattern may look awkward adjacent to the last row of another. In cases like these, smooth the transition by using a few rows of stockinette, reverse stockinette, or garter as a visual intermediary.

▲ *Work out shaping.* The swatch also provides an opportunity to work out details of shaping while maintaining the pattern stitch. If your garment will have shaping for armholes or a round neck, make a curved edge on your swatch that mimics them. When the swatch is square, bind off about 1" (2.5 cm) at the beginning of a right-side row. Decrease 1 stitch at the beginning of the next few right-side rows, until you've removed about another inch (2.5 cm) of stitches, then work even for a couple of inches. Test the borders by adding one along this curved edge. Try out any straight borders along the straight side or bottom edges. (For discussions of sizing borders properly, see pages 240 and 287.)

{Developing the Pattern}

Use the schematic with measurements in conjunction with the gauge from the fabric you designed to calculate each garment measurement in stitches or rows and add the stitch and row counts to your diagram.

Adjusting for pattern stitches. If a change in pattern stitch requires increases, decreases, or a change in needle size, note this at the point where it occurs. Don't forget the stitch count for any ribbing or other borders that are knit as part of each piece. You may need to adjust the width a bit to fit in pattern repeats agreeably. There is also the disheartening possibility that you'll discover your pattern stitch doesn't fit comfortably into the available number of stitches for the size you want to make. If there are too few stitches, you may need to modify your pattern to make it narrower or find a thinner yarn and start your fabric design over. If there are too many stitches, you may need to add a partial pattern repeat at both edges, add more pattern repeats overall, enlarge motifs within the pattern, add side panels in a different pattern, or find a thicker yarn.

Estimating row counts. Row calculations are not always necessary. In a straight piece of the garment using a small repeating pattern, you can just work until the piece is the required length, always allowing for any expected stretching. When shaping pieces such as tapered sleeves or raglan armholes, when working sideways sweaters, or when there are large pattern motifs, you'll need to calculate the number of rows to make sure everything will fit. For complex patterns, you may find it most useful to draw the shape of the garment on graph paper (allowing one square for each stitch), then fill in the patterns within the garment shape and add symbols to indicate shaping details such as increases and decreases. Indicate the direction of the knitting using arrows, if you think you'll become confused.

Time to knit! When you're ready to begin knitting, start at the cast-on edge of each piece, cast on the required number of stitches, and then work the shape according to the schematic or graph that you've made. If you feel uncomfortable just working from the drawing, you may write out the instructions in words.

Design as you go. A great advantage to knitting from your own designs is that you can make adjustments to the design as you work. If there's something that looked good in the swatch, but doesn't in the full-sized garment, change it. Are you bored with the pattern stitch? You could work some sections plain or in a different pattern. Check the measurements of your knitting against your schematic. If it's not coming out the correct size, figure out why and make modifications. Perhaps your knitting has become tighter or looser and you need to change needle size to match the proper gauge. Is the neckline the wrong size? Adapt by making a wider or narrower border than you originally planned. Look critically at your work as you knit: you'll either love what you see, or you'll discover problems early so you can fix them.

{Putting It All Together}

The structure of the garment dictates at least some of the finishing. For example, if the fronts, back, and sleeves are worked separately, then you need to join them somehow. While you were knitting, you may have had ideas for embellishments. Before you put the pieces together, consider whether any of these will be easier to add before seaming. If so, embellish first, then put the pieces together and add the borders. You'll find methods of joining and adding borders in chapter 8.

Getting the Borders Right

Of all the aspects of finishing that influence the success of a design, the borders are the most important. They are embellishments that add a finishing touch to any project. They prevent the edges from curling. But, most significantly, they are absolutely crucial to the stability of the garment because they support it, preventing it from stretching out of shape.

▲ *Neck borders* are especially critical because they must be elastic enough to go over the wearer's head easily, the inner edge should connect smoothly to the body of the garment, and the border must be firm enough to prevent the entire top of the garment from drooping. Working samples, measuring for gauge, and calculating the number of required stitches at both the outer and inner edges of the borders can make it possible to create perfect finishes on the first attempt. See chapter 8 for more information on curved borders.

▲ *Ribbing at the cuffs and bottom* needs to stretch easily, but it must also return to its original width after stretching or the edge of the garment will look loose and sloppy. Assuming you're working in wool, when adding ribbing to the bottom of a stockinette body or sleeve, use needles two sizes smaller and 10 percent fewer stitches for the border. For other fibers that aren't as elastic and tend to stretch out of shape, you may want to use even smaller needles and as much as 15 or 20 percent fewer stitches. Another option for these problematic fibers is to design bottom borders that don't need to stretch and return to their original width. Instead of the ubiquitous ribbing, consider substituting garter stitch, a decorative scalloped edge, or picot or lace borders. In this case, you might not use a smaller needle or reduce the number of stitches, because you want the border to hang smoothly from the bottom of the garment without pulling in. As always, test these on your swatch to be sure that the proposed border won't be too tight or too loose.

Other decorative borders. Worked in multiple colors and in pattern stitches other than ribbing, decorative borders require additional experimentation: knit swatches in the border pattern, measure its gauge, and calculate how many stitches will make the border the correct length. This ensures that the borders will be both effective visually and functional in the actual garment. Remember that each pattern stitch and color technique has its own special properties, so don't expect them to all behave the same way.

{Problem Solving}

If you've no experience with knitting design, you may expect the design process to work this way: You begin with a comprehensive plan for what you want to make and the perfect yarn to make it with. The pattern you design fits perfectly into the width and height that produces a garment in the correct size. The colors cooperate perfectly within the pattern. In other words, everything works out perfectly from start to finish, without any frustrations or adjustments.

Realistically, you may have yarn and no idea what to do with it, or you have a great idea but can't find an appropriate yarn or can find only one of the colors you need. When this happens, as it inevitably will, don't despair. Save the ideas that didn't work for future projects and begin experimenting. Sometimes the most innovative and satisfying creations grow directly out of frustration during the design process, and the end result is an unexpected triumph.

If your yarn doesn't behave the way you expect, take some time to figure out what would make it look its best, then design your garment to accomplish this. If the colors don't interact the way you want, analyze why they don't. Would they interact better if the areas of color were larger or smaller? If one color were removed? If another were added? If the scale of the yarn doesn't cooperate with the scale of the pattern stitch to fit into your garment properly, is there a way to redesign the pattern or the garment so that it will fit?

It's very rare for even an experienced designer to conceive, plan, and execute a design without rethinking or reworking some aspect of it. The creative process is not a linear one — it's a cycle. You can expect to first develop a preliminary plan for your design, trying to make the decisions discussed above. As you work out the details, problems with your design and limitations imposed by your materials will force you to rethink those answers. When you attempt to actually knit something according to your plan, you'll discover difficulties that didn't become apparent until it was on your needles. You may need to make several attempts, with modifications of the plan in between, to arrive at a finished product that satisfies you. So don't be disheartened when you have to circle back and make changes. The process itself is the creative challenge; knitting the project is just the final validation of the design.

Color, texture, pattern, composition, fiber, and fit — there are so many glorious aspects of knitting design that it never loses its fascination! Whether you take your inspiration from nature, from art, from your own imagination, or from other designers, the information and techniques in this book will provide you with the knowledge and flexibility to do more in your knitting than you ever thought possible, to see the interactions of these design elements in a new light, and, even if you can't fully control them, to manipulate and experiment with them both to your heart's delight and your knitting hands' contentment.

APPENDIX

{Glossary of Techniques}

Bind Off

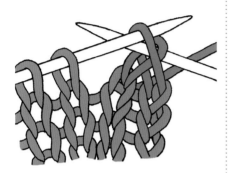

Standard bind off. K1, *K1, insert the left needle into the stitch on the right, pass it over the other stitch and off the needle; repeat from *. At the end of the row, cut the yarn and pull through the last stitch to prevent it from unraveling.

Buttonhole Stitch

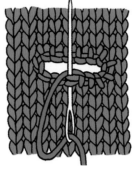

Sewing stitch used to secure buttonholes to prevent fraying.

Cast Ons

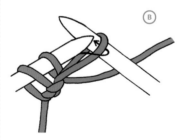

Cable cast on. A firm cast on with a ropelike edge. Cast on 2 stitches using the knitted cast on. *Insert the right needle between the 2 stitches (A). Knit up a stitch, leaving the 2 original stitches on the left needle (B). Insert the left needle up into the new stitch from the front and slip it off the right needle. Repeat from *, knitting each new stitch between the last 2 stitches cast on.

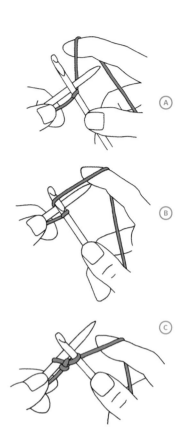

Crocheted cast on. Also called the bind-off cast on, because its chain mimics a bound-off edge. It may be used as a provisional cast on if worked in waste yarn or as a decorative cast on if worked in a contrasting yarn. You need a crochet hook in addition to one of your knitting needles and yarn. Make a slip knot and place it on the crochet hook. Cross the crochet hook in front of the knitting needle (A). *Bring the yarn behind the knitting needle (B), chain a stitch with the crochet hook (C). Repeat from *. Note that the yarn may be held in either hand.

If this is worked in a contrasting yarn, either as a decorative or a provisional cast on, repeat until the desired number of stitches is on the needle, cut the contrasting yarn and pull it through the last chain stitch to secure. Change colors and begin knitting as usual. To remove the waste yarn later, pick this tail back out, unravel the chain, and place the stitches on a knitting needle.

If this is worked to put a chain across the bottom edge and is not in contrasting yarn, stop when there is one less than the desired number of stitches, transfer the final chain stitch from the crochet hook to the knitting needle. Do not cut the yarn — just continue knitting with it.

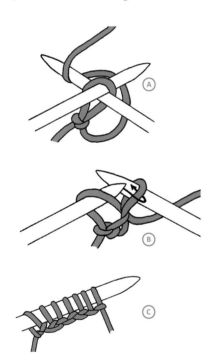

Knitted cast on. A loose cast on, useful when edges need to be stretchy or when loops are desired for fringe. Make a slip knot, leaving a short tail and place it on your left needle. *Knit a stitch, leaving the original stitch on the needle (A). Insert the left needle up into the new stitch from the front (B), tighten up the stitch. Repeat from * until you have enough stitches (C).

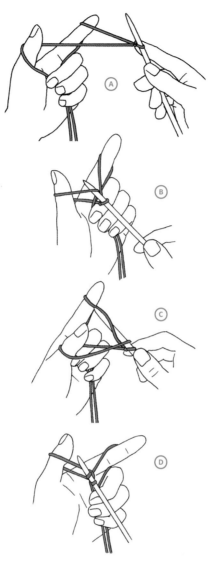

Long-tail cast on. Pull out a length of yarn for the long tail, about three times as long as the width of your knitting, plus a few inches. Make a slip knot at this point and place it on the needle. Hold the needle in your right hand with the index finger on the slip knot to prevent it from sliding off. Arrange the yarn in your left hand, with the tail over your thumb and the working yarn over your index finger (A). *Insert the needle up through the loop around your thumb (B), bring it over and behind the front

strand on your index finger (C), then back out through the thumb loop to form a stitch (D). Drop the thumb loop, place your thumb behind the long tail and use it to tighten the loop. Repeat from *.

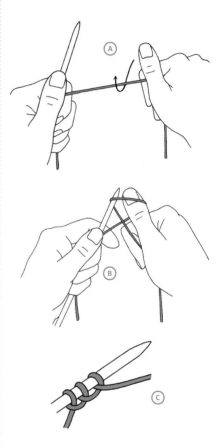

Loop cast on. A very simple, very loose cast on, useful when you want to be able to adjust the tension easily after the knitting is completed. It is just a series of half-hitches placed on the needle. This is only one of many ways to work this cast on: Hold the cut end of the yarn against your left palm. *Bring your thumb to the front under the yarn (A). Slip the needle up into the loop on your thumb (B). Slip your thumb out (C). Repeat from *.

Cast Ons (continued)

Ribbed cable cast on. Work as for the cable cast on (see page 292), but alternately knit and purl between the last two stitches. To purl, insert the needle between the two stitches from the back.

Circular Knitting

A method of knitting that makes a tube. Larger tubes, such as bodies of sweaters, are made on circular needles; smaller tubes, such as socks and mittens, on sets of 4 or 5 double-pointed needles (dpns) or on two circular needles.

Circular needles. Cast on as usual, then spread the stitches from point to point on the needle. Make sure that the cast-on row doesn't spiral around the needle at any point. Join the beginning and end of round as described below (see page 295), then work continuously around.

Double-pointed needles (dpns). Cast on all stitches on one needle, then slip some of the stitches to two or three other needles. Arrange the needles to form a triangle or square. Make sure the right side is facing you and the cast-on row doesn't spiral around any needle at any point. Join the beginning and end of the round using one of the methods described below (see page 295). Using an empty needle, knit across the first cast-on needle. When you are finished, you have emptied a needle. Use this to knit across the second needle. Continue around, working each needle in succession, using the needle you just emptied as the new working needle.

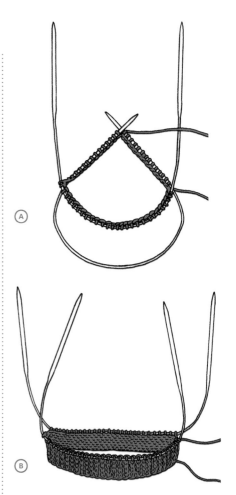

Ⓐ

Ⓑ

Two circular needles. Cast on half the stitches on one needle and half on the other. Bring the needle points with the first and last cast-on stitches together, being careful not to twist or untwist the cast on where the other ends of the two needles come together, and check to make sure that the knitting doesn't spiral around either needle at any point (A). Join the beginning and end of round as described below (see page 295). Holding both ends of the first needle, work all of those stitches onto that same needle. Put down the first needle and pick up both ends of the second needle. Work all of the stitches on the second needle onto itself. Continue around, alternating needles (B).

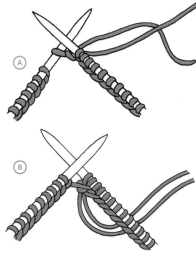

Joining into a round. There are several options:

» Cast on one extra stitch. Arrange your knitting so the last cast on stitch is on the right-hand needle. Slip this stitch to the left needle (A). Knit the first two stitches on the left needle together, using the working yarn and the cast-on tail held together (B). Drop the cast-on tail and continue with the working yarn only. On the next round, treat the double strand of the first stitch as a single stitch. When working K2, P2 ribbing, knit the second stitch using the doubled strands as well.

» Cast on the number of stitches needed. Slip the first stitch from the right needle to the left needle. Insert the right needle into the next stitch on the left needle and pass it over the first stitch. The two stitches have traded places.

Decreases

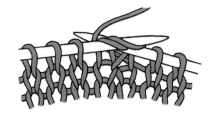

Knit 2 together (K2tog). Insert the right needle into the first two stitches knitwise and knit them together.

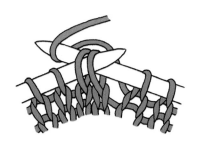

Knit 2 together through the back loop (K2tog tbl). Insert the right needle into the back of the first two stitches knitwise and knit them together.

Purl 2 together (P2tog). Insert the right needle into the first two stitches and purl them together.

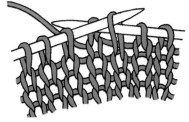

Slip 1, knit 1, pass slipped stitch over (skp). Slip 1 stitch knitwise, knit 1, pass the slipped stitch over the knitted one and off the needle.

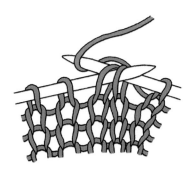

Slip, slip, knit (ssk). Slip 1 stitch knitwise, slip another stitch knitwise, insert the left needle into these two stitches and knit them together.

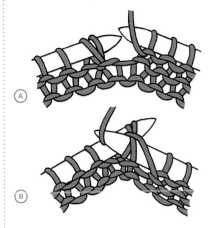

Slip, slip, purl (ssp). Slip 1 stitch knitwise, slip another stitch knitwise, insert the left needle into these two stitches knitwise and slip them back to the left needle together (A). Reinsert the right needle purlwise and purl the two stitches together (B).

Double Decreases

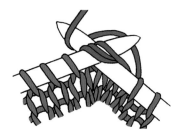

Knit 3 together (K3tog). Insert the right needle into the first 3 stitches knitwise and knit them together.

Purl 3 together (P3tog). Insert the right needle into the first 3 stitches purlwise and purl them together.

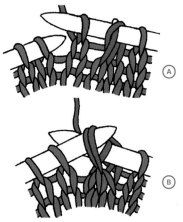

Raised double decrease (Slip 2, K1, p2sso). Insert the right needle knitwise into the first two stitches, as if to knit them together, and slip them to the right needle. Knit 1 (A). Pass the two slipped stitches over the knit stitch and off the needle (B).

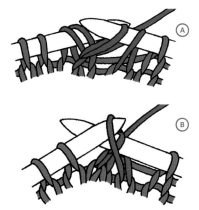

Slip 1, knit 2 together, pass slipped stitch over (slip 1, K2tog, psso). Slip 1 knitwise. Knit 2 together (A). Pass the slipped stitch over (B).

Duplicate Stitch

A method of embroidering with yarn on the surface of the knitting that follows the structure of the knitted stitch.

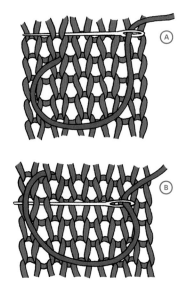

Knit side, horizontal rows. Bring the point of the yarn needle up through the bottom of the stitch. *Sew behind two strands along the top of the stitch (A). Sew back through the bottom of the stitch and under two strands to the bottom of the

next stitch (B). Repeat from *. You may work from either right to left or left to right. Single stitches are also worked using this method.

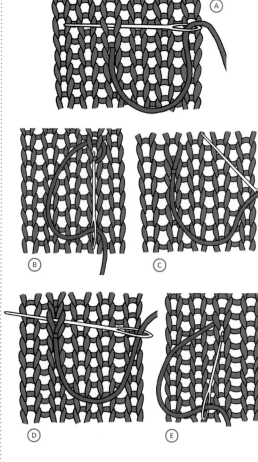

Knit side, vertical columns. Start with the top stitch. Bring the point of the yarn needle up through the bottom of the stitch. Sew behind two strands along the top of the stitch (A). Sew back through the bottom of the stitch and pull the yarn through to the back of the fabric (B). *Bring the needle and yarn up through the center of the next stitch below (C). Sew behind the base of the stitch above, under just the two strands of duplicate stitch (D). Sew back through the bottom of the stitch and pull the yarn through to the back of the fabric (E). Repeat from *.

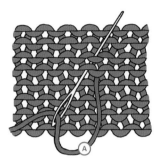

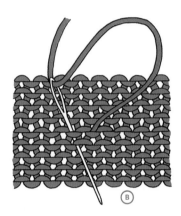

Purl side. The yarn should not show on the knit side of the fabric. This technique is used only for working in ends invisibly or to adjust the tension and alignment of the stitches to improve the appearance of the right side of the fabric. *Sew under two purl bumps from bottom to top (A). Sew under the next two purl bumps from top to bottom (B). Repeat from *. Work right to left or left to right.

Gauge

The tightness (or looseness) of your knitting. This is usually measured in stitches or rows per 4" (10 cm).

Half Hitch

A simple knot formed from a twisted loop. The half hitch is used in the loop cast on and the Make 1 increase. The working yarn can also be tied in a half hitch around a ball of yarn to allow it to be dangled in the air and untwisted.

Increases

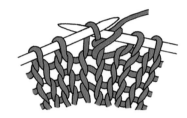

Knit into the front and back. Knit into the stitch, leaving it on the left needle. Bring the right needle to the back of the work, knit into the back loop of the stitch and slip it off the needle.

Make 1 (M1). There are many ways to work the M1 increase:

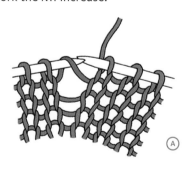

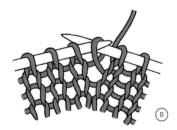

Left slant: lifted. Insert left needle from front under the top strand between the two needles (A), then knit into the back of the stitch to twist it (B).

Left slant: working yarn. Make a small loop of the working yarn close to the needle, twist it clockwise and place it on the needle.

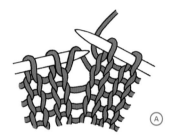

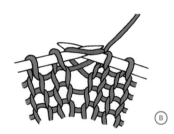

Right slant: lifted. Insert left needle from back under the strand between the two needles (A), then knit into the front of the stitch to twist it (B).

Right slant: working yarn. Make a small loop of the working yarn close to the needle, twist it counterclockwise, and place it on the needle.

Increases *(continued)*

Open. Insert the left needle from the front under strand then knit this new stitch. This makes an increase that is open like a yarn over, but doesn't leave as large a hole.

Yarn over. Work a yarn over on the increase row, then knit into the back of this stitch on the following row to twist it. This makes a left-slanting increase and is useful when the first two options are too tight to work easily. (See also Yarn Over, page 303.)

Double Increases

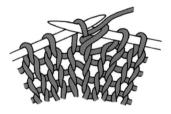

Knit-purl-knit into a stitch. Knit into the stitch as usual, but leave it on the left needle. Bring the yarn to the front, purl into the stitch, yarn back, knit into the stitch, and slip it off the needle.

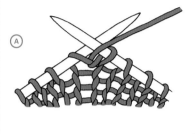

Knit-yo-knit into a stitch. Knit into the stitch as usual, but leave it on the left needle (A). Yarn over, knit into the stitch again, and slip it off the needle (B).

Kitchener Stitch

Hold the two pieces of knitting with wrong sides together. If you are right-handed, point the needles to the right; if you are left-handed, reverse them. Use a yarn needle

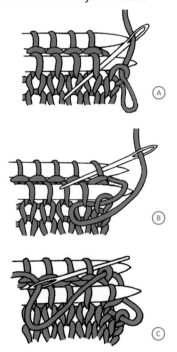

threaded with matching yarn. If the working yarn is hanging at the edge, cut it to a comfortable length and use it.

*Insert the yarn needle knitwise into the first stitch on the front knitting needle and slip it off. Insert the yarn needle into the next stitch on the front knitting needle purlwise, leave it on the knitting needle (A) and gently pull up the slack in the yarn. Insert the yarn needle into the first stitch on the back knitting needle purlwise (B) and slip the stitch off. Insert the yarn needle into the next stitch on the back knitting needle knitwise (C), leave it on the knitting needle and pull up the slack in the yarn. Repeat from *. As you work, adjust the tension of the sewn stitches to match the rows above and below.

These instructions are for stockinette stitch. For garter stitch, repeat the instructions for the front needle on the back needle.

Knit Backward

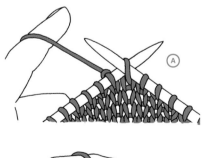

Yarn in left hand. With the knit side facing you, the stitches to be worked on the right-hand needle, and the yarn in back, insert the left needle knitwise (through the front of the stitch to the back of the right needle) into the first stitch on the right needle (A). Bring the yarn over the left (back) needle tip to the front, then under it to the back (B). You may need to let go of the left needle in order to wrap the yarn. Lift the loop of the old stitch over the tip of the left needle with the right needle, or pull it through with the left needle. Slide the right needle out of the loop.

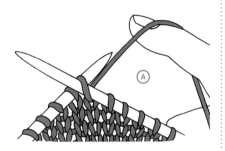

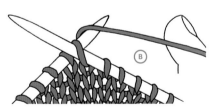

Yarn in right hand. With the knit side facing you and the yarn in back, insert the left needle knitwise (through the front of the stitch to the back of the right needle [A]). Bring the yarn around the left (back) needle tip from back to front (B). Lift the loop of the old stitch over the tip of the left needle with the right needle, or pull it through with the left needle. Slide the right needle out of the loop.

Knit Stitch

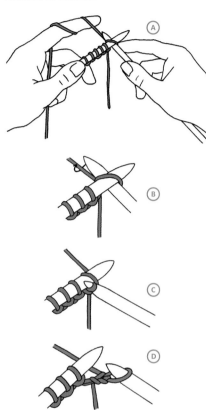

Yarn in left hand. *Insert right-hand needle into the stitch (A). Bring the tip of the needle over and behind the working yarn or use the left hand to wrap the yarn around the needle (B). Hook the yarn back through the stitch with a twist of the right-hand needle (C). Slip the old stitch off the left needle (D). Repeat from *. Keep the yarn near the first joint of your index finger while you work. If it slides up and down, wrap it around the finger once to keep it in place. If the tension on the working yarn is too loose, wrap it once around your index or any other finger to control it. Once you get used to it, this will become a smooth in-and-out movement, rather than separate steps. (See also Purl Stitch, page 301.)

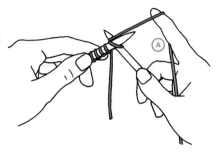

Yarn in right hand. *Insert right-hand needle into the front of the stitch. Wrap the yarn around the needle counterclockwise (A). Pull it through the stitch with tip of needle (B). Slip the old stitch off the left needle (C). Repeat from *. With practice, you will work more quickly and this will become a smooth in-out-and-off motion, rather than separate steps. If you find it difficult to hold the yarn, try wrapping it once around one of your fingers or holding it against your palm with the little and ring fingers. (See also Purl Stitch, page 301.)

Mattress Stitch

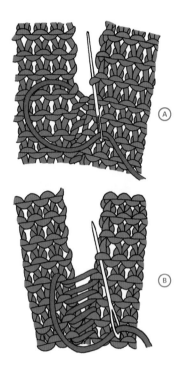

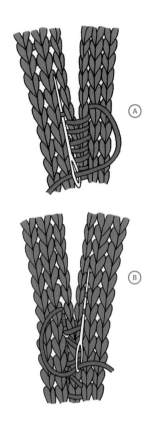

For garter edge stitches. Lay the two pieces side by side on a flat surface with the right side facing you. Thread a yarn needle with matching yarn. Work from bottom to top, sewing through just the bumps at the edge of the fabric. This seam has very little bulk and is reversible (A). For a neater, more substantial but nonreversible seam, sew through the tops of the stitches (curved like a frown) just in from the edge (B). Regardless of which technique you use, pull the yarn tight enough that the sewn lengths are about the same length as the stitches on either side.

For Stockinette edge stitches. Work as for mattress stitch on garter stitch edges, but sew between the edge stitch and the one next to it, under just one strand (A). To make a less bulky seam, sew under two strands with every stitch (B). Work alternately on one side of the seam and then the other, always inserting the needle at the point where the yarn emerges from the previous stitch. Pull the yarn tight enough to draw the two edges together and hide the sewing yarn but loose enough that the seam will stretch a little.

Moss Stitch

A simple pattern stitch that produces a small checkerboard of purled and knitted squares, each 2 stitches wide and 2 rows tall.

CAST ON A MULTIPLE OF 2 STITCHES.

ROW 1: *K2, P2; repeat from *. End with either K2 or P2.

ROW 2: Knit the knit stitches and purl the purl stitches.

ROW 3: Knit the purl stitches and purl the knit stitches.

ROW 4: Knit the knit stitches and purl the purl stitches.

Pick Up

Throughout this book, the terms "pick up" and "pick up and knit" are used interchangeably.

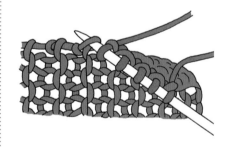

Along garter edges. Insert your needle through the tiny bumps at the end of each garter stitch ridge. Wrap the yarn around the needle and knit the stitch out to the front. This works best on straight edges. For curved edges, like armholes and neck openings, pick up a whole stitch from the edge for a smoother finish, as described for stockinette (below).

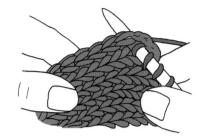

Along stockinette edges. Insert the tip of your needle through the fabric to the back, a whole stitch in from the edge. Wrap the yarn around it and knit the stitch out to the front.

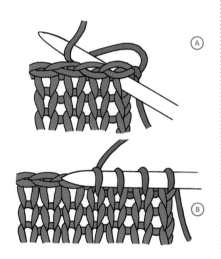

Along the top or bottom. Insert the needle directly into a stitch, wrap the yarn, and knit up a stitch (A). If your knitting is upside down, this is actually the space between 2 stitches, but it looks just like a stitch (B).

Purl Stitch

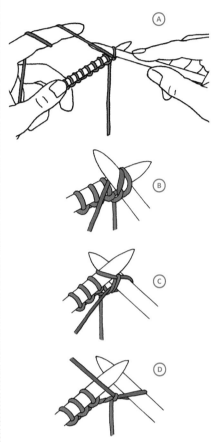

Yarn in left hand. Hold the yarn pulled taut (but not too tight!) in front of the left needle. Insert right-hand needle into the stitch from right to left. Make sure the tip of it is behind the yarn stretching up to your index finger (A). Move your left index finger down and to the front so the yarn is taut over the tip of the right needle (B). Hook the yarn back through the stitch with the right needle (C). Slip the original stitch off the left needle (D). (See also Knit Stitch, page 299)

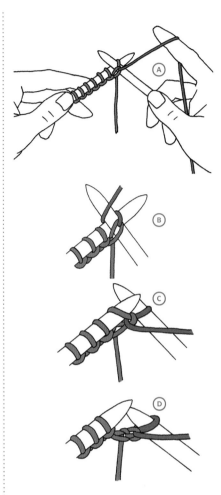

Yarn in right hand. Hold the yarn in front of the needles. Insert the right-hand needle into the stitch from right to left (A). Wrap the yarn around the needle counterclockwise (B). Pull it through the stitch with the right needle tip (C). Slip the original stitch off the left needle (D). (See also Knit Stitch, page 299.)

Seed Stitch

A simple pattern stitch that can be worked on any number of stitches. Repeat K1, P1 across the first row. On subsequent rows, knit the purl stitches and purl the knit stitches. This produces a checkerboard of knits and purls.

Short Row

A method of shaping that involves working partway across a row and then turning back before finishing the row. A series of short rows makes it possible to shape a piece seamlessly or to manipulate the grain of the fabric to make it appear to have been made in separate pieces.

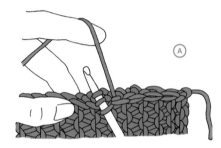

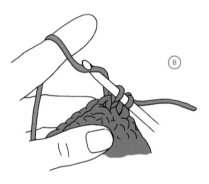

Single-Crochet Seam

For the seam to show on the outside, place the wrong sides of the pieces together. Begin with a slip knot on your crochet hook. *Insert the crochet hook through both layers and hook up a new loop (A), then chain another loop through the two now on your hook (B). Repeat from *. To make the chain lie directly above the seam rather than to one side, alternately hook new stitches up from one side of the seam, then the other. Adjust the tension to match your knitting.

Skein

A length of yarn wound in a loose coil. This term is also sometimes used to refer to a commercially wound center-pull ball of yarn.

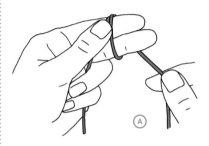

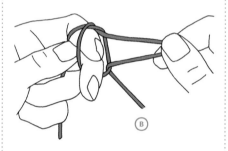

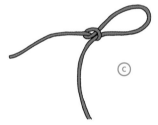

Slip Knot

Holding the end of the yarn in your hand, wrap it around two fingers, and then a little further to end at the back (A). Pull a loop of the working yarn through between your fingers (B). Slip your fingers out and tighten by pulling the cut end and the loop (C).

Through the Back Loop (tbl)

An alternative method of inserting the needle when working a stitch, causing it to twist. This can be done when knitting or purling, and when working knit 2 together (K2tog) or purl 2 together (P2tog).

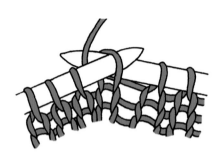

Knitting through the back loop. Insert the right needle from right to left into the section of the stitch that lies behind the left needle.

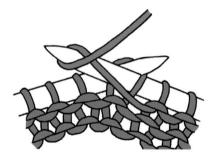

Purling through the back loop. Insert the right needle from left to right into the section of the stitch that lies behind the left needle.

Waste Yarn

Yarn used while casting on that is later removed so stitches can be picked up seamlessly at the cast-on edge of the fabric. It is also used in the middle of the fabric where live stitches are needed for adding a section of knitting later, such as a mitten thumb, a sock heel, or a pocket. Waste yarn should be smooth, nonfuzzy, contrast-color yarn the same thickness as the working yarn, so that it knits up at the same gauge as the working yarn and can be removed easily without leaving residue.

Working Yarn

The yarn that is attached both to the most recently worked stitch and to the ball of yarn currently in use. The term may be used to differentiate between the yarn in use and another not currently in use, between the yarn attached to the ball and the cut tail of yarn at the cast on, or between the project yarn and waste yarn.

Yarn Over (yo)

A stitch worked between two existing stitches that produces an eyelet, which can be closed if desired by working into the back loop on the following row. Note that the yarn always travels over the top of the right needle. If the next stitch will be a knit, the yarn over must end with the yarn in back. If the following stitch will be a purl, the yarn must continue under the needle from back to front in preparation to purl.

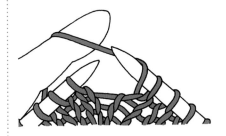

Yarn in left hand. Either wrap counterclockwise around the needle with your index finger, or take the right needle around the back and under the yarn.

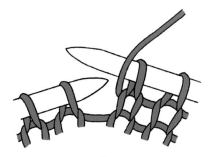

Yarn in right hand. Wrap counterclockwise once around the right needle.

{Using Charts}

Knitting charts are laid out in a grid, with one square or rectangle representing each stitch. They can represent textured pattern stitches, colored pattern stitches, and shaping, all in relation to each other. You'll find examples of charts for color patterns in chapters 2, 5, and 6; charts for stitches that combine color and texture in chapter 3; and charts for textured patterns in chapter 4. Charts for mosaic knitting follow a different set of rules, which is explained in the section on this technique in chapter 7.

Squares versus rectangles. The cells in knitting charts are sometimes rectangular because the individual stitches in stockinette stitch are wider than they are tall. This is important for intarsia charts, because the image would end up too wide and too short if it were charted in square cells and then knitted in stockinette. Charts for stranded knitting, however, have square cells because the strands on the back of the fabric pull it in just a bit horizontally, making the stitches almost square (see page 168). Charts for patterns worked in anything other than stockinette stitch may have square or rectangular cells because there is no attempt to match the proportion of the chart to the proportion of the knitting.

Repeats. Intarsia charts may or may not depict patterns that repeat across the knitting. Large motifs or pictures that cover most of the fabric are worked only once. Smaller motifs may be used only once, repeated across the knitting, or scattered at random. If it's not clear from the chart itself, related instructions should explain whether any repeats are necessary, or it may be obvious from illustrations of the finished project. Intarsia charts frequently show entire pieces of the garment, including any shaping, which can be very helpful in staying oriented while working a complex design.

In stranded knitting, charts frequently show only one repeat of a pattern. Large motifs may be worked only once in the center of the knitting, but small motifs are worked repeatedly across the fabric. Garment shaping is not usually shown in charts for stranded knitting. An exception to this, however, is charts for circular sweater yokes and the shaped crowns of hats (see page 173). You'll find more information on this type of chart in Working from Charts, below.

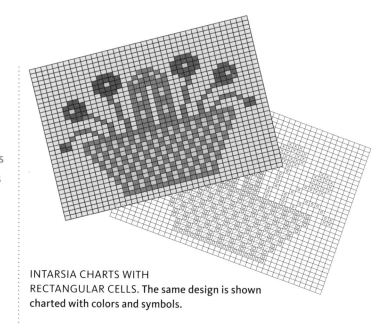

INTARSIA CHARTS WITH RECTANGULAR CELLS. **The same design is shown charted with colors and symbols.**

Sometimes charts show a single pattern repeat plus additional stitches to center the pattern on the fabric. The repeating section of the chart is frequently indicated by a wide bracket across the bottom of the chart. In this book, the pattern repeat for both stitches and rows is indicated by the boxed area in the chart. If there is no pattern repeat indicated, check supporting text instructions for clarification.

Symbols. Color charts may be produced in the actual colors, with symbols representing each color (see above), with plain black and white squares (see page 168), or with blank squares for the background color and a symbol representing the foreground color. When more than one symbol is used, there should be a key identifying the color corresponding to each symbol unless, of course, the designer is leaving the color choice to you.

Charts also portray textured pattern stitches using individual symbols for the various stitch manipulations, such as purls, cables, yarn overs, increases, and decreases. In this book, the key to symbols appears below each chart; for abbreviations, see page 308.

Working from charts. Each horizontal row of a chart represents a row of your knitting. Each cell across the row represents an individual stitch. Because the first row hangs at the bottom of your knitting, the first row of a chart is the bottom row. Read across the row from right to left, which is the direction you work when you knit. For a large motif or an image worked in intarsia, work just once across the chart.

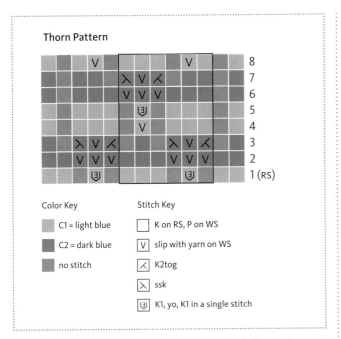

Thorn Pattern

Color Key

- ▢ C1 = light blue
- ▢ C2 = dark blue
- ▢ no stitch

Stitch Key

- ▢ K on RS, P on WS
- Ⅴ slip with yarn on WS
- ⋋ K2tog
- ⋌ ssk
- ⊎ K1, yo, K1 in a single stitch

Charting the Thorn Pattern required color, symbols for stitch manipulations, and "no stitch" because the number of stitches changes.

If you are working circularly, repeat the pattern as necessary around, working the stitches depicted in the chart over and over until you get to the end of the round. Move up one row on the chart and work it from right to left, repeating as necessary until you again reach the end of round. Read from right to left on every row and continue moving up one row in the chart each time you begin a new round.

If you are working flat, work any edge stitches at the beginning of the row, repeat the repeating section of the pattern across, and end with any edge stitches at the end of the row. Turn your knitting and begin working across on the wrong side, reading the next higher row from left to right. Work any edge stitches, repeat any repeating sections, and end with any edge stitches. Continue moving up one row on the chart each time you complete a row of your knitting. Be sure to read the right-side rows from right to left and the wrong-side rows from left to right. If there are textured patterns, when working on the wrong side you also must remember to reverse these, purling when you want a knit stitch to appear on the right side of the knitting and knitting when you want a purl stitch to appear.

Some charts for stranded knitting may not have the same number of stitches on every row. This happens when working a piece with shaping, such as the yoke of a circular sweater or the crown of a hat. If there are decreases, there are fewer stitches on your needle and correspondingly fewer stitches on that row of the chart. If there are increases, there are more stitches on both the chart and the needle. Charts for shaped knitting usually have stairstep edges, rather than straight edges, to accommodate the change in stitch count from row to row. On any given row, the number of stitches on your needles should be a multiple of the stitches in the pattern repeat on the chart.

If there is shaping in the middle of a garment piece or a pattern repeat, or the pattern stitch itself has a different number of stitches on some rows, you may see a black or gray square that means "no stitch." This mysterious name means that, while there's a place holder in the chart for a stitch which has disappeared or will appear on a subsequent row, there's currently no corresponding stitch on your needle. When you come to "no stitch" in the chart, skip over it, do absolutely nothing to the stitches on the needle, and begin working again with the next stitch on the chart and on your needle.

Keeping your place. It can be difficult to read charts (especially if they are small) and to keep track of your place in them. Here are some hints to make it easier:

» Enlarge the chart. Take it to a copy center and have them enlarge it, or scan it yourself and print it out.

» Use a sticky note placed just above the row you're working on and move it up as you complete each row.

» Use a highlighter to mark each row as it's completed. When working a complicated design, you may want to mark sections of the row as you complete them. To use the same chart multiple times, use different-colored highlighters.

» Print the chart on a transparency and use a water-soluble highlighter to mark each row. Wash it off afterwards so you can reuse it. Note that inkjet print is usually water soluble, so turn it over and make your markings on the back.

» Use a metal board with a long horizontal magnet to hold your chart and keep your place in it at the same time. These are available from needlework suppliers and office supply stores.

Creating your own. Techniques for creating intarsia charts are covered in detail in chapter 6. You may find some of them helpful for transferring images to charts for other knitting techniques.

Charts can be drawn by hand, using either regular graph paper or knitter's graph paper with rectangular cells. Knitter's graph paper is available from machine knitting suppliers or can be printed in various sizes from Internet sites. You can begin by outlining the shape of each garment piece, then filling in the design. This is especially useful if the motif is large in proportion to the garment. Or you can design the pattern then draw the outline of the garment piece around it. With small repeating patterns, you may not need to superimpose them on the shape of the knitted piece, but may still find it helpful to do so when working out details around shaped openings like necklines and armholes. To guard against loss or destruction, if you create your chart by hand, make a color copy at a copy center, or scan and save a copy on your computer.

Charting software is also available and, depending on the product you purchase, may have several advantages over hand-charting.

» Copying and "stamping" sections over and over very quickly to make a large chart, which gives a better feel for the proportions overall.

» Flipping patterns horizontally and vertically, which allows you to easily create the second half of a symmetrical motif or to make charts for matching fronts or sleeves.

» Exchanging symbols for colors or replacing one color with another.

» Counting all the stitches in each color to give you an idea of how much yarn of each color will be needed.

» Printing out multiple copies and replacements if your original is lost or damaged.

» Converting text instructions to symbols and vice versa.

{Garment Sizing Guidelines}

Reprinted from *Standards & Guidelines for Crochet and Knitting,* (April 2003), with permission of the Craft Yarn Council of America.

FIT

When sizing sweaters, the fit is based on actual chest/bust measurements, plus ease (additional inches or centimeters). The following chart recommends the amount of ease to add to body measurement, depending on your preference

VERY-CLOSE FITTING: Actual chest/bust measurement or less

CLOSE-FITTING: 1–2" (2.5–5 cm)

STANDARD-FITTING: 2–4" (5–10 cm)

LOOSE-FITTING: 4–6" (10–15 cm)

OVERSIZED: 6" (15 cm) or more

LENGTH FOR CHILDREN

WAIST LENGTH: Actual body measurement

HIP LENGTH: 2" (5 cm) down from waist

TUNIC LENGTH: 6" (15 cm) down from waist

LENGTH FOR WOMEN

WAIST LENGTH: Actual body measurement

HIP LENGTH: 6" (15 cm) down from waist

TUNIC LENGTH: 11" (28 cm) down from waist

LENGTH FOR MEN

Men's length usually varies only 1–2" (2.5–5 cm) from the actual "back hip length" measurement *(see chart at right)*

HEAD CIRCUMFERENCE CHART

	Infant/Child				Adult	
	Premie	Baby	Toddler	Child	Woman	Man
in.	12	14	16	18	20	22
cm	30.5	35.5	40.5	45.5	50.5	56

» For an accurate head measure, place a tape measure across the forehead and measure around the full circumference of the head. Keep the tape snug for accurate results.

BODY SIZE CHARTS

Baby's size		3 mo.	6 mo.	12 mo.	18 mo.	24 mo.
Chest	in.	16	17	18	19	20
	cm	40.5	43	45.5	48	50.5
Center Back (Neck-to-Cuff)	in.	10½	11½	12½	14	18
	cm	26.5	29	31.5	35.5	45.5
Back Waist Length	in.	6	7	7½	8	8½
	cm	15.5	17.5	19	20.5	21.5
Cross Back (Shoulder to Shoulder)	in.	7¼	7¾	8¼	8½	8¾
	cm	18.5	19.5	21	21.5	22
Sleeve Length to Underarm	in.	6	6½	7½	8	8½
	cm	15.5	16.5	19	20.5	21.5

Child's size		2	4	6	8	10	12	14	16
Chest	in.	21	23	25	26½	28	30	31½	32½
	cm	53	58.5	63.5	67	71	76	80	82.5
Center Back (Neck-to-Cuff)	in.	18	19½	20½	22	24	26	27	28
	cm	45.5	49.5	52	56	61	66	68.5	71
Back Waist Length	in.	8½	9½	10½	12½	14	15	15½	16
	cm	21.5	24	26.5	31.5	35.5	38	39.5	40.5
Cross Back (Shoulder to Shoulder)	in.	9¼	9¾	10¼	10¾	11¼	12	12¼	13
	cm	23.5	25	26	27	28.5	30.5	31	33
Sleeve Length to Underarm	in.	8½	10½	11½	12½	13½	15	16	16½
	cm	21.5	26.5	29	31.5	34.5	38	40.5	42

Woman's size		X-Small	Small	Medium	Large	1X	2X	3X	4X	5X
Bust	in.	28–30	32–34	36–38	40–42	44–46	48–50	52–54	56–58	60–62
	cm	71–76	81–86	91.5–96.5	101.5–106.5	111.5–117	122–127	132–137	142–147	152–158
Center Back (Neck-to-Cuff)	in.	27–27½	28–28½	29–29½	30–30½	31–31½	31½–32	32½–33	32½–33	33–33½
	cm	68.5–70	71–72.5	73.5–75	76–77.5	78.5–80	80–81.5	82.5–84	82.5–84	84–85
Back Waist Length	in.	16½	17	17¼	17½	17¾	18	18	18½	18½
	cm	42	43	43.5	44.5	45	45.5	45.5	47	47
Cross Back (Shoulder to Shoulder)	in.	14–14½	14½–15	16–16½	17–17½	17½	18	18	18½	18½
	cm	35.5–37	37–38	40.5–42	43–44.5	44.5	45.5	45.5	47	47
Sleeve Length to Underarm	in.	16½	17	17	17½	17½	18	18	18½	18½
	cm	42	43	43	44.5	44.5	45.5	45.5	47	47

Man's size		Small	Medium	Large	X-Large	XX-Large
Chest	in.	34–36	38–40	42–44	46–48	50–52
	cm	86–91.5	96.5–101.5	106.5–111.5	116.5–122	127–132
Center Back (Neck-to-Cuff)	in.	32–32½	33–33½	34–34½	35–35½	36–36½
	cm	81–82.5	83.5–85	86.5–87.5	89–90	91.5–92.5
Back Hip Length	in.	25–25½	26½–26¾	27–27½	27½–27¾	28–28½
	cm	63.5–64.5	67.5–68	68.5–69	69.5–70.5	71–72.5
Cross Back (Shoulder to Shoulder)	in.	15½–16	16½–17	17½–18	18–18½	18½–19
	cm	39.5–40.5	42–43	44.5–45.5	45.5–47	47–48
Sleeve Length to Underarm	in.	18	18½	19½	20	20½
	cm	45.5	47	49.5	50.5	52

{Abbreviations and Symbols}

C1, C2, C3, etc	Indicates various colors used in pattern stitch instructions.
cm	Centimeter
inc	Increase
K	Knit
K2tog	Knit 2 together
K3tog	Knit 3 together
m	Meter
MC	Main color. Used when one color predominates or serves as a background color.
P	Purl
p2sso	Pass 2 slipped stitches over (this is a double decrease)
P2tog	Purl 2 together
P3tog	Purl 3 together
psso	Pass slipped stitch over (this is a decrease)
RS	Right Side
skp	Slip 1, knit 1, pass slipped stitch over (this is a decrease)
Sl	Slip
ssk	Slip slip knit. This is a decrease, worked as follows: Slip 1 knitwise, slip a second stitch knitwise, insert the left needle into these two stitches and knit them together.
ssp	Slip slip purl. This is a decrease, worked as follows: Slip 1 knitwise, slip a second stitch knitwise, insert the left needle into these two stitches knitwise and slip back to the left needle together, and purl them together.
st(s)	Stitch(es)
Tbl	Through the back loop. For example, K1 tbl is "Knit 1 through the back loop." P1 tbl is "Purl 1 through the back loop."
WS	Wrong Side
wyib	With yarn in back (i.e., with yarn held behind the knitting while you work the stitch)
wyif	With yarn in front (i.e., with yarn held in front of the knitting while you work the stitch)
yo	Yarn over
[], ()	Brackets or parentheses around instructions are used to indicate that the actions form a group. The group may be repeated several times or the actions may all be worked in one stitch.
*	An asterisk indicates the beginning of a section that is to be repeated.

{Bibliography}

Chapter 1: Color Basics

Albers, Josef. *Interaction of Color,* Revised and Expanded Edition (Yale University Press, 2006). A classic work on color theory.

Goethe, Johann Wolfgang von, trans. Charles L. Eastlake. *Theory of Colours* (Dover Publications, 2006). A classic work on color theory.

Itten, Johannes. *The Elements of Color: A Treatise on the Color System of Johannes Itten Based on His Book* The Art of Color (Van Nostrand Reinhold, 1971). A classic work on color theory.

Melville, Sally. *The Knitting Experience Book 3: Color* (XRX Books, 2005). Color theory, plus musings on using color in knitting and instructions for projects.

Menz, Deb. *Color in Spinning* (Interweave Press, 1998). Information on color theory, with detailed studies of dyed and blended color in yarn.

Menz, Deb. *Color Works: The Crafter's Guide to Color* (Interweave Press, 2004). Provides excellent information on color theory and on working with color in fiber crafts. Contains a cardboard scale of shades from white to black and instructions for using it to determine the value of colors.

Morton, Jill. *Color Logic* (Color Voodoo #4) (COLORCOM, 1998). Just one of the excellent e-books available at *www.colorvoodoo.com,* with practical information and understandable examples.

Chapter 3: Pattern Stitches

When researching this chapter, I surveyed many of the pattern stitch dictionaries available, looking for stitches that used multiple colors and those that might lend themselves to color changes. I found a great deal of overlap among these sources, so you'll find many of the patterns included here are featured in several books. Some are my own inventions, but chances are other knitters invented the same patterns in the past and may have included them in their own books. There was no way to include all the pattern stitches that work well with multiple colors in this single chapter, and so you may find the following list of additional sources useful.

Knight, Erika, ed. *Harmony Guide: Knit and Purl: 250 Stitches to Knit* (Interweave Press, 2007). Pattern stitch reference.

Modesitt, Annie. *Confessions of a Knitting Heretic* (ModeKnit Press, 2004). Explanation of standard versus non-standard stitch position and styles of knitting.

Norbury, James. *Traditional Knitting Patterns from Scandinavia, the British Isles, France, Italy and other European Countries* (Dover Publications, 1973). Collection of traditional pattern stitches.

Radcliffe, Margaret. *The Knitting Answer Book* (Storey Pubishing, 2005). Explanation of standard versus non-standard stitch position and styles of knitting.

Vogue Knitting Magazine Editors. *Vogue Knitting Stitchionary Volume Three: Color Knitting* (Sixth&Spring Books, 2006). Pattern stitch reference.

Walker, Barbara G. *A Treasury of Knitting Patterns and A Second Treasury of Knitting Patterns* (both Schoolhouse Press, 1998). Pattern stitch reference.

Zilboorg, Anna. *Knitting for Anarchists* (Feet on the Ground Press, 2002). Explanation of standard versus non-standard stitch position and styles of knitting.

Chapter 5: Stranded Knitting

Blanchard, Nanette. *Stranded Color Knitting,* 2nd edition (Self published, www.lulu.com, 2005). Practical how-to.

Bourgeois, Ann and Eugene Bourgeois. *Fair Isle Sweaters Simplified* (Martingale and Company, 2000). Practical how-to.

Christoffersson, Britt-Marie. *Swedish Sweaters: New Designs from Historical Examples* (The Taunton Press, 1990). A gallery of traditional garments, followed by instructions for new designs.

Don, Sarah. *Fair Isle Knitting* (revised edition) (Dover Publications, 2007). Excellent source of pattern charts.

Feitelson, Ann. *The Art of Fair Isle Knitting: History, Technique, Color and Patterns* (Interweave Press, 1996). Covers history, traditions, techniques, design considerations, and color interaction, in addition to instructions for garments.

Gibson-Roberts, Priscilla A. *Salish Indian Sweaters: A Pacific Northwest Tradition* (Dos Tejedoras Fiber Arts Publications, 1989). Documents the history, traditions, and patterns of these sweaters.

Hansen, Robin. *Favorite Mittens* (Down East Books, 2005). Republication of selected mittens from *Fox and Geese and Fences* (Down East Books, 1983) and *Flying Geese and Partridge Feet* (Down East Books, 1986). Traditional Maine mittens, including stranded patterns.

Keele, Wendy. *Poems of Color: Knitting in the Bohus Tradition* (Interweave Press, 1995). Inspirational history of the Bohus knitting cooperative and its designs.

Lind, Vibeke, trans. Annette Allen Jensen. *Knitting in the Nordic Tradition* (Lark Books, 1997). A survey of knitting in the region organized by type of garment, with lots of pictures.

McGregor, Sheila. *Traditional Fair Isle Knitting* (Dover Publications, 1981) and *Traditional Scandinavian Knitting* (Dover Publications, 2004). Both books document history and traditional techniques and serve as a reference for pattern charts and garment shaping.

Norbury, James. *Traditional Knitting Patterns from Scandinavia, the British Isles, France, Italy and other European Countries* (Dover Publications, 1973). Collection of traditional pattern stitches.

Pagoldh, Susanne, trans. Carol Huebscher Rhoades. *Nordic Knitting: Thirty-Patterns in the Scandinavian Tradition* (Interweave Press, 1991). Organized by country, this book includes historical information as well as new designs.

Schurch, Charlene. *Knitting Marvelous Mittens* (Lark Books, 1998). A collection of ethnic mitten designs from Russia.

Starmore, Alice. *Alice Starmore's Book of Fair Isle Knitting* (The Taunton Press, 1988). The best resource for Fair Isle from start to finish, including history, technique, designing sweaters and other garments, pattern placement, and a large section of pattern charts.

Upitis, Lizbeth. *Latvian Mittens* (Schoolhouse Press, 1997). Traditional designs and techniques, including history and locale.

Zilboorg, Anna. *45 Fine and Fanciful Hats to Knit* (Lark Books, 1997). Bright colors, wonderful patterns, lessons in shaping. A great source of inspiration.

Zilboorg, Anna. *Fancy Feet* (Lark Books, 1994). Documents traditional patterns and sock construction of Turkey. Republished as *Simply Socks* in 2001.

Chapter 6: Intarsia

Cartwright-Jones, Catherine, and Roy Jones. *Enchanted Knitting: Charted Motifs for Hand and Machine Knitting* (Interweave Press, 1997) and *The Tap-Dancing Lizard* (Interweave Press, 1992). Source of charts for intarsia.

Duckworth, Susan. *Susan Duckworth's Knitting* (Ballantine Books, 1988). Original designs and a source of inspiration for combining color and texture.

Fassett, Kaffe. *Glorious Knits* (Clarkson N. Potter, Inc., 1985) and *Kaffe's Classics* (Little, Brown and Company, 1993). Collection of designs by the master of knitted colorwork.

Fassett, Kaffe and Zoë Hunt. *Family Album* (Taunton Press, 1989). More intarsia inspiration.

Galley, Sarah. "Rock around the Block," in her blog Let Me explaiKnit (explaiknit.typepad.com/let_me_explaiknit/2006/08/rock_around_the.html, August 4, 2006). Discussion of intarsia in the round and explanation of joining using the interlocks at color changes.

Liljegren, Lucia. "Hand Knit Seamless Argyle Socks with Short Row Heels," in her blog The Knitting Fiend (www.thedietdiary.com/cgi-bin/Argyle.pl). Uses the basic concept of working the upper half of argyle diamonds separately, then filling in between them with a new color, joining the new area to the old using wrapping and slipped stitches.

Neatby, Lucy. *A Knitter's Companion: Intarsia Untangled: 1 and 2* (DVD) (Tradewind Knitwear Designs, Inc., 2008). Personal instruction from this incomparable teacher; includes everything you need to know, plus lots of tips and tricks to make the intarsia experience more pleasurable.

Stuever, Sherry, and Keely Stuever. *Intarsia: A Workshop for Hand and Machine Knitting* (Sealed With A Kiss, Inc., 1998). The best practical reference in print for intarsia techniques.

Thomas, Mary. *Mary Thomas's Knitting Book* (Dover Publications, 1972). Source of information on working intarsia circularly, under "Festive Knitting."

Thompson, Suzann. "Argyles without Seams," *Knitting around the World* (Taunton Press, 1993). Explains a method of knitting argyle one diamond at a time, while joining to the adjacent diamonds (pp. 38–41).

Chapter 7: Other Techniques

Bartlett, Roxana. *Slip-Stitch Knitting* (Interweave Press, 1998). Mosaic pattern stitches.

Christoffersson, Britt-Marie. *Swedish Sweaters: New Designs from Historical Examples* (Taunton Press, 1990). Includes a few examples of entrelac sweaters.

Dandanell, Birgitta, and Ulla Danielsson, trans. Robin Orm Hansen. *Twined Knitting: A Swedish Folkcraft Technique* (Interweave Press, 1989). The best source of information available on twined knitting and the best explanations of this technique. Lots of historical background.

Duckworth, Susan. *Susan Duckworth's Knitting* (Ballantine Books, 1988). Innovative explorations of entrelac.

Høxbro, Vivian. *Domino Knitting* (Interweave Press, 2002). The European take on modular knitting.

Høxbro, Vivian. *Shadow Knitting* (Interweave Press, 2004). The source for both technical explanations and pattern instructions.

Ling, Anne-Maj, trans. Carol Huebscher Rhoades. *Two-End Knitting* (Schoolhouse Press, 2004). Includes wonderful contemporary designs in twined knitting.

Luters, Ginger. *Module Magic* (XRX Books, 2004). A guide to modular knitting that is both practical and inspirational.

McGregor, Sheila. *Traditional Scandinavian Knitting* (Dover Publications, 2004). Includes information on entrelac.

New, Debbie. *Unexpected Knitting* (Schoolhouse Press, 2003). Goes way beyond the usual knitting concepts to explore the frontiers, especially in the realm of free-form modules and complex geometries.

Schreier, Iris. *Modular Knits: New Techniques for Today's Knitters* (Lark Books, 2005). Complete how-to lessons on knitting modules all in one piece so no joining is necessary.

Schulz, Horst. *New Patchwork Knitting: Fashion for Children* (Saprotex, 2000) and *Patchwork Knitting: Pullovers, Jackets, Waistcoats* (Saprotex, 2000). Modular knit from the German master.

Walker, Barbara G. *Mosaic Knitting* (revised edition) (Schoolhouse Press, 2006). The bible for mosaic knitting techniques and charts.

Zilboorg, Anna. *Knitting for Anarchists* (Feet on the Ground Press, 2002). Methods of working with strip knitting.

Chapter 8: Finishing Touches

Thompson, Gladys. *Patterns for Guernseys, Jerseys and Arans* (Dover Publications, 1979). Source for the best bobble anywhere (page 171).

Wiseman, Nancie. *The Knitter's Book of Finishing Techniques* (Martingale and Company, 2002). Absolutely the best guide to perfect finishing.

Zilboorg, Anna. *Knitting for Anarchists* (Feet on the Ground Press, 2002). Strip knitting techniques particularly adaptable to adding edging.

Chapter 9: Design Workshop

Budd, Ann. *The Knitter's Handy Book of Patterns* (Interweave, 2002) and *Knitter's Handy Book of Sweater Patterns* (Interweave, 2004). Excellent sources of basic patterns for sweaters and other garments.

Bush, Nancy. *Folk Socks: The History and Techniques of Handknitted Footwear* (Interweave Press, 1994). History, techniques, and instructions for traditional socks. This book also includes an introductory section that allows you to design your own socks.

Fee, Jacqueline. *Sweater Workshop* (Down East Books, 2002). Design your own sweater.

Gibson-Roberts, Priscilla A. *Simple Socks: Plain and Fancy* (Nomad Press, 2001). Design your own socks, with short row heels and toes.

Gibson-Roberts, Priscilla A., and Deborah Robson. *Knitting in the Old Way: Designs and Techniques from Ethnic Sweaters* (expanded edition) (Nomad Press, 2004). Lessons in simple traditional sweater designs, so you can do it yourself.

Hansen, Robin. *Knit Mittens!* (Storey Publishing, 2002). Patterns for mittens, plus information on fitting your own.

Newton, Deborah. *Designing Knitwear* (Taunton, 1998). Everything a knitwear designer needs to know from an expert in the field.

Righetti, Maggie. *Sweater Design in Plain English* (St. Martin's Griffin, 1990). Down to earth, practical introduction to sweater design and fitting.

Starmore, Alice. *Alice Starmore's Book of Fair Isle Knitting* (Taunton Press, 1988). The best source available for designing stranded sweaters and tams.

Turner, Sharon. *Teach Yourself Visually Knitting Design* (Visual, 2007). Provides master patterns for a variety of simple projects.

Vogue Knitting Magazine Editors. *Vogue Knitting: The Ultimate Knitting Book* (updated edition) (Sixth&Spring Books, 2002). A complete knitting reference book that includes information on designing various sweater shapes, including armholes and sleeve caps, necklines, and details like collars, pockets, and borders.

Walker, Barbara G. *Knitting from the Top* (Schoolhouse Press, 1996). Guide to designing your own top-down sweaters.

Zilboorg, Anna. *Knitting for Anarchists* (Feet on the Ground Press, 2002). Completely details how to knit a sweater in strips without using a pattern.

Zimmermann, Elizabeth. *Knitting without Tears* (Fireside, 1971; reprinted in 1995). Encouraging, conversational source of information on designing circular sweaters, socks, mittens, and hats.

{Acknowledgments}

Numerous people aided and abetted me in the conception and completion of this project, and they deserve my heartfelt thanks.

First and foremost are the knitters who gave generously of their time and expertise to create the samples that illustrate this book. You brought to this project unflagging enthusiasm, helpful suggestions, a willingness to confront unfamiliar techniques, and the ability to combat frustration with humor, for which I am eternally grateful: Debbie Brame, Carol Haskell, Nancy Lutz, Leanne Mitchell, Lawre O'Leary, Pat Polentz, Cecilia W. Riegert, Jeanne Rippere, Phil Sponenberg, Christy Straight, Joanne Strauch, Cheryl Sweeney, Linda Tegarden, Tracy Watson, Darcy Whitlock, Corrie B. Whitmore, Catherine Wingfield-Yeatts, and one who shall remain anonymous.

Thank you also to all my colleagues who took the time to answer my questions about specific knitting problems and techniques, especially Joan Schrouder and Leigh Witchel.

The colorful, lustrous mohair and wool yarn used throughout the book was generously provided by Kid Hollow Farm in Free Union, Virginia, owned by Pat and Steve Harder (www.kidhollow.com). The yarn is a blend of their own kid mohair with fine wool, spun to their specifications and dyed by hand at the farm. I am very grateful to Pat and Steve for their support and enthusiasm, and especially to Pat for responding repeatedly to my desperate calls for more yarn, some of it custom-dyed.

In addition, the following businesses generously supplied additional yarn, equipment, and other supplies used in the creation of this book: Adriafil SRL (www.adriafil.com), Black Water Abbey Yarns (www.abbeyyarns.com), Briggs & Little Woollen Mills Ltd (www.briggsandlittle.com), Brown Sheep Company, Inc. (www.brownsheep.com), Cascade Yarns (www.cascadeyarns.com), Cherry Tree Hill Yarn (www.cherryyarn.com), Coughlin's Homespun Yarns (717-896-9066), Ellen's ½ Pint Farm LLC (www.ellenshalfpintfarm.com), Honeypot Yarns (www.honeypotyarns.com), Kathleen Hughes Hand Dyed Originals (801-277-5318), Lawre's Laine (www.lawreslaine.com), Lorna's Laces (www.lornaslaces.net), Mountain Colors (www.mountaincolors.com), Plymouth Yarn Company Inc. (www.plymouthyarn.com), Strauch Fiber Equipment Company (www.strauchfiber.com), Tess Designer Yarns (www.tessyarns.com), Yarns International (www.yarnsinternational.com).

I offer my sincere appreciation to the authors and teachers whose work has expanded my knitting knowledge and specifically informed this book: Gladys Thompson, Deborah Newton, and Barbara Walker for bobbles; Sherry and Keely Stuever and Lucy Neatby for intarsia; Alice Starmore for wrapped steeks; Rick Mondragon for crocheted steeks; Joan Schrouder for knitted bindings; Merike Saarniit for Estonian pattern stitches; and, of course, Barbara Walker for mosaic knitting and more pattern stitches than could possibly be included.

Many thanks also go to my editor, Gwen Steege, who immediately saw the potential for this book when I suggested it and nurtured it through writing, editing, and production with understanding and excited anticipation, and my project editor, Erin Holman, whose knitting knowledge complemented, and whose editorial expertise far exceeds, my own. Thanks, too, to the team of designers, photographers, artists, and models who contributed to its success.

I am very grateful to my agent and fellow knitter, Linda Roghaar, whose knowledge of knitting and of publishing has helped me to accomplish current goals and to catch a glimpse of the future.

Last, but certainly not least, I thank my family — David, Anna, and Allegra — who listened, sympathized, and encouraged, over and over again.

{Index}

Page numbers in *italics* indicate photographs; **bold** indicates pattern instructions and charts.

More Books by Margaret Radcliffe

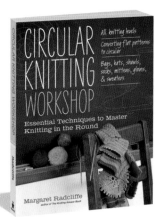

Circular Knitting Workshop
Master the art of circular knitting techniques like Fair Isle, twined helix, tubular, and more, with photographic sequences and 35 demonstration projects.
320 pages. Paper. ISBN 978-1-60342-999-3.

The Knitting Answer Book, 2nd Edition
This fully updated essential reference has answers to every knitting quandary, for knitters of all levels and all types of projects.
440 pages. Flexibind with cloth spine.
ISBN 978-1-61212-404-9.

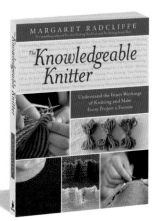

The Knowledgeable Knitter
Learn the "whys" and "hows" behind every knitting technique to make every project a success.
296 pages. Paper. ISBN 978-1-61212-040-9.
Hardcover. ISBN 978-1-61212-414-8.